RETHINKING THE UNITY AND RECEPTION OF LUKE AND ACTS

RETHINKING THE UNITY AND RECEPTION OF LUKE AND ACTS

EDITED BY
ANDREW F. GREGORY AND C. KAVIN ROWE

The University of South Carolina Press

Published by the University of South Carolina Press
Columbia, South Carolina 29208

www.sc.edu/uscpress

Manufactured in the United States of America

19 18 17 16 15 14 13 12 11 10 9 8 7 6 5 4 3 2 1

Library of Congress Cataloging-in-Publication Data

Rethinking the unity and reception of Luke and Acts / edited by Andrew F. Gregory and C. Kavin Rowe.
p. cm.
Includes bibliographical references and index.
ISBN 978-1-57003-916-4 (cloth : alk. paper)
1. Bible. N.T. Luke—Criticism, interpretation, etc. 2. Bible. N.T. Acts—Criticism, interpretation, etc. I. Gregory, Andrew F. II. Rowe, Christopher Kavin, 1974-
BS2589.R48 2010
226.4'065—dc22

2010005708

This book was printed on Glatfelter Natures, a recycled paper with 30 percent postconsumer waste content.

CONTENTS

FOREWORD

François Bovon

This book owes its origin primarily to the intellectual impetus of Richard I. Pervo, Mikeal C. Parsons, C. Kavin Rowe, Markus Bockmuehl, and Andrew F. Gregory. Pervo and Parsons invited New Testament scholars to rethink the unity of Luke-Acts, a unity largely accepted for more than eighty years, from Henry J. Cadbury and Martin Dibelius until today. Rowe and Bockmuehl criticized the unity of the Lukan work and suggested that the Gospel and the Book of Acts could be read as two independent literary works. Gregory, in his monograph on the reception of Luke-Acts in the second century, and in several additional articles, contributed first indirectly then directly to the discussion on the unity of Luke-Acts. He argued that, with the exception of Irenaeus of Lyons and the authors of the Muratorian canon, Christian authors of the second century did not manifest an interest in the unity of Luke-Acts.

To be frank, even after more than forty years of working on the *Wirkungsgeschichte* of Luke-Acts, on the theology of the double work, and on the philological, literary, and historical interpretation of the two books, I did not pay sufficient attention to the new and original theses of these scholars. Part of the explanation for my lack of attention was the comfortable consensus I had accepted. I had such admiration for the two veteran scholars Cadbury and Dibelius, and such respect for my two mentors, Hans Conzelmann and Jacques Dupont, that any attempt to shake the unity of Luke-Acts seemed to me a fanciful, if not a desperate, endeavor to find a new interesting topic. Today, however, I am presenting my mea culpa and recommending this book. Of course, as with any serious scholarly project, there remain some critical questions.

But first of all I would like to acknowledge the quality of the central statement of this collective volume: the fact that Luke and Acts were written by the same author (accepted by virtually all scholars) does not necessarily imply that these two books were written together, nor that they should be considered as the two parts of the same work. There are indeed differences between Luke and Acts, particularly on the ethical level. As Brigitte Kahl has shown in her dissertation, "Armenevangelium und Heidenevangelium" (1987), the socio-critical Gospel—for example, "Blessed are the poor" (Luke 6:20)—will lead to a Book of Acts less eager to bring the believers to a counter-cultural position and path of poverty.

When New Testament scholars attempt to deal with the question of unity and diversity in Luke and Acts, they have to face four major issues. First is the theological one. As my example above makes clear, the explanation can be, as Luise Schottroff has suggested, that the Gospel draws an ideal portrait of Jesus and his requirements, while the Book of Acts enters more prosaically into the Freudian *Wirklichkeitsprinzip*. Second, the scholar has to compare the language of the Gospel and the language of Acts. In an age of philological indifference, he or she has to rely on the formidable investigations of previous scholars such as Sophie Antoniadis, Henry J. Cadbury, Adolf Schlatter, or Walter Radl. The result is impressive and proves that Luke and Acts belong together and were written by the same author (although it still leaves the door open to the question of a total unity). Third—and the present generation is particularly competent in this matter—the New Testament scholar must ask in what proportion the analysis of the composition contributes to the problem of the unity of Luke-Acts. From Roland Meynet to Robert C. Tannehill, many scholars have discovered similar patterns, an identical genre (or two complementary genres—a biographical gospel and an historical monograph), and many intentional parallels between the two works. One example, in my opinion, is the correspondence of the Jerusalem conference (Acts 15) to the parable of the prodigal son (Luke 15). There is also the influence of the Hebrew Bible/Septuagint on the author of Luke-Acts: the prophecy of Isaiah 2 (the ascension to Jerusalem and the descent from Jerusalem) probably explains the composition of the Gospel (to Jerusalem) and of the Acts (from Jerusalem). And when writing to the same Theophilos, at the beginning of Acts, the author refers to the Gospel as his "first book" (Acts 1:1). It is therefore logical to believe that the two books belong together, and this from the beginning. Such is my opinion, but I respect the "disbelievers" and the "dysbelievers."

The discussion of the history of reception is a particularly interesting aspect of this volume. I admit to sharing some of Luke Timothy Johnson's reservations and am uncertain that the patristic interpretation can really help in this matter. Also, the power of orality, underscored by Helmut Koester, seems to be neglected by some recent reflection on the reception history of the Gospels. In my judgment, not just one, but two distinct influences can be tracked on the Gospel of Luke and the Book of Acts in the second century. There is, on the one hand, the Lukan prose used or imitated by authors eager to create additional new stories (see the *Protevangelium of James* or the *Questions of Bartholomew*), and, on the other hand, there is a respectful exegesis of Luke or Acts considered as an authoritative text on its way to canonization. If the theological interpretation is here well treated, the same cannot be said of the impact of Luke-Acts on the noncanonical and apocryphal literature (see the *Epistula apostolorum* or the *Letter of Peter to Philip*).

Another significant issue discussed in this book is the canonization of the four Gospels. What is not sufficiently emphasized, however, is the discovery made as early as 1880 by Franz Overbeck in his short study *Zur Geschichte des Kanons.* When Christian readers canonized a text, they attributed a fully new value and, logically, a new meaning to the documents concerned. Overbeck even went so far as to claim that the canonizing Christians finally lost the understanding of the text they cherished. The second century's progressive canonization of the Gospels widened the distance between the Gospel and Acts. The different history of reception for the two books, as well as the different history of textual transmission, are dependent upon that difference in the canonical treatment. As an example of the slow canonization of the Book of Acts, we may note that Cyprian of Carthage usually does not call the Book of Acts *scriptura.*

The authors of this volume legitimately underscore the importance of the manuscript evidence. It is true that not a single Greek manuscript contains the Gospel of Luke and the Book of Acts side by side. All the more interesting, therefore, are the remarks given here on Acts as a follow-up of the Gospels (plural) or as an overture to the Epistles (Pauline or Catholic). Still, as interesting as they are, these insights do not necessarily apply to the first two or three generations, between 70 and 110 C.E., the time of the birth of the Gospel of Luke and of the Acts of the Apostles.

The reader of this foreword should not believe that the authors of these essays all agree. On the contrary, I congratulate them for accepting the challenge of different opinions and intellectual disputes. My role, therefore, is less to shake, like Samson, the doors of the city gate and more to play the role of the scribe who mediates between the authors and the readers.

PREFACE

Ancient readers of the Gospel of Luke and the Acts of the Apostles were confident that these two texts were written by the same person. Modern scholars have usually agreed.[1] But within the last one hundred years, they have also claimed much more. Not only are Luke and Acts written by the same author, but they also constitute two parts of a single story. In order to interpret these texts with the greatest degree of comprehension, therefore, readers of Luke and Acts should read them together as parts 1 and 2 of a unified literary work: Luke-Acts. Only so, it is maintained, can we fully grasp the literary, historical, and theological contour of this two-volume text.

Of course—as with any scholarly consensus—there have been challengers, most notably Mikeal C. Parsons and Richard I. Pervo, whose *Rethinking the Unity of Luke and Acts* was first published in 1993 and republished with additional bibliography in 2007. Parsons and Pervo did not question the authorial unity of Luke and Acts but argued that the common authorship of the two texts and their literary unity are quite different things. From the fact that Luke wrote both books it follows neither that he set out to do so nor that they are two volumes of one work. Conceptually speaking, Luke and Acts can be seen as two discrete, although interrelated, narratives. Quite against the scholarly stream Parsons and Pervo thus foregrounded not the continuities but the discontinuities between Luke and Acts, particularly in matters of genre, narrative, and theology. Despite gaining widespread attention, however, their challenge has done little to provoke a significant rethinking of dominant interpretive paradigms.

This lack of impact upon the guild was not due to the insignificance of the question. Rather, more fundamentally, it may have been because Parsons and Pervo paid relatively little attention to the one particular issue that could move the discussion forward: the early and strikingly different reception history of Luke and Acts. Such histories are precisely the starting point and focus of this book. The present volume thus marks a new stage in the modern debate about the unity of Luke-Acts exactly because of its point of departure: the historical evidence for the reception of Luke and Acts and the methodological consequences of reflecting on the hermeneutical implications of such evidence.

As Patrick E. Spencer has recently observed, this increased interest in the early reception of Luke and Acts has played an important role in reigniting the debate about the unity of these two narratives—indeed to the extent that a question the majority of scholars had taken to be closed can now be described as the new "storm center" in the study of Luke and Acts.[2] In the course of his analysis Spencer singles out for particular attention two recent publications, each written by one of the editors of this collection. The first is the monograph by Andrew F. Gregory, *The Reception of Luke and Acts in the Period before Irenaeus.* The second is an article by C. Kavin Rowe, "Literary Unity and Reception History: Reading Luke-Acts as Luke and Acts," included here as one of six essays that previously appeared in the *Journal for the Study of the New Testament.*

Gregory's monograph is historical in its focus: it sets out to address the question of which ancient authors and/or texts make demonstrable use of Luke and/or Acts. Gregory recognizes that Luke and Acts have been read as separate texts for much of the time since they were written and that such a reading practice entails the fact that a reader's knowledge of one volume need not imply knowledge of the other. For this reason Gregory investigates the early reception of each work as a separate text, concluding that there is "no evidence other than that of Irenaeus and the Muratorian Fragment to demonstrate that Luke and Acts were read as two volumes of one work."[3] What Gregory does not do, however, is to move beyond these historical conclusions to engage the hermeneutical questions raised by his monograph for contemporary scholarship on Luke and Acts. More specifically, although he notes that Luke-Acts is a modern construct, he does not address the question of whether this construct is challenged by the evidence that he presents. This is precisely the point that Rowe addresses and which this collection of essays takes further.

Rowe's essay begins from Gregory's conclusions but argues that there is no need to see either Irenaeus or the Muratorian Fragment as recognizing anything other than the authorial unity of Luke and Acts—that is, that they were two books written by the same author, not two parts of one text that were to be read in the light of each other and to the exclusion of other texts by other authors. Rowe thus employs the reception history of Luke and Acts to deconstruct hermeneutically the grounding assumptions with which modern scholars have worked on "historical" interpretation of Luke-Acts. In light of Gregory's work Rowe asks "whether our [post-Cadbury] interpretations that depend in principle on the unity of Luke-Acts are in fact not as historical as we might suppose, at least in the sense that the texts would not have been heard together in the way we read them today."[4] In short, explicating the historical significance of Gregory's work for the New Testament guild entailed the hermeneutical conclusion that literary and authorial unity could no longer be equated with the historical reception of the texts and the reading practices that accompanied such reception. The academic demand to read Luke and Acts as Luke-Acts may well have a solid basis in the authorial skill, or literary dynamics, of the two texts, but the move toward conclusions about an actual ancient readership of one literary work Luke-Acts is contradicted by the vast majority of known evidence from antiquity. The aporia is thus clear: historical-critical work on Luke-Acts has been, so Rowe argues, neither historical nor critical enough.

The present book constitutes the next phase in the larger discussion of how best to read the two Lukan works. In order both to present clearly the current shape of the argument and to facilitate further debate, the book is divided into three parts. Part 1 consists of two essays that survey the history and contemporary landscape of scholarly approaches to the unity of Luke-Acts. It therefore provides the overall context from which future discussion of this question will take its bearings. Part 2 reprints in chronological succession five articles from the two rounds of the most recent published debate. The second part of the book thus gathers together and conveniently displays both the conceptual contours and the specific points of dispute in the current discussion: the precise nature and range of the ancient evidence, the hermeneutical consequences of that evidence, and the resultant scholarly practices that have arisen from the inevitable particularity of the decisions made at the intersection of ancient history and hermeneutics. Part 3 presents five new essays that react to and develop various facets of the recent debate. In that they offer a wide-ranging extension and interpretive application of the insights that have emerged from the present discussion, these new essays both demonstrate the fruitfulness of reception history for multiple dimensions of New Testament interpretation and help to set the agenda for future work.

Taken together, parts 1, 2, and 3 form a coherent interpretive project capable of being read at two different levels. The first rather obvious level is that of scholarship on the question of the reception and unity of Luke and Acts and how best to construe the relation of these two books both to one another and to other ancient Christian texts. The second level is that of the methodological usefulness of reception history as a way to generate insight into historical interpretation of the New Testament texts. As is only to be expected, not all of the contributors to this volume are always in agreement with each other, and points of difference between them will naturally offer fruitful starting points for further discussion. All authors, however, are concerned with both these matters and with the proper way to think about their intersection.

Of course these two levels are finally not fundamentally different modes of thinking. They are instead but useful ways of characterizing the present book in order to direct our attention to different dimensions of unified interpretive endeavors—the constructive proposals of the essays. Still, speaking of the book's concerns in this twofold way emphasizes its potential to engender work beyond the Gospel of Luke and the Acts of the Apostles. Luke-Acts is without a doubt the textual center of the debate about the importance of reception history for New Testament hermeneutics. But Luke-Acts is hardly where that debate should remain. If the essays in this book are rightly read they constitute a methodological resource from which biblical scholars can draw in their interpretive explorations in other textual fields. There is much to learn in these pages about Luke-Acts in particular, and there are also insights that may be taken and applied to other New Testament texts and the history of their reception.

NOTES

1. A recent exception is Patricia Walters, *The Assumed Authorial Unity of Luke and Acts: A Reassessment of the Evidence* (SNTSMS 145; Cambridge: Cambridge University Press, 2009). This monograph was not yet available when the manuscript of the present book was completed.

2. Patrick E. Spencer, "The Unity of Luke-Acts: A Four-Bolted Hermeneutical Hinge," *CBR* 5/3 (2007): 341–66, on pp. 342 and 346–47; quotation on p. 359.

3. Andrew F. Gregory, *The Reception of Luke and Acts in the Period before Irenaeus: Looking for Luke in the Second Century* (WUNT 2/169. Tübingen: Mohr Siebeck, 2003), 352.

4. C. Kavin Rowe, Abstract of "History, Hermeneutics and the Unity of Luke-Acts," *JSNT*, 28/2 (2005): 131.

ACKNOWLEDGMENTS

Though it provides much intellectual pleasure, editing a collection of essays is no easy task. Our greatest gratitude goes to Judith Heyhoe, senior editor at Duke University's Divinity School, whose works of supererogation would be impossible to enumerate. Jim Denton, our editor at the University of South Carolina Press, has been outstanding both because of his overall professionalism and his particular interest in this project. Linda Fogle of the press has also been very helpful, as has the copyediting and book production staff.

The following essays were previously printed in the *Journal for the Study of the New Testament* and are here reprinted by permission of Sage Publications, all rights reserved:

Michael F. Bird, "The Unity of Luke-Acts in Recent Discussion"; C. Kavin Rowe, "History, Hermeneutics, and the Unity of Luke-Acts"; Luke Timothy Johnson, "Literary Criticism of Luke-Acts: Is Reception History Pertinent?"; Markus Bockmuehl, "Why Not Let Acts Be Acts? In Conversation with C. Kavin Rowe"; C. Kavin Rowe, "Literary Unity and Reception History: Reading Luke-Acts as Luke and Acts"; and Andrew F. Gregory, "The Reception of Luke and Acts and the Unity of Luke-Acts."

PART ONE

THE UNITY OF LUKE-ACTS IN RECENT DISCUSSION

Michael F. Bird

The unity of Luke-Acts has been an axiom in modern scholarship ever since Henry J. Cadbury's 1927 work on the subject. Although much has been written about the authorship, history, genre, and theology of Luke-Acts, the basic premise of some kind of unity between Luke's Gospel and his subsequent history of the early church has been a pillar of Lukan scholarship.[1] This consensus was cemented further by Robert C. Tannehill's two-volume monograph on the narrative unity of Luke-Acts, which demonstrated, with great success, the overarching cohesion of the two works in light of thematic repetition, cross-links, systematic parallels, and other literary phenomena.[2]

But a consensus is there to be challenged. Mikael C. Parsons and Richard I. Pervo do exactly that in *Rethinking the Unity of Luke and Acts.*[3] The authors complain that the unity of Luke-Acts is an assumption that needs to be questioned and/or justified. In support they draw attention to the differences in genre, narrative, and theology between Luke and Acts and highlight a number of authorial and canonical questions posed by Luke and Acts. At stake is whether we link Luke and Acts with a hyphen (Luke-Acts = a close connection) or with a forward slash (Luke/Acts = a loose connection). They contend that "the theological unity of Luke and Acts is not a foregone conclusion."[4] On another front, Andrew Gregory[5] and C. Kavin Rowe[6] have raised some questions about the unity of Luke-Acts through reception history, noting that second-century writers did not, as far as is known, read Luke and Acts in unison or treat them as a single literary unit. The aim of this study, then, is briefly to highlight the contours of debate concerning the unity of Luke-Acts in scholarship since 1993, and to identify what is at stake in the current discussion.[7]

NIPPING AT THE HEELS OF A CONSENSUS: The Challenge of Parsons and Pervo to the Unity of Luke-Acts

The burden of the study of Parsons and Pervo was to suggest that, although the one author created Luke and Acts, the two works possess "very distinct narratives embodying different literary devices, generic conventions, and perhaps even theological concerns."[8] It is the effect and aftermath of their study on which I wish to focus in this section.

For the most part we can say that monographs on Luke, Acts, or Luke-Acts (typically published dissertations) continue to assume and affirm the significance of the unity of the Lukan volumes.[9] In some cases there is a tacit acknowledgement of the objections of Parsons and Pervo, but with a continued resistance to their hypothesis. For instance, in a monograph on the Isaianic New Exodus in Acts, David W. Pao recognizes the gravity of the issues raised by Parsons and Pervo but goes on to announce that in his study the unity of Luke-Acts is simply "assumed and affirmed," especially in light of a common Isaianic story underlying both works and the possibility of a "scriptural unity" between both volumes.[10]

Beyond the published dissertation genre, other volumes have given more consideration to the basis for the unity of Luke-Acts. I. Howard Marshall has presented a rigorous defense of the unity of Luke-Acts in light of the work by Parsons and Pervo.[11] After presenting a taxonomy of views, Marshall states that there really are only two viable options: "The one is that the Gospel was written before and independently of Acts. The other is that Luke produced the two books as part of the one work, with some shaping and adaptation of each in a process which cannot now be reconstructed in detail."[12]

Marshall draws on three arguments for postulating a unity between Luke and Acts: (1) evidence garnered from the prologues in Luke 1:1–4 and Acts 1:1 that signifies that we have two parts of the one work; (2) material in the Gospel as a whole, such as complexes that have been sourced or redacted in light of what follows in Acts, omissions of material or themes from the Gospels where the material or themes are paralleled in Acts, material that is prophetic of what is to happen in Acts, and alterations to the Gospel that reflect knowledge of traditions in Acts; (3) the ending of the Gospel, which shows signs of adaptation to allow for a sequel. Marshall therefore concludes: "The weight of these considerations points strongly in our opinion to the hypothesis that the Gospel was published as the first part of a two-volume composition, whatever be the process by which it came into its present form."[13]

Joel B. Green also advances a forthright case for the unity of Luke-Acts. Green employs a comprehensive narrative, rhetorical, and sociological approach to both volumes and is consequently sensitive to the matter of unity.[14] Green is aware of the divide between Luke and Acts in the New Testament canon, he is cognizant of the second-century use of Luke among the other Gospels, and he admits that Luke could have completed and made both works available separately. Even so, Green does not regard the composition of Acts as an afterthought; instead, the narrative that Luke developed was intended to link the story of Jesus' earthly ministry to the continuation of Jesus' mission in the life of the church.[15] Green states: "Luke's agenda is not to write the story of Jesus, followed by the story of the early church . . . Rather, his design is to write the story of the continuation and fulfillment of God's project—a story that embraces both the work of Jesus and of the followers of Jesus after his ascension. From start to finish, Luke-Acts brings to the fore one narrative aim, the one aim of God."[16]

Thus, according to Green, "seen against this purpose, the Gospel of Luke is incomplete in itself, for it opens up possibilities in the narrative cycle that go unrealized in the Gospel but do materialize in the Acts of the Apostles."[17] Against the objections of Parsons and Pervo, Green regards it as both possible and necessary to postulate a narrative unity in which the two volumes progress from "possibility" to "realization" and then "result" in the unfolding story. It is within this narrative cycle that one discovers the aim of God in Luke's thinking.[18] Green responds more specifically to Parsons and Pervo in an article on the Acts of the Apostles, where he finds their arguments "difficult to sustain."[19] Regarding the apparently different genres of Luke and Acts, he supposes that generic unity is a red herring, since generic forms were fluid in antiquity. Further, Luke wrote his Gospel constrained by the evolving Gospel genre, and he may have approached his project by composing something for which previous models or forms proved inadequate. Additionally Green finds unconvincing the claim that Luke has a different textually constructed narrator for each work. The application of narratology in either volume brings to light multiple narrators and various levels of narration. For Green unity exists not in narration but in narrative purpose. The division of Luke-Acts into two parts, he argues, was also a matter of "physical expediency," given the fact that Luke's work could not fit on a single papyrus roll. The separation into two parts does not signify that one work has ended and another has begun. Green appeals also to the prologues, which he regards as supporting a narrative continuation. In fact he regards the unity of Luke-Acts as "hermeneutically necessary in order to understand the purpose of the Lukan writings and the way in which the incidents in Acts are prefigured in the Gospel."[20]

The manifold and magisterial studies of C. K. Barrett have frequently involved analysis of the unity of the writings attributed to Luke. Nearly fifty years ago, Barrett wrote, "Luke's is a two-volume work. This observation, naively simple at first sight, is of great importance, and marks Luke off from all other New Testament writers, and Luke-Acts from all other New Testament books."[21] In Barrett's estimation Luke was building a bridge between two periods, since his volumes overlap. The ascension marks the end of the ministry of Jesus and the commencement of the church, with the result that "the end of the story of Jesus is the Church; and, the story of Jesus is the beginning of the Church."[22] For Luke, the father of church history, the story of Jesus is about the establishment of a new religion. The church did not emerge spontaneously but was the outcome of the life of Jesus.[23] In an essay for the Frans Neirynck Festschrift, Barrett catalogued forty-one instances which demonstrate that Luke was preparing for

Acts in the composition of his Gospel. These connections between Luke and Acts warrant the conclusion that Acts confirms the Gospel as much as the Gospel introduces Acts.[24] More recently Barrett has proposed that Luke-Acts functioned somewhat like a New Testament in miniature for Luke's readers, since it connected the Old Testament Scriptures to the story of Jesus and the church. The result is that for Luke the Christian movement is the climax of the history of Israel and the fulfillment of the Old Testament promises.[25] The separation of the Gospel from Acts in the second century was inevitable when Luke joined its partners Matthew, Mark, and John, but was also detrimental to Acts, which ceased to be a "confirmation of the gospel." Instead the question of what to do with Acts became a problem for the church in the first half of the second century, and it was only its utility in combating Gnosticism that guaranteed its survival and afforded its place in the canon.[26]

Charles H. Talbert also finds assorted reasons for postulating the unity of Luke-Acts. In his view: (1) with their prefaces, Luke and Acts are analogous to Josephus's *Against Apion,* a work consisting of two books with prefaces involving dedication; (2) the architecture of Luke-Acts corresponds to the literary unity of works from the Homeric tradition; (3) the narrative and theological connections between the two volumes also offer sound evidence that the two volumes are part of one story. Thus Talbert infers: "To have heard Luke-Acts read as a continuous whole would have been to hear it as a narrative of fulfillment. When, in Luke 1:1, the author says that he is composing a 'narrative of the things that have been fulfilled . . . among us,' he gives a clue to the nature of the upcoming narrative. Luke-Acts is an account of the life of Jesus and the beginnings of the early church told as the fulfillment of prophecy."[27]

A volume edited by David P. Moessner, *Jesus and the Heritage of Israel: Luke's Narrative Claim upon Israel's Legacy,* contains several essays pertinent to the question of unity, and some are worth highlighting here.[28] The opening essay by Moessner and David L. Tiede commends a growing consensus that "Luke as the interpreter of Israel presents a carefully crafted argument *in two parts* to lay claim to a culmination of Israel's traditions in Jesus of Nazareth, Messiah of Israel."[29] Richard I. Pervo takes the opportunity to reiterate the generic objection to the unity of Luke-Acts. He does not deny that Luke and Acts should be read together, but objects to the "ultra-unitarian approach" that fails to take seriously the possibility of differences in genre and to entertain questions about composition that do not support literary unity.[30] For Pervo, Luke and Acts are both exercises in "legitimating narrative," yet Acts is more like a sequel than a second volume to Luke's Gospel.[31] William Kurz highlights the promise-fulfillment theme in Luke-Acts, which is said to be similar to other Jewish literature such as 1 and 2 Maccabees.[32] Gregory E. Sterling argues that Luke deliberately withheld the Gentile mission until Acts, so that "the two-volume work was planned as a single work in two parts rather than two separate works or a first independent work with a sequel."[33] Charles H. Talbert and J. H. Hayes draw attention to foreshadowing and correspondences between Luke and Acts.[34] Robert C. Tannehill defends his narrative-unity approach against criticism by Parson and Pervo, and he maintains that "Luke and Acts are a unified narrative because the different events reported relate to a single underlying purpose, God's purpose of bringing salvation to all flesh."[35] I. Howard Marshall continues his criticism of Parson and Pervo by postulating a theological unity built around five key elements of thematic continuity between Luke and Acts, including Jesus as proclaimer and proclaimed, apostles and witnesses, kingdom and messiah, discipleship, and salvation for Jews and Gentiles.[36]

Most major commentaries on Luke and Acts continue to reassert the unity of Luke-Acts. For example Beverly Roberts Gaventa touches briefly on the subject in her commentary, proposing that "Acts would make little or no sense without some understanding of the Gospel."[37] Luke's Gospel assumes that the reader is familiar with the "things fulfilled among us," making Luke and Acts mutually dependent.[38] François Bovon argues that the prologue in Luke 1:1–4 "opens the entire work and not merely the Gospel"; and, further, "according to the prologue of Acts, the Gospel is the 'first book' of the entire work."[39] Luke Timothy Johnson has composed consecutive commentaries on Luke and Acts in the Sacra Pagina series, and has attempted to systematically exploit the significance of the designation Luke-Acts in both of his volumes.[40]

Several scholars, however, while not fully convinced by Parsons and Pervo, concede the legitimacy of their argument and posit the unity of Luke-Acts with far greater reserve and caution than was ordinarily done in the past. In her comparison of the Lukan prefaces with the scientific treatises Loveday Alexander operates with the assumption that Luke and Acts are "two parts of a single work";[41] but toward the end of her study she concludes: "The connection between two successive works of a corpus linked by recapitulations is not always as tight as we might expect," and thus there remains a genuine "possibility that Luke did not have the narrative of Acts immediately in mind when he wrote Luke 1:1–4."[42] More recently, though, Alexander has abandoned her agnosticism on the subject, with a "reluctant . . . conversion to authorial unity."[43] She was convinced by her own study of the ending of Acts "that a case can be made out for the proposition that Luke conceived his work from the outset as a two-volume set in which the Gospel story would be balanced and continued with the stories of the apostles."[44] The stimulus for change was her observation that the first four chapters of Luke's Gospel exhibit elements of strong narrative coherence with the ending of Acts and that these two units may be thought of as a narrative frame providing a prologue and epilogue for the two-volume work. The narrative coherence is largely retrospective, in that (ideal) readers approach the text with some tacit knowledge of the ending of the story and are able to interpret it in light of that knowledge. Consequently Alexander thinks that the prologue to Luke and the ending of Acts possess a unity evident only in a "paratextual framework," the significance of which appears in rereading both volumes.[45]

In a study on the Holy Spirit in Luke-Acts, Ju Hur says that, while he is inclined toward unity, he concedes that it "cannot be regarded as an absolute assumption." A solution to the issue derives from one's preunderstanding and is validated by one's method and subject matter. As a result Hur feels that one needs to read Luke-Acts "flexibly."[46] Despite this caution Hur differs from Parsons's postulation, based on Parsons's distinction between narrative and discourse, of two different narrators of the Gospel and Acts. In Hur's opinion the narrator consistently applies a "divine frame of reference" (or what I would call a symbolic universe) pertaining to angels, visions, Scripture, and the activity of the Spirit, and this frame of reference reinforces the narrative reliability of the narrator precisely at the level of discourse.[47] In this way Hur is able to retain unity at the level of both narrative *and* discourse.

Ben Witherington acknowledges the work of Parsons and Pervo,[48] and he readily admits both that Luke can indeed stand on its own and that Luke 24 does bring some sort of closure to the Gospel. The questions, though, are: was Acts meant to be read with the first book in mind, and did Luke pen his Gospel with a sequel in mind?[49] In addition, Witherington writes, "We must be careful when we use the terminology *Luke-Acts* to make clear what sort *of unity* we have in mind by this term. Does the term *Luke-Acts* refer to authorial or compositional or narrative or generic or theological or thematic unity, or several of these sorts of unity all at once?"[50] Nevertheless Witherington is compelled by the similar literary patterns to opt for the unity of Luke-Acts. He bases this especially on the observation that many of the inclusions (like the promise of being a light to the Gentiles in Luke 2:32 and 3:6) and exclusions (like food and purity from Mark 7:1–23) in the Gospel of Luke are best explained on the grounds that Luke intended a second volume. He goes on to state: "In short, the first volume was likely written with at least one eye already on the sequel. In other words, there is indeed some sort of compositional unity to Luke-Acts, and this raises the question about the generic unity of the two volumes."[51] Witherington suggests that the preface in Luke 1:1–4 includes both Luke and Acts, and that Luke has composed a two-volume historiographical work in continuous narrative about the remarkable phenomenon of early Christianity.[52]

More sympathetic to Parsons and Pervo is F. Scott Spencer. On the one hand Spencer acknowledges a concrete relationship between the two works, given the correlation between the missionary agenda of the risen-ascended Lukan Jesus in Luke 24 and the global proclamation intended in Acts 1. There is also a connection through the characterization of the witnesses in Acts that matches the profile of the Lukan Jesus. This observation stands in "favor of Acts as a direct extension of the Gospel."[53] On the other hand Spencer finds reasons for "loosening the hyphen" in Luke-Acts since: (1) we have no record of conjoining the works in canonical lists; (2) each work stands on its own as a complete narrative; and (3) there are differences between the Lukan Jesus and the character of the Acts missionaries. Spencer's final thought, then, is: "While the two Lukan volumes may be profitably correlated, specific links must be demonstrated rather than assumed and distinctive nuances appreciated rather than flattened."[54]

Jacob Jervell believes that a lapse of some years transpired between the composition of Luke and Acts. The new preface in Acts 1:1–2 was necessary precisely because of such a lapse, and similar recapitulating prefaces were common in works that were drawn together (for example, Josephus, *Against Apion* 1.1. with the reference to *Antiquities).* Accordingly: "The Gospel and Acts are two works of the same author, and not two parts of one book. They are also not written as one book, but between the two works Luke has allowed some years to elapse." Even if one consents to a similar authorship for both works that does not establish a narrative unity, "because we have here to do with two different kinds of literature and because Acts was written several years later than the Gospel, so that the preface of Luke 1:1–4 only applies to the Gospel."[55]

In his *New Testament Christology,* Frank J. Matera demurs from the modern conception of a narrative unity that binds Luke-Acts together. Matera notes that Luke extends the story of Jesus by recounting the role of the risen Lord in the life of the church, but quickly adds: "But is there a narrative unity between the Gospel of Luke and the Acts of the Apostles? Can we speak of a single, uninterrupted story, or do these writings represent different stories: the story of Jesus *and the* story of his church?"[56] Matera states that in Acts Luke is resuming the narrative begun in the Gospels. He also asks: "But is it the same story? The answer to this question is not so clear." On the one hand he finds a narrative unity apparent in so far as Acts completes the themes that the Gospel introduces. The risen Lord instructs his disciples to remain in Jerusalem until they have received the Holy Spirit (Luke 24:49), and this request is fulfilled at the day of Pentecost (Acts 2:1–12). Alternatively Luke and Acts each has a literary integrity of its own. The Gospel concludes with Jesus' ascension on Easter (Luke 24:50–53), yet Acts begins with a new account of the ascension forty days after the resurrection (Acts 1:6–11). One ascension account brings literary closure, while the other inaugurates a whole new narrative. According to Matera, Luke and Acts each has its own story, and their narrative unity exists only insofar as the person of Jesus is the indispensable character of both writings.[57] He thus writes: "In Luke-Acts we are dealing with two stories that have a narrative unity rooted in the person of Jesus. One relates the ministry, death, resurrection, and ascension of the earthly Jesus; the other recounts the church's witness to the risen Lord."[58]

Todd C. Penner eschews many of the efforts made to demonstrate the overall unity of Luke-Acts, especially the volumes *The Unity of Luke-Acts* edited by Joseph Verheyden[59] and *Witness to the Gospel: The Theology of Acts* edited by I. Howard Marshall and David Peterson.[60] He alleges that both volumes "offer a predominantly theologized (i.e. Christian) understanding and assessment of Lukan discourse."[61] He takes issue with the volume edited by Verheyden in particular, on the grounds that it attempts to prove the unity of authorship, purpose, and theological conception, and to demonstrate clear links between Luke and Acts. Penner appears to be suspicious of anyone pursuing unity, since this may constitute a tacit attempt to engage in biblical apologetics.[62]

Parsons and Pervo made a bold move in questioning such an ingrained assumption in Lukan scholarship. They correctly pointed out that the unity of Luke-Acts is something that has been more or less assumed rather than demonstrated and that the evidence garnered in support of unity is somewhat more ambiguous than many have realized. Even so, despite warranting a frequent mention in the footnotes of scholarly monographs, they have not convinced the majority of Lukan scholars and have not overturned the consensus. Verheyden could state at the end of the 1990s that the "majority of scholars still holds to the view that Luke intended to write a work that covered both the story of Jesus and that of his disciples, and that he has composed this work in such a way that what is said about the history of Jesus contains all that which was regarded as important for continuing that history by the community that had committed itself to Jesus. This means that the Gospel is the introduction to Acts and the basis upon which Acts is built, but also that the Gospel, in a sense, needs Acts and calls for the continuation in which its message is realized in the world, and consequently that Luke and Acts together constitute one work."[63]

Why, then, have Parsons and Pervo failed to win a wide following? This is not because of a failure to point out the problems and complexities posed by unity. Rather it is due to the success of Cadbury, and others such as Tannehill, who have constructed arguments that are both persuasive on the textual level and that resonate with the current interests of scholarship in literary-critical studies. If the unity of Luke-Acts is to be challenged further, that challenge must come from another quarter of scholarship.

FINDING LUKE AND ACTS IN THE SECOND CENTURY

Pervo pointed out that the essential unity of Luke-Acts was generally not observed in early Christian history. In his words "Luke-Acts is essentially without support from the ancient manuscripts and commentary traditions."[64] This same observation is meticulously developed in a significant contribution to the debate by Andrew Gregory in a volume on the reception of Luke-Acts in the second century.[65] Gregory investigates to what degree Luke and Acts were known in the period prior to Irenaeus. When it comes to the question of unity, Gregory writes:

> Behind this question lies the modern assumption that *Luke* and *Acts* are two volumes of one longer work, each of which was written by the same author. Therefore it is important to realise that *Luke-Acts* as an object of study, two separate texts linked by a hyphen, is in fact a modern construct. Of course this is not to deny that Luke wrote two successive volumes—and perhaps even set out to write two successive volumes—each of which largely coheres with and informs the other. Rather, it is simply to note that for much of their subsequent history Luke's two volumes have not been read in this way and, consequently, that it is not possible to assume that the knowledge and use of one of these texts by a subsequent reader or text need in itself require or indeed make probable the knowledge and use of the other. Nor do we know if ever they circulated together in this period, for once Luke released each volume he would have had no control over its circulation and copying.[66]

With the exception of Irenaeus and the Muratorian Fragment there is no evidence that Luke and Acts were read together, nor does it appear that it was typical to do so in the period either before or after Irenaeus. Gregory finds no grounds for maintaining use of Luke alongside Acts by Marcion, Tatian, Justin, and the longer ending of Mark.[67] Gregory does not deny that Luke may have written his Gospel and Acts as part of one work, but he makes the point that the way we understand the textual phenomenon of Luke and Acts must take into account its reception and collection in the second century. More recently Gregory has stated: "Luke as it is known to modern readers is available only as it has been transmitted within the fourfold gospel: not as a text that circulated independently by itself or even as part of a two-volume work by one author. It may be only an accident of history that we have no direct access to Luke in any form earlier than the form in which it was transmitted as part of the fourfold gospel—there is no reason to believe that earlier 'stand alone' copies were suppressed—but the point remains that Luke as it has been transmitted to us has been transmitted only as part of a construct of the second-century church."[68]

There have been several responses to Gregory's monograph, both positive and negative.[69] C. Kavin Rowe thinks that Gregory has not taken the evidence far enough, and he contests whether Irenaeus and the Muratorian Fragment actually testify to Luke-Acts being read as one literary unit.[70] While Irenaeus coordinates the end of Luke with the beginning of Acts, this may have been perceived by Irenaeus as a form of "chain-link" with no literary intent to read the volumes in light of each other. Irenaeus's awareness of a common authorship is not the same as admitting a particular practice of reading the two works in unison. Acts was read alongside the *Tetraevangelium,* not just alongside the Gospel of Luke. Likewise the Muratorian Fragment's only claim is to a common authorship for Luke and Acts, not a decisive reading strategy for both works.[71]

Moving from the second century to the text of Acts itself, Rowe examines the preface of Acts 1:1–2 in light of this conclusion: (1) Luke alludes to his earlier book with the presumption that understanding its contents does not depend on Acts, meaning that Luke's Gospel is self-sufficient; (2) the Acts preface presupposes a chronological separation between the two works; (3) the assumption of an early division of Luke from Acts must be rejected, since this assumption derives exclusively from the preface of Acts, and such recapitulatory prefaces in antiquity did not require a close literary unity with other volumes;[72] and (4) Luke and Acts were never placed beside each other in any ancient manuscript.[73] Rowe argues that we should not confuse literary unity with historical unity, and he notes: "it is doubtlessly true on a literary level that Luke-Acts *can* 'be read as a *single* story.' The problem is that historically it hardly ever—if ever—was."[74]

Luke Timothy Johnson, who has written extensively on Luke-Acts, rigorously opposes Rowe's argument. He suggests that "the fact that there is no evidence that Luke-Acts was received or read as a literary unity in late second-century compositions does not answer the question of how the first readers might have read and understood Luke's writing."[75]

Johnson contends, first, that we have little evidence for how any New Testament document was read in the second century, and the fact that Luke-Acts was not read as a unified composition is no more surprising than it is for any other New Testament writing. In addition the second-century writers were approaching the New Testament compositions as a collection of authoritative writings read in the context of the church, something that was not possible for the original audiences. The gap between the composition of Luke-Acts and its later reception is not only temporal but also situational. The original audience(s) of Luke-Acts would have heard it as a discrete literary composition and not merely as part of a scriptural collection. It is the task of historical-critical exegesis then to fill in that gap by trying to identify the author's "rhetorical intentionality."[76] Furthermore Johnson denies Rowe any leverage from the prologue in Acts 1:1–2, since the brevity of the prologue implies familiarity with the preceding volume and not necessarily a significant passage of time elapsing between the composition of the two documents. Finally Johnson is willing to admit the value of reading Acts together with the Epistles and of reading Luke alongside the other Gospels, and likewise he grants that the various criticisms (source, redaction, tradition, reception) all have their place. Even so, in his opinion a literary-critical perspective is most useful for illuminating Luke's "literary and theological voice." Reception history has its limitations, and reading texts alongside patristic authors is not a substitute for reading the texts "within the frame of first-century social reality and rhetoric."[77]

Markus Bockmuehl, in contrast to Johnson, is relatively positive about Gregory and Rowe's reception-history approach. Bockmuehl maintains that "the critical construct that sees these two biblical works as an indissoluble literary integrity runs against the historical reality that no known ancient readers copied, read or interpreted them together. The evangelist may have intended his two-volume work to be read as one, but the consistent practice of all known ancient readers was to read the first volume as integral to the fourfold Gospel and the second as the story of the apostolic church."[78]

Bockmuehl points out that in the manuscript collections where Acts is found, it introduces the *Apóstolos* (Catholic Epistles) or occasionally the Pauline corpus, but never runs as a sequel to Luke and very rarely to the Gospels (the exceptions perhaps being P^{45} and P^{53}).[79] Bockmuehl then raises four separate issues. (1) He asks whether the continued division between "authorial intent" and "actual use" is helpful. It is not obvious that Luke intended to write a two-volume work that was designed to be read as an integral whole. In Bockmuehl's view, deliberate pointers forward to Acts are only general. (2) He proposes that reception history may be even more pertinent to the question of authorial intention than Rowe realizes. Reception history may not give us insight into the mind of the author, but it does provide a range of plausible meanings for the original intention of texts. (3) Bockmuehl is also decidedly agnostic about the value of Luke-Acts in illuminating a Lukan community. If there was a community which read Luke in tandem with Acts, we have no trace of its existence. (4) Whatever Luke's historical intention, Luke became part of the fourfold Gospel, and Acts an introduction to the *Apóstolos.* Hence "scholarly investigation of Acts may be enriched by affirming both the literary and historical insight, each in its place."[80]

It is important to note that, in contrast to Parsons and Pervo, neither Gregory nor Rowe nor Bockmuehl denies a literary unity between Luke and Acts.[81] In many respects Gregory's study is entirely compatible with the concerns raised by Johnson, since Gregory does not forfeit interest in the "rhetorical intentionality" of Luke's composition as it develops across both volumes.[82] The contention of Rowe and Bockmuehl, building on the work of Gregory, is that the history of reception, canonical placement, and textual transmission of Luke and Acts provide little evidence, if any, for the unity of the two volumes in early Christianity. They maintain that the best evidence available indicates that Luke and Acts were largely read independently of each other. The literary unity of Luke-Acts did not translate into the dissemination and interpretation of Luke and Acts together as one integral composition. This in turn requires a reassessment of strategies for reading Luke and Acts, so that the implied readers of literary criticism are juxtaposed with the real readers of the second century.

Thus in the state of research as it currently stands the unity of Luke-Acts—an embedded assumption of modern scholarship—is now under siege on two fronts: the barrage from Parsons and Pervo with their authorial, canonical, generic, narrative, and theological objections; and the reception-history perspective, particularly as advanced by Rowe and Bockmuehl. Importantly the marauding scholarly forces have trained their sights on the most critical and vulnerable point of the Luke-Acts hypothesis: the hyphen. Whether the "Luke-Acts" hypothesis can repel this pincer movement is yet to be seen. Nevertheless the time is ripe for a volume on the "Re-making of Luke-Acts," the intention of which might be either to pursue the thesis of Parsons and Pervo to its logical conclusion, or alternatively to present a renewed and revised defense of Cadbury's hypothesis.

I suggest that the battleground in future studies will be: (1) the extent to which each Lukan prologue presupposes the act of reading the other volume as a prequel or sequel; (2) the genres of Luke and Acts, including their differences and capacity to sustain an overarching purpose; (3) the validity of the suggested interconnections between Luke and Acts; (4) the ending of Luke's Gospel and its utility to mark a transition to Acts; (5) the meaning of unity and the different types of unity that can exist—this debate would lend itself most naturally to a rigorous criticism of certain conceptions of unity and the development of criteria by which unity can be determined; (6) the value of second- and third-century authors for determining first-century authorial intention and audience reception; and finally (7) further research into the claim that Luke and Acts became separated relatively early in the dissemination of both works.

WHAT IS AT STAKE IN THE RECENT DISCUSSION?

What differences does the unity or lack of unity between Luke and Acts make for interpretation?[83] In this last section I wish to identify the consequences of this debate for Lukan studies and to suggest several factors that warrant further consideration.

1. *The interpretation of Luke and Acts will depend on with what other literature they are read.* Should Luke and Acts be read together as one unit in a mutually interpretive two-part treatise on Jesus and the church? Or should we read Luke canonically, that is, beside the other Gospels, and read Acts alongside the Epistles? For instance is the Lukan eschatological discourse (Luke 21:5–36) better understood in juxtaposition to the Markan and Matthaean versions (Mark 13; Matthew 24), or does it look ahead to Acts and provide the beginning of the clash between the Kingdom of God and the Roman Empire, and does the discourse look toward the fulfillment of the times of the Gentiles in the post-Pentecost era (Luke 21:24)? This debate opens up several vistas of study, which historical and

literary critics must now ponder—namely, the influence of Luke and Acts on the canon,[84] as well as the benefits of reading these documents canonically.[85]

2. *The prologue of Luke's Gospel will be interpreted differently according to alternative conceptions of the relationship between Luke and Acts.* Up for grabs is the scope of the prologue in Luke's Gospel and whether it introduces the Gospel alone or Luke-Acts as a whole. Taken as a preface to Luke-Acts the prologue would imply that the traditions handed down by witnesses and servants of the word included the Jesus tradition and traditions about the early church—and also that Luke's claim to careful composition extends to Acts. The things that Theophilus (as person or symbol) has been taught would have included some elements of the post-Easter story as well.

3. *The genre of Luke and Acts postulated by scholars is informed in some way by what is made of their literary relationship.* If they are read as independent documents then it is possible to view Luke as a *bios* or a *vita* and Acts as a historical monograph, historical fiction, or historical romance; and the difference in genre and form poses no such problem. But when Luke and Acts are integrated into a single literary composition the differences in genre can become problematic and raise a number of questions. Do we have in Luke-Acts one work with two genres, a two-part "historical monograph,"[86] a "succession narrative,"[87] a "scientific treatise,"[88] or a *sui generis* for the "beginnings of Christianity."[89] Those who advocate the unity of Luke-Acts have to solve the genre question that Parsons and Pervo have posed.[90]

4. *Any attempt to devise a structure of Luke and Acts will again be influenced by prior convictions about the relationship and the type of relationship between them.* If one holds to a narrative and theological unity of Luke-Acts then one may attempt to identify correspondences in content and sequence, thematic development, theological outlook, and shared rhetorical features that imply an overarching literary plan and purpose. That stands in contrast to independent structures for Luke and Acts as separate volumes.

5. *Any conclusion made regarding the unity or disunity of Luke and Acts invariably affects how Luke's overarching literary and theological purposes are understood.* The two volumes can be read as a biography of a religious leader and a separate history of a religious movement loosely related around a shared subject matter. Alternatively a deliberate unity means that Luke intended to narrate the geographical expansion of the Christians from Bethlehem to Rome and to forge tangible links between Israel, Jesus, and the early church. Such a project situates the new religious movement in the wider geographical and political context of the Roman Empire and makes the church the fulfillment of God's promises to Israel. But scholars need to be conscious of the fact that many of the purposes proposed for Luke-Acts are contingent on a prior assumption of literary and theological

unity. If that assumption is either stripped away or undermined, then the apparent purpose or thematic cohesion of Luke-Acts becomes open to question.[91] Likewise the argument that the Gospel and Acts were composed for two completely different reasons can become equally artificial if it can be effectively shown that the volumes do exhibit an intentional form of unity on some horizon or other. This creates a methodological conundrum as to whether or not one should start with an affirmation of unity and then pursue the purpose of Luke-Acts, or pursue the purpose(s) of Luke and Acts without any prior commitment to unity.[92]

6. *By addressing the issue of the unity of Luke and Acts we are forced to evaluate a variety of methodological approaches to New Testament study.* How does one integrate findings from literary criticism, canonical approaches, and reception history into a study of the New Testament and employ those insights in order to solve contentious topics such as the unity of Luke-Acts? Perhaps a solution to the unity of Luke-Acts will depend in part upon privileging a single methodology, be it literary criticism or reception history. The questions being asked here demand that we determine the value, limits, and weight of these methodologies. For example, in reception history to what extent do we allow the second- and third-century authors to inform us of the authorial intention, initial reception, and interpretation of a first-century writing? How close is Irenaeus to the mind of Luke; and can the absence of evidence that Luke and Acts were read together be taken as the evidence of absence? How much continuity should we posit between first-century and second-century readings of these documents? Alternatively how much of the purported unity of Luke-Acts exists only in the mind of the beholder? I think that many of the apparent scriptural echoes and thematic connections identified between the two volumes are evident only to those who read Luke-Acts through a computerized search engine. Perhaps more caution is warranted in efforts to reconstruct an *intentional unity* of the author and the *perceived unity* evident to the first readers of Luke-Acts. Finally everyone agrees that a holistic and broad methodological approach is in order, but that leads us no further when these methodologies conflict in their conclusions. Consequently the limitations, value, and weight assigned to these methodologies need to be more clearly assessed.

7. *The relationship between Luke and Acts will determine one's approach to New Testament theology.* In the discourse of New Testament theology judgments on the unity of Luke-Acts determine whether one undertakes a "theology of Luke" and a separate "theology of Acts" or engages in a "theology of Luke-Acts."[93] If one opts for the Luke-Acts path, it raises the issue of demonstrating an authorial, narrative, and theological unity and also requires (something very rarely touched on in my view) a description of the exact nature of the unity between the two volumes and a justification of its hermeneutical significance.

NOTES

An earlier form of this paper was delivered to the joint Acts and Synoptics seminar at the British New Testament Conference in Sheffield, September 2006. I am grateful to C. Kavin Rowe, Andrew F. Gregory, Rick Strelan, I. Howard Marshall, Mikael C. Parsons, and Steve Walton for feedback in preparing this version of the essay.

1. For a survey of the few dissenters, see I. Howard Marshall, "Acts and the 'Former Treatise,'" in *The Book of Acts in its First Century Setting: Volume 1—Ancient Literary Setting* (ed. Bruce W. Winter and Andrew D. Clark; Carlisle, U.K.: Paternoster, 1993), 165–69.

2. Robert C. Tannehill, *The Narrative Unity of Luke-Acts: A Literary Interpretation* (2 vols.; Minneapolis: Fortress, 1986, 1990), and "The Story of Israel within the Lukan Narrative," in *Jesus and the Heritage of Israel: Luke's Narrative Claim upon Israel's Legacy* (ed. David P. Moessner; Harrisburg.: Trinity Press, 1999), 325–39; and more recently Paul Borgman, *The Way According to Luke: Hearing the Whole Story of Luke-Acts* (Grand Rapids, Mich.: Eerdmans, 2006).

3. Mikeal C. Parsons and Richard I. Pervo, *Rethinking the Unity of Luke and Acts* (Minneapolis: Fortress, 1993); cf. earlier Mikeal C. Parsons, "The Unity of Lukan Writings: Rethinking the *Opinio Communis,*" in *Steadfast Purpose: Essays on Acts in Honor of Henry Jackson Flanders* (ed. N. H. Keathley; Waco, Tex.: Baylor University Press, 1990), 29–53.

4. Parsons and Pervo, *Rethinking,* 89.

5. Andrew F. Gregory, *The Reception of Luke and Acts in the Period before Irenaeus: Looking for Luke in the Second Century* (WUNT 2/169; Tübingen: Mohr Siebeck, 2003).

6. C. Kavin Rowe, "History, Hermeneutics, and the Unity of Luke-Acts," in this volume, 43–65 (first published in *JSNT* 28/2 [2005]: 131–57). Subsequent references are to this essay as it appears in this volume.

7. For a more global survey of the debate reaching back to Cadbury, see Joel B. Green and Michael C. McKeever, eds., *Luke-Acts and New Testament Historiography* (IBR Bibliographies 8; Grand Rapids.: Baker, 1994), 33–39, and Joseph Verheyden, "The Unity of Luke-Acts. What Are We Up To?" in *The Unity of Luke-Acts* (ed. Joseph Verheyden; BETL 142; Leuven: Leuven University Press, 1999), 3–56; the present study in contrast focuses on more recent strategies for approaching the unity of Luke-Acts since the publication of the volume by Parsons and Pervo.

8. Parsons and Pervo, *Rethinking,* 18.

9. Cf., for example, Manfred Korn, *Die Geschichte Jesu in veränderter Zeit: Studien zur bleibenden Bedeutung Jesu im Lukanischen Doppelwerk* (WUNT 2/51; Tübingen: Mohr Siebeck, 1993); John T. Squires, *The Plan of God in Luke-Acts* (SNTSMS 76; Cambridge: Cambridge University Press, 1993); William H. Shepherd, *The Narrative Function of the Holy Spirit as a Character in Luke-Acts* (SBLDS 147; Atlanta: Scholars, 1994); Jon A. Weatherly, *Jewish Responsibility for the Death of Jesus in Luke-Acts* (JSNTSup 106; Sheffield: Sheffield Academic Press, 1994); Mark L. Strauss, *The Davidic Messiah in Luke-Acts: The Promise and Its Fulfilment in Luke's Christology* (JSNTSup 110; Sheffield: Sheffield Academic Press, 1995); H. Douglas Buckwalter, *The Character and Purpose of Luke's Christology* (SNTSMS 89; Cambridge: Cambridge University Press, 1996); Thomas J. Lane, *Luke and the Gentile Mission: Gospel Anticipates Acts* (New York: Peter Lang, 1996); O. Wesley Allen, *The Death of Herod:*

The Narrative and Theological Function of Retribution in Luke-Acts (SBLDS 158; Atlanta.: Scholars, 1997); Scott Smith Cunningham, *'Through Many Tribulations': The Theology of Persecution in Luke-Acts* (JSNTSup 142; Sheffield: Sheffield Academic Press, 1997); Rebecca I. Denova, *The Things Accomplished Among Us: Prophetic Traditions in the Structural Pattern of Luke-Acts* (JSNTSup 141; Sheffield: Sheffield Academic Press, 1997); Robert M. Price, *The Widow Traditions in Luke-Acts: A Feminist-Critical Scrutiny* (SBLDS 155; Atlanta: Scholars, 1997); S. John Roth, *The Blind, The Lame, and the Poor: Character Types in Luke-Acts* (JSNTSup 144; Sheffield: Sheffield Academic Press, 1997); A. W. Zwiep, *The Ascension of the Messiah in Lukan Christology* (NovTSup 87; Leiden: Brill, 1997); Günter Wasserberg, *Aus Israels Mitte - Heil für die Welt: Eine narrativ-exegetische Studie zur Theologie des Lukas* (BZNW 92; Berlin: Walter de Gruyter, 1998); Marianne Palmer Bonz, *The Past as Legacy: Luke-Acts and Ancient Epic* (Minneapolis: Fortress, 2000); David W. Pao, *Acts and the Isaianic New Exodus* (WUNT 2/130; Tübingen: Mohr Siebeck, 2000); Matthias Wenk, *Community-Forming Power: The Socio-Ethical Role of the Spirit in Luke-Acts* (Sheffield: Sheffield Academic Press, 2000); Richard B. Harms, *Paradigms from Luke-Acts for Multicultural Communities* (New York: Peter Lang, 2001); Ju Hur, *A Dynamic Reading of the Holy Spirit in Luke-Acts* (JSNTSup 211; Sheffield: Sheffield Academic Press, 2001); Edward J. Woods, *The 'Finger of God' and Pneumatology in Luke-Acts* (JSNTSup 205; Sheffield: Sheffield Academic Press, 2001); Christopher N. Mount, *Pauline Christianity: Luke-Acts and the Legacy of Paul* (NovTSup 104; Leiden: Brill, 2002); Guy D. Nave, *The Role and Function of Repentance in Luke-Acts* (Atlanta: Scholars, 2002); Alexandru Neagoe, *The Trial of the Gospel: An Apologetic Reading of Luke's Trial Narratives* (SNTSMS 116; Cambridge: Cambridge University Press, 2002); Todd Klutz, *The Exorcism Stories in Luke-Acts: A Sociostylistic Reading* (SNTSMS 129; Cambridge: Cambridge University Press, 2004); Martin W. Mittelstadt, *The Spirit and Suffering in Luke-Acts: Implications for a Pentecostal Pneumatology* (New York: T & T Clark, 2004); Clare K. Rothschild, *Luke-Acts and the Rhetoric of History: An Investigation of Early Christian Historiography* (WUNT 2/175; Tübingen: Mohr Siebeck, 2004); Kenneth D. Litwak, *Echoes of Scripture in Luke-Acts: Telling the History of God's People Intertextually* (JSNTSup 282; London: T & T Clark, 2005); and Diane G. Chen, *God as Father in Luke-Acts* (New York: Peter Lang, 2006).

10. Pao, *New Exodus,* 19.

11. Marshall, "'Former Treatise.'"

12. Ibid., 171.

13. Ibid., 176.

14. Joel B. Green, *The Theology of Luke* (NTT; Cambridge: Cambridge University Press, 1995); "Internal Repetition in Luke-Acts: Contemporary Narratology and Lucan Historiography," in *History, Literature and Society in the Book of Acts* (ed. Ben Witherington; Cambridge: Cambridge University Press, 1996), 283–99; *The Gospel of Luke* (NICNT; Grand Rapids, Mich.: Eerdmans, 1997); "Acts of the Apostles," in *Dictionary of the Later New Testament and Its Developments* (ed. Ralph P. Martin and Peter H. Davids; Downers Grove, Ill.: InterVarsity Press, 1997), 724.

15. Green, *Gospel of Luke,* 67.

16. Ibid., 47.

17. Ibid., 10.

18. Ibid., 89.

19. Green, "Acts of the Apostles," 12.

20. Ibid., 12–13; Green, "Internal Repetition," 284–89.

21. C. K. Barrett, *Luke the Historian in Recent Study* (London: Epworth, 1961), 53.

22. Ibid., 57.

23. Ibid., 58–60.

24. C. K. Barrett, "The Third Gospel as a Preface to Acts?" in *The Four Gospels 1992: Festschrift Frans Neirynck* (ed. F. Van Segbroek et al.; 3 vols.; BETL 100; Leuven: Leuven University Press, 1992), 2:1451–66.

25. C. K. Barrett, "The First New Testament?" *NovT* 38 (1996): 102; *Acts 15–28* (ICC; London: T & T Clark, 1998), lxviii.

26. Barrett, "First New Testament?"10–34; *Acts 15–28,* lxx.

27. Charles H. Talbert, *Reading Acts: A Literary and Theological Commentary on the Acts of the Apostles* (New York: Crossroads, 1997), 3.

28. David P. Moessner, ed., *Jesus and the Heritage of Israel: Luke's Narrative Claim upon Israel's Legacy* (Harrisburg: Trinity Press, 1999).

29. David P. Moessner and David L. Tiede, "*Two* Books but *One* Story?" in *Jesus and the Heritage of Israel,* 23.

30. Richard I. Pervo, "Israel's Heritage and Claims Upon the Genre(s) of Luke and Acts: The Problems of a History," in *Jesus and the Heritage of Israel,* 127–29.

31. Ibid., 136–37, 142.

32. William Kurz, "Promise and Fulfillment in Hellenistic Jewish Narratives and in Luke and Acts" in *Jesus and the Heritage of Israel,* 147–70.

33. Gregory E. Sterling, "'Opening the Scriptures': The Legitimation of the Jewish Diaspora and the Early Christian Mission," in *Jesus and the Heritage of Israel,* 215; cf. 217.

34. Charles H. Talbert and J. H. Hayes, "A Theology of Sea Storms in Luke-Acts," in *Jesus and the Heritage of Israel,* 280–83.

35. Tannehill, "Story of Israel," 339.

36. I. Howard Marshall, "'Israel' and the Story of Salvation: One Theme in Two Parts," in *Jesus and the Heritage of Israel,* 340–57.

37. Beverly Roberts Gaventa, *Acts* (ANTC; Nashville: Abingdon, 2003), 52.

38. Ibid., 52–53.

39. François Bovon, *Luke 1: A Commentary on the Gospel of Luke 1:1–9:50* (ed. Helmut Koester; trans. Christine M. Thomas; Hermeneia; Minneapolis: Fortress, 2002), 24.

40. Luke Timothy Johnson, *The Gospel of Luke* (SacPag 3; Collegeville, Minn.: Liturgical Press, 1991), 1; *The Acts of the Apostles* (SacPag 5; Collegeville, Minn.: Liturgical Press, 1992), 1–2, 12–13.

41. Loveday C. A. Alexander, *The Preface to Luke's Gospel: Literary Convention and Social Context in Luke 1.1–4 and Acts 1.1* (SNTSMS 78; Cambridge: Cambridge University Press, 1993), 2 n. 1.

42. Ibid., 146.

43. Loveday C. A. Alexander, "Reading Luke-Acts from Back to Front," in *The Unity of Luke-Acts* (ed. Joseph Verheyden; BETL 142; Leuven: Leuven University Press, 1999), 439.

44. Ibid., 438.

45. Ibid., 440–41.

46. Ju Hur, "The Unity, Genre and Purpose of Luke-Acts Revisited," *Korea Theological Journal* 3 (2000): 87–88 n. 2; *Dynamic Reading,* 227–58.

47. Hur, *Dynamic Reading,* 91–92 n. 12.

48. Ben Witherington, *The Acts of the Apostles: A Socio-Rhetorical Commentary* (Grand Rapids, Mich.: Eerdmans, 1998), 5 nn. 12–13,

49. Ibid., 4–5.

50. Ibid., 5.

51. Ibid., 8.

52. Ibid., 21.

53. F. Scott Spencer, *Acts* (Sheffield: Sheffield Academic Press, 1997), 15.

54. Ibid., 15.

55. Jacob Jervell, *Die Apostelgeschichte* (KEK 17; Göttingen: Vandenhoeck & Ruprecht, 1998), 57 n. 23. ("Das Evangelium und die Apostelgeschichte sind also zwei Werke von demselben Verfasser, und nicht zwei Teile eines Buches. Sie sind auch nicht als ein Buch geschrieben, sondern zwischen den beiden Werken des Lukas vergingen offenbar einige Jahre . . . weil wir mit zwei verschiedenen Literaturarten zu tun haben und weil die Apg mehrere Jahre später als das Evangelium geschrieben worden ist, so dass das Vorwort Lk 1,1–4 nur für das Evangelium gilt." My thanks to Dr. Jim West for checking my translation.)

56. Frank J. Matera, *New Testament Christology* (Louisville.: Westminster John Knox, 1999), 49.

57. Ibid., 50.

58. Ibid., 50–51.

59. Joseph Verheyden, ed., *The Unity of Luke-Acts* (BETL 142; Leuven: Leuven University Press, 1999), 3–56.

60. I. Howard Marshall and David Peterson, eds., *Witness to the Gospel: The Theology of Acts* (Grand Rapids, Mich.: Eerdmans, 1998).

61. Todd C. Penner, "Contextualizing Acts," in *Contextualizing Acts: Lukan Narrative and Greco-Roman Discourse* (ed. Todd C. Penner and Caroline Vander Stichele; SBLSS 20; Leiden: Brill, 2004), 9 n. 31.

62. Ibid., 8–9.

63. Verheyden, "The Unity," 56.

64. Pervo, "Israel's Heritage," 128.

65. Gregory, *Reception.* Analogous to Gregory's approach is that of Christine M. Thomas, who proposes the use of ancient reception history and investigation into the implied readers of ancient documents for studying the relationship between fact and fiction in ancient historiography. Thomas's approach shows that reception history is potentially applicable to a whole range of historical, literary, and hermeneutical issues pertaining to Luke and Acts (*The* Acts of Peter, *Gospel Literature, and the Ancient Novel: Rewriting the Past* [New York: Oxford University Press, 2003], 102). On textual criticism and reception history see also Barbara Aland, "Welche Rolle spielen Textkritik und Textgeschichte für das Verständnis des Neuen Testaments? Frühe Leserperspektiven," *NTS* 52 (2006): 303–18.

66. Gregory, *Reception,* 2.

67. Ibid., 352.

68. Andrew F. Gregory, "Looking for Luke in the Second Century: A Dialogue with François Bovon," in *Reading Luke: Interpretation, Reflection, Formation* (ed. Craig Bartholomew, Joel B. Green, and Anthony C. Thiselton; Scripture and Hermeneutics; Carlisle, U.K.: Paternoster, 2005), 411.

69. Contrast the reviews of James Carleton Paget (review of Andrew F. Gregory, *The Reception of Luke and Acts in the Period before Irenaeus, JEH* 55/4 [2004]: 742–44), and J. K. Elliott (review of Gregory, *Reception, NovT* 48/1 [2006]: 201–2), with I. Howard Marshall (review of Gregory, *Reception, SJT* 59/1 [2006]: 121–24).

70. Rowe, "History, Hermeneutics."

71. Ibid., 43–46.

72. Cf. on this point Parsons and Pervo, *Rethinking,* 42.

73. Rowe, "History, Hermeneutics," 46–48.

74. Ibid., 148.

75. Luke Timothy Johnson, "Literary Criticism of Luke-Acts: Is Reception-History Pertinent?" in this volume, p. 66 (first published in *JSNT* 28/2 [2005]: 159). Subsequent references are to this essay as it appears in this volume.

76. Ibid., 67.

77. Ibid., 68.

78. Markus Bockmuehl, "Why Not Let Acts Be Acts? In Conversation with C. Kavin Rowe," in this volume p. 70 (first published in *JSNT* 28/2 [2005]: 163). Subsequent references are to this essay as it appears in this volume.

79. Ibid., 70. In fact P^{53} contains Matt. 26:29–40 and Acts 9:33–10.1, which provides empirical evidence for Matthew-Acts as opposed to Luke-Acts. Of course due to the incompleteness of the manuscript one cannot be certain what was or was not part of the original text (see further Rowe, "History, Hermeneutics," 43–65.)

80. Bockmuehl, "Why Not Let Acts Be Acts?" 72.

81. See Gregory, *The Reception of Luke and Acts,* 2; Rowe, "History, Hermeneutics," 43, 50–51, 54–55; Bockmuehl, "Why Not Let Acts Be Acts?" 70.

82. Johnson, "Literary Criticism," 67.

83. Cf. Marshall, "Acts and the 'Former Treatise,'" 171–72, 177–82; Green, "Acts of the Apostles," 13; Moessner and Tiede, "*Two* Books but *One* Story?" 3; Rowe, "History, Hermeneutics," 48–51.

84. Cf. David E. Smith, *The Canonical Function of Acts: A Comparative Analysis* (Collegeville, Minn.: Liturgical Press, 2002).

85. Cf. Robert W. Wall, "The Acts of the Apostles," in *New Interpreter's Bible* (ed. Leander E. Keck; 12 vols.; Nashville: Abingdon, 2002), 10:26–32. See also his "A Canonical Approach to the Unity of Acts and Luke's Gospel" in this volume, 172–91.

86. David E. Aune, *The New Testament in Its Literary Environment* (LEC 8; Philadelphia: Westminster Press, 1987).

87. Charles H. Talbert, *Literary Patterns, Theological Themes and the Genre of Luke-Acts* (SBLMS 20; Missoula, Mont.: Scholars Press, 1974).

88. Alexander, *The Preface to Luke's Gospel.*

89. Marshall, "Acts and the 'Former Treatise,'" 180.

90. See recently Pervo, "Israel's Heritage," and Thomas E. Phillips, "The Genre of Acts: Moving Towards a Consensus," *CBR* 4 (2006): 365–96.

91. Cf. Rowe, "History, Hermeneutics," 50–51.

92. Cf. Verheyden, "The Unity," 8.

93. See on Luke, Green, *The Theology of Luke;* Christopher M. Tuckett, *Luke* (NTG; Sheffield: Sheffield Academic Press, 1996); on Acts, J. C. O'Neill, *The Theology of Acts in Its Historical Setting* (2d ed.; London: SPCK, 1970); I. Howard Marshall, *The Acts of the Apostles* (NTG; Sheffield: Sheffield Academic Press, 1992); Jacob Jervell, *Theology of the Acts of the Apostles* (Cambridge: Cambridge University Press, 1996); Marshall and Peterson, *Witness to the Gospel;* and on Luke-Acts, Hans Conzelmann, *The Theology of Saint Luke* (trans. Geoffrey Buswell; London: Faber & Faber, 1961); I. Howard Marshall, *Luke: Historian and Theologian* (3d ed.; Exeter: Paternoster, 1988) and *New Testament Theology: Many Witnesses, One Gospel* (Downers Grove, Ill.: InterVarsity Press, 2004); Frank Thielman, *Theology of the New Testament: A Canonical and Synthetic Approach* (Grand Rapids: Zondervan, 2005).

FOURTEEN YEARS AFTER

Revisiting *Rethinking the Unity of Luke and Acts*

Richard I. Pervo

One supposes that all scholarly authors experience some disappointment with the reception of their books. In the case of *Rethinking the Unity of Luke and Acts,*[1] disappointment has not been in the form of the failure of Hollywood to offer millions for the movie rights but of critics to take seriously the nature of the book as probing rather than probative, as an attempt to raise questions rather than to provide firm answers.[2] It is surprising that, in the face of such statements as "We therefore deemed it timely to subject [Cadbury's] idea to a thorough scrutiny, not with the intention of either canonizing or deposing the prevalent view, but of providing it with suitable nuance," the project has sometimes been described as an assault upon the very notion of unity. The title was not, after all, *Rejecting the Unity of Luke and Acts* but *Rethinking the Unity of Luke and Acts.* Its object was to transform "the unity of Luke-Acts" from a dogma into a hypothesis. If hypotheses are the currency of scholarship, dogmas are protective tariff barriers.

I. Howard Marshall grasped our purpose: Parsons and Pervo, he writes, "have rightly challenged scholars to examine the basis for what was in danger of becoming an unquestioned and unexamined assumption." He continues: "Nevertheless, it is safe to say that their challenge has probably led to a stronger, because better defended, case for the unity of Luke-Acts." If correct, that judgment would mean that our little book was a success. Marshall adds this qualification: "That case has been made largely on *literary* grounds."[3] The qualification is important and will receive further attention.

Pervo, for one, thinks that the majority of scholars have continued to assume, rather than argue for, unity.[4] Insofar as claims for unity are based upon broad literary grounds, they have limited relevance to the questions posed in *Rethinking the Unity of Luke and Acts,* for Parsons and Pervo did not deny this connection and relationship.[5] The suggestion that the hyphen "be spelled, at least now and then, by a far from superfluous 'and'" is not a demand for disjunction.[6] The merits of reading the two books together are patent.[7] *Rethinking the Unity of Luke and*

Acts did not attempt to condemn such projects. It did, however, seek to refine sweeping pronouncements.

The presupposition of *Rethinking the Unity of Luke and Acts* was that studies of Luke and Acts must both account for their similarities and explain their differences. The nearly seven-decade dominance of the former had made it difficult to give serious attention to the latter. Eight full decades after Henry J. Cadbury's *The Making of Luke-Acts* the situation has not changed, despite considerable advances in narrative method, theological analysis, and the study of ancient genres.[8] To those three areas Parsons and Pervo directed their probes.

The outstanding question, fourteen years later, is whether "Luke-Acts" is a modern *discovery* or a modern *invention.* Literary critics dominate the scene today. If at one time literary critics complained about the privileged position of redaction criticism,[9] today one might ask whether it is appropriate to assign that privilege to literary criticism.[10] The enthymeme, implicit or explicit, is that since literary analysis validates the unity of Luke and Acts, it has thereby revealed the author's intention. Literary criticism, in distinction from historical criticism, is normally suspicious of the "intentional fallacy," focusing not upon what authors might have thought but what they *wrote.* Analysis of a work's structure, for example, may or may not reveal the actual author's plan. The issue is whether a certain structural plan facilitates (contemporary) understanding and appreciation of the work in question. Historical and literary criticism may coincide to a degree, as when a proposed literary plan is grounded in recognized ancient techniques.[11] Literary criticism thwarts claims that Luke and, in particular, Acts are historically accurate accounts, since, while history may repeat itself, it rarely does so in the artistic manner proposed—often with good reason—for Luke and/or Acts. History, in the form of reception history, constitutes the most recent spanner to be thrust into the wheel of Luke-Acts. Before taking up that matter, it is appropriate to review briefly the status of the issues to which *Rethinking the Unity of Luke and Acts* devoted its central chapters.

THEOLOGICAL UNITY

The chapter on theological unity in *Rethinking the Unity of Luke and Acts* was the most tentative of the several probes and the most misunderstood.[12] Authors must bear some responsibility if their efforts are not understood; in this case the major reason was the presumption of readers that the chapter constituted an attack upon the theological unity of the two books.[13] The chapter began by noting the lack of unity in much theological analysis of Luke and Acts and then explored one line that promised to reflect unity: anthropology.[14] That subject raised the question of how anthropology correlates with christology.[15] The summary closed with the statement that "Pursuit of the theological unity of Luke and Acts remains a good idea."[16]

Fourteen years have reinforced the conviction that Lukan theology is not fully consistent. One can identify overarching themes, such as the continuity of salvation history, the Plan of God, and the role of Providence within that plan, but the details do not fall into neat compartments. Luke was not a systematic theologian.[17] He picked up elements from various sources that were not always carefully integrated into a governing model. Affirmations of the theological unity of Luke/Acts have not terminated efforts to attempt a theology of Acts.[18] One of those affirmations will be reviewed.

Marshall proposed to defend the theological unity of Luke and Acts upon five grounds.[19] The first of these is "proclaimer and proclaimed," a concept he probably picked up from Parsons and Pervo.[20] The Jesus of Luke is the proclaimer of God's reign. In Acts he is the proclaimed, the object of the message rather than its spokesperson. In this sense Acts is more like Paul and his theology than like Luke. For a theologian whose central message was the continuity of salvation history, this tension required resolution. Marshall points first to Luke 4:18–19 as an announcement of who Jesus is.[21] Granting this far from explicit identification, the proclaimer is a prophet announcing salvation. It is not christological in the sense of "I am the messiah who will bring all this to pass." In Luke 4:41 the demons know that Jesus is "the son of God," but this proclamation of the proclaimer is suppressed. Luke 4:43 describes Jesus as a proclaimer. Luke 5:15 is not relevant to the issue. Luke 5:21 is an unanswered question (also, like 4:41, from opponents) about Jesus' identity. Luke 6:5 is a statement about the authority of the Son of Man. All but Luke 4:18–19 derive from Mark. Marshall's conclusion that "Jesus is the object of his own activity" is not tantamount to an identification of proclaimer and proclaimed.

Two comments: first, Luke solves Bultmann's dichotomy by having Jesus announce his change of role, as it were, in his farewell messages (Luke 24:44–49; cf. 24:13–35; Acts 1:8). The risen one teaches his followers to understand his status and proclaim it as his witnesses. Second, the Jesus of Luke 1:1–2:40 is the object of announcement and proclamation. This was necessitated by circumstances, to be sure, since Jesus was in the womb or an infant, but it points to the particular character of the Infancy Narrative, the theology of which is distinct from that of Acts, which does not characterize him as messiah/savior from birth. Even the most ardent proponent of the unity of the two books must grant that the christology of Acts differs considerably from that of Luke.

Marshall's next category is "Apostleship and Witness."[22] He notes that *sending* (the verb from which *apostle* derives) is prominent in the Gospel, whereas *witness* is largely restricted to Acts.[23] "Apostles are thus transformed into witnesses." This is more of a distinction than an identification. Marshall stresses the qualifications for apostleship (Acts 1:21–22), but these are not Lukan in origin and play a very limited role in Acts. Paul and Stephen (22:15, 20) are also witnesses. His subsequent pair, *kingdom* and *messiah* (= the message), also reveals different usage.[24] Proclamation about God's reign in Acts is equivalent to preaching about Jesus. None of the thirty-two references to "Kingdom of God" in the Gospel can so be interpreted. The phrase encapsulates the difference between proclaimer and proclaimed. "Disciple and community" is Marshall's next category.[25] Again there is a difference. *Disciple* in Luke has its basic meaning of pupil, whereas in Acts it usually means believer.[26] The final categories "salvation" and "Israel"[27] do exhibit general coherence, but Marshall's evidence is far from overwhelming.

It remains possible to list a number of theological categories on which Luke and Acts are in essential agreement—not to mention categories of general agreement with much of early Christian literature. Another possibility is to identify topics where difference is apparent.[28] The scholarly task is not to prepare one or the other of these lists and announce a conclusion. Both similarities and differences require attention. One example will provide transition. Scholars since Jacques Dupont[29] have noted links between the close of Acts and the beginning of Luke (as well as the opening of Acts). This constitutes a strong plank in the platform of literary unity, yet, as noted above, the christology of Acts ignores the claims of Luke 1–2: Jesus' status is based upon his resurrection and exaltation.

NARRATIVE UNITY

No one to my knowledge has offered a detailed refutation of the chapter on narrative unity in *Rethinking the Unity of Luke and Acts.*[30] This probe investigated narrative at a range of levels, including fine points of style, technical literary critical issues, differences of form, and technique.[31] Martin Dibelius's recognition that the form-critical methods that yielded fruitful results in the study of the Synoptic Gospels had limited applicability to Acts led him to inaugurate, in 1923, a literary approach to Acts that has profoundly impacted most subsequent studies.[32] Although the sayings of Jesus are often presented as speeches in Luke,[33] the speeches of Acts are more explicitly Greco-Roman in organization and form. If both books use travel as a theme and a symbol, the journeys in Luke are filled with teaching and contain little information about routes, while the journeys in Acts abound in geographical detail and are characterized by adventure.[34] In Acts Luke displays an ability to write lengthy, connected episodes that is rivaled in Luke only by the Passion Narrative—where he was following Mark. At the very least Luke and Acts exhibit different narrative techniques. Even if this is because new occasions teach new duties, it still remains new.

Alternative positions have taken the form of arguing that the Gospel cannot be understood without Acts, and, vice versa, specifically that Luke anticipates Acts.[35] C. K. Barrett's investigation is often cited in this regard. Barrett set himself the task of exploring passages in the Gospel of Luke that could be viewed as presaging Acts and thus indicating the possibility that Luke was written with Acts in mind and therefore showing that a two-volume work was envisaged from the beginning.[36] Barrett was, in fact, dubious about many of the forty-one possibilities that he lists and was quite tentative in his conclusions.[37] The following comments take up those passages about which Barrett was least reserved.

References to the Gentile mission are definitely present in the Gospel, but these do not per se demonstrate that Acts was in mind.[38] Luke was, even if he were an ethnic and once-practicing Jew (a hypothesis not widely endorsed), a *product* of the Gentile mission; therefore, his desire to associate this enterprise with Jesus is scarcely surprising. He found support for that view in both Mark and Q.[39] Matthew is not only aware of the (increasing) presence of Gentiles in the ranks of the Jesus movement; he also reports the risen Lord as commanding his disciples to baptize non-Jews (28:16–20). One does not, however, on the basis of these forecasts conclude that Matthew (as well as Mark, Q, and John) wrote, or intended to write, a second volume. Greater precision is required to show that some of these issues reflect common themes in Luke and Acts. The existence of such themes does not establish a plan. It does show that the books share concepts. The relative frequency of allusions to the Gentile mission in Luke is due, in part, to the widely accepted view that a major purpose of his work was to demonstrate the legitimacy of the Gentile, specifically the Pauline, mission.[40]

The expansion of the Isaiah quote of Mark 1:2 in Luke 3:6 to include 40:5, "all flesh shall see the salvation of God,"[41] is an example of Lukan diligence. For readers of the canonical text this theme was first clearly announced in the *Nunc Dimittis* (2:29–32).[42] Luke 4:16–30 also shows the consistency of Lukan thought and method. Luke 4:28–30 is the prototype of many episodes in Acts: "the Jews" seek to kill the herald of good news, who narrowly escapes. Those who read Luke and Acts in sequence would rightly view this as foreshadowing, but Luke is not the only evangelist who says that the fate of disciples will be that of the master (for example, Mark 13:9–13). Luke's positive view of the family of Jesus[43] is not derived from a plan to write a second volume.[44] The Q parable of the banquet (Luke 14:15–24) is a somewhat allegorized salvation-historical portrait of the Gentile mission, but that understanding is even more pronounced in Matt. 22:1–14.[45] The so-called Prodigal Son (Luke 15:11–32) certainly expresses Luke's views of the story of salvation (Jews: no; Gentiles: yes), but it does not require Acts to be understood.[46]

Luke 22:32 envisions a rehabilitation of Peter. This was not to prepare the way for Acts but to recognize and explain Peter's prominence among the early followers of Jesus, a subject about which Matt. 16:17–19 is much more emphatic.[47] Luke 23:6–12 is interesting, for it sheds light on the history of composition, since Acts 4:25–28 reveals the source of a passage from the Gospel.[48] A difficulty is that neither Luke nor Acts otherwise assign Herod a role in the execution of Jesus. The similarities among the trials of Jesus and those of Stephen and Paul are among the most obvious parallels between the two books. In general they show that Luke was exploiting his Gospel in the composition of Acts. These parallels are among the best indicators that the two books go well together and may be taken to show that Luke wished them to be read in tandem. It is also true that readers of Matthew, Mark, and even John would be able to grasp many of the connections. Luke and Acts portray similar ambivalence about the temple.[49] Note that neither Jesus nor any follower of him, *except* Paul (21:26), is portrayed as engaging in the temple cult. Jesus and the Twelve teach there (Luke 19:47; Acts 5:12).[50]

Eschatology is not a major theme of Acts.[51] In discussing Luke 17:20–22 Barrett asks whether the period "in which men long for the parousia of the Son of Man" might be the "period described in Acts." The answer must be negative, for, although Acts speaks of future judgment (10:42; 17:31), nothing is said about longing for the Parousia. With this proposition Barrett's discussion of Luke 21:7–11 agrees. Likewise Luke 21:12–19 expresses the theme of delay.[52]

The overlap between the end of the Gospel and the beginning of Acts is, despite Barrett,[53] also among the better arguments for some separation of the two books.[54] This doublet constitutes a major disruption in the continuity between the volumes.[55] If it be said that the ascension is both the end of one story and the beginning of another, the conclusion will be that there are, in some sense, two stories. Barrett's negative evidence is important. He asks why Acts does not look back upon Luke, why, in effect, it does not cite the words of Jesus in support of its message.[56] For Luke the Gospel is the message *of* Jesus, while Acts speaks *about* Jesus.[57]

The prefaces to Luke and Acts do not resolve the issue of narrative unity.[58] Those who emphasize unity are likely to find that the preface to Luke embraces Acts also, while scholars who see some distinction are inclined to find otherwise.[59] These prefaces are too brief and too conventional to permit definite conclusions. The circumstances of their composition are not clear. Luke may have completed the canonical Gospel text, composed a preface, then, at some point, written Acts, at which point he composed or revised the preface to Luke, and so forth. Loveday C. A. Alexander, the foremost contemporary student of the prefaces, concludes: "Acts may be read either as 'Volume II' of a unified composition, or as an independent monograph which simply reminds the reader that its narrative is a sequel to the earlier work."[60]

One drawback of the insistence upon unity is the implicit or explicit assumptions that the author planned to write two volumes and completed them in prompt succession. "We speak of Luke's 'Two-volume work' as if it were certain that he intended from the beginning to produce a book in two parts. It may be that he did not. Many an author has written a book which he intended to stand on its own, but then decided, on grounds historical or literary—sometimes economic—to produce a sequel. It may have been so with Luke; at least, we cannot *a priori* exclude the possibility."[61] Nor can the possibility be excluded that a gap of as much as a decade may have intervened between the composition of the two volumes.[62] Luke's mind cannot be read. Only his writings exist.

GENERIC UNITY

"To classify Luke's work seems therefore the beginning of wisdom."[63] The question of generic unity or difference is another impasse.[64] Those who argue that Luke and Acts represent a single literary genre—a perfectly legitimate position—rarely engage in dialogue with those who propose an alternative. The assertion of David E. Aune, "Luke and Acts *must* be affiliated with one genre,"[65] with which the chapter on generic unity in *Rethinking the Unity of Luke and Acts* opens,[66] epitomizes the dogmatic approach. Because Luke and Acts are Luke-Acts, *secundum non datur.* The relevant chapter of *Rethinking the Unity of Luke and Acts* does not seek to resolve the genre question. Its object is to survey the range of proposals, with some attention to the problems of generic unity: "If the argument for generic unity is pressed vigorously, Luke must be regarded as nothing more than half of a work rather than as a Gospel."[67] Critics have not always read that chapter carefully, in part because some decided to view it through the lens of Pervo's *Profit with Delight.*[68]

If Luke alone had survived, generic classification would not be an issue. It would be recognized as a kind of biography. Had Acts alone survived, it would be viewed as some kind of history, be that called a monograph, apologetic historiography, novelistic history, or historical novel.[69] Both books, however, do survive.[70] Literary unity of some type is quite possible even if the works more closely approximate different genres. The question is, granting that much has been gained from hypotheses based upon a single genre as well as hypotheses preferring two genres, which approach will best explain the differences between the books, as well as their similarities.

The judgment of ancient canon lists and full manuscripts of the New Testament is rather clear. "The proposal that Acts became separated from Luke because of the four-gospel collection begs the question, for genre was the grounds for that putative separation."[71] Canon lists and New Testament manuscripts arrange the books by genres. Gospels come first. Acts may follow, then Pauline letters to communities and individuals, the Catholic Epistles, and (if present) Revelation. The position of Acts may vary, but it is distinct from both Gospels and letters. One may deploy cogent arguments for refuting this enduring judgment, but it does deserve more attention than it has received.[72]

RECEPTION HISTORY

The focus of *Rethinking the Unity of Luke and Acts* is upon issues internal to the volumes. Although Parsons and Pervo note that the history of reception (including "canonical unity," a category that, like authorial unity, was deemed closed),[73] they did not have the wisdom or foresight to devote a short chapter to the subject. In a letter to Parsons of February 3, 1995, Pervo wrote: "We did score some points on the question of *Rezeptionsgeschichte* and unity, and there are others." Indeed there are. Andrew F. Gregory launched the current phase of the discussion in his *Reception of Luke and Acts in the Period before Irenaeus.*[74] The title was not intended as a provocation. A dissertation treating the reception of Luke-Acts before Henry J. Cadbury would not be particularly voluminous. Gregory's investigation, which is more noteworthy for its thoroughness and methodological rigor than for the novelty of its conclusions, exposes the gap between the modern construct Luke-Acts and the treatment of Luke and Acts in the early church.[75] If a unified reading of Luke and Acts can be justified by the results, it cannot claim to have proved the author's original intention. Studies of the reception show that, beginning with Irenaeus, authorial unity was recognized.[76]

Irenaeus, unlike Justin, associated the four accepted Gospels with particular authors, notably Luke, whom he identified as the author of Luke and Acts and as an "inseparable companion" of Paul. In support he appeals to Col. 4:14 and 2 Tim. 4:11 (*A. H.* 3.14.1). The earliest argument for Luke the physician and companion of Paul as the writer of Acts, and therefore of the Third Gospel, is arguably based upon deductions from these post-Pauline epistles. No independent or external tradition was evidently available to Irenaeus, who may have been the originator of the claim. For Irenaeus the Lukan authorship of Acts was crucial, for, if the author of Acts also wrote the Gospel, Marcion's interpretation of Luke could not stand. Acts was, in some ways, more central to Irenaeus's heresiological program than was Luke. When Luke and Acts appear on the scene as clearly attested with an identified author, authorial unity is vastly more important than any literary concerns. Luke Timothy Johnson overstates the matter when he says that Irenaeus viewed Acts as elements in a collection of writings read in Christian assemblies.[77] Irenaeus had to argue for the *Tetraevangelium* rather than assume his readers' familiarity with these texts through worship.

The evidence that Marcion rejected Acts is dubious.[78] His use of an extant edition of the Third Gospel is certain. The hypothesis that he knew an edition of Luke that was not associated with Acts is no less probable than the alternative: that he knew both and rejected the latter while editing the former. Acts, an adventurous scholar might propose, could have supplied him with abundant data of how false apostles corrupted the pristine gospel, making him a sort of forerunner of P. Vielhauer.[79] Marcion's silence about Acts does not prove that he never encountered it, but it lends no support to assertions that he knew it.

Dibelius believed that Luke was read in churches, but that Acts was not. He concluded that the text of the Gospel was carefully preserved, but that Acts, which was not read in church, existed only in the "book trade" and thus suffered a different textual fate.[80] His view of the book trade wants correction, and his argument about the careful preservation of the Gospel text is overstated, but he understood that the distinct textual characteristics of Acts were due to a different reception. Since the D-Text (= "Western Text") is already attested by Irenaeus and is arguable for the *Acts of Paul*,[81] the gap[82] between the composition of Acts and evidence of its earliest reception narrows considerably.[83] Pervo has argued in considerable detail that Acts is to be dated ca. 115.[84] The *Acts of Paul* is not much later than ca. 170.[85] The fog between composition and reception is, by these hypotheses, about two generations in length.[86]

Another element that illuminates reception is the compositions of imitations, sequels, and incorporations.[87] Acts of various apostles continued to be written for centuries, eventually merging with hagiography.[88] The authors of the major apocryphal acts of Andrew, John, Peter, Paul, and Thomas, at least, viewed the canonical Acts as a separate book worthy of emulation, supplementation, and improvement.[89] The same may be said of the author of one source of the Pseudo-Clementines.[90] The agglomeration and harmonization of various gospels and their constituent elements began with Matthew and Luke, insofar as is known, and continued, in the second century, with the work of Justin and Tatian.[91] The so-called *Protevangelium Jacobi,* a sort of gospel about Mary the mother of Jesus, was issued, ca. 175, to imitate, supplement, and correct Luke. For that author the Third Gospel was not a sacred text immune from tampering.[92]

A wide range of second-century authors, from the vigorously proto-orthodox to the thoroughly "heretical" did not acknowledge the literary unity of Luke and Acts. For Irenaeus Acts succeeded the *Tetraevangelium.*[93] His painstaking arguments for the fourfold Gospel prevented him from espousing another view.[94] If the author intended these books to be a stand-alone œuvre of two volumes, he did not succeed. One reason for his lack of success was that each of the books can stand on its own, a fact to which the history of reception has given abundant witness.[95] That same observation cannot be applied to the *Against Apion* of Josephus.[96]

CONCLUSION

Patrick E. Spencer sought to secure the "four bolts" (genre, narrative, theology, reception) that form the hinge unifying Luke and Acts.[97] *Hinge* may be an unfortunate metaphor, since hinges link two different items, such as a door and its frame or a box and its lid. Although satisfied with his repairs, Spencer has more aptly exemplified the thesis that those who assume unity will find it. Broad literary unity has not, since Cadbury, been in dispute. The issue, raised by Parsons and Pervo, is whether this factor should quash discussion of other issues.

In one of his many insightful articles, Daniel Marguerat finds the unity of Luke and Acts to reside not in the text itself, but in the process of reading.[98] This presumes an implied reader who will investigate the texts together more than once and discover the various links and cross-references. We (those of the guild who specialize in Lukan studies) have done just that and perceive that Marguerat's thesis is valid. His metaphor, congenial to Spencer, is a diptych, two images connected with a hinge. Irenaeus would not disagree, although the left side of his diptych would contain images of all four evangelists. Others would join Acts to Pauline or other epistles, placing it on the left side. Diptychs can be rearranged. Metaphors aside, Marguerat's implied reader was not joined by any known actual readers in early Christianity. His reading does not absolutely establish the author's intention, although it is far from improbable. Diptychs do involve *two* images. "What," an impudent questioner might ask, "is the better grammatical equivalent to the hinge: a hyphen or a conjunction?"

Study of reception history has revealed that the literary construct "Luke-Acts" cannot claim to be more than a hypothetical reconstruction, analogous to the partition of 2 Corinthians into a number of fragments. This observation does not degrade the claim, for the occasionally defended view of 2 Corinthians as a unity is also a hypothesis. Hypotheses, to reiterate, are discussable. What Parsons and Pervo have learned is that questioning the utility of Luke-Acts unleashed ire not unlike that which emanated from conservative scholars when the authenticity of the Pastoral Epistles was questioned in earlier generations or that of Colossians in more recent times. Some—far from all—of the defense of Luke-Acts shows that this expression has become more of a dogma than a rewarding tool for the study of these two books.

Genre provides the most cogent illustration. Were it not for Luke-Acts, little, if any, effort would have been devoted to discovering a common form for these two books, and that activity would not have been driven by a δεῖ ("must").[99] The quest for a single genre has produced valuable and illuminating observations, findings that might have been better had they not arisen from compulsion. So, too, in regard to discussions of Lukan theology and narrative technique, discussions that can take place without a priori insistence upon total unity.

Rethinking the Unity of Luke and Acts sought to establish the position that the unities of Luke and Acts are best viewed as questions to be pursued rather than as presuppositions to be exploited. Its leading thesis, that Acts is best viewed as a sequel to Luke, rather than as a continuation based upon the size of scrolls or the energies of the reader, has met broad acceptance. For the rest, let the conversation continue.

NOTES

1. Mikeal C. Parsons and Richard I. Pervo, *Rethinking the Unity of Luke and Acts* (Minneapolis: Fortress, 1993; repr. with additional bibliography, 2007).

2. Another disappointment was the conference at Leuven in July 1998 that resulted in Joseph Verheyden, ed., *The Unity of Luke-Acts* (BETL 142; Leuven: Leuven University Press, 1999). The authors may be forgiven for suspecting that their short book played some part in generating this colloquy. Neither, however, was invited to participate in the conference. One explanation for this appears in Verheyden's introductory survey in that volume, "The Unity of Luke-Acts. What Are We Up To?" 356. This useful review summarizes a number of works, generally without comment. Negative judgment is all but exclusively reserved for Parsons and Pervo, whose work is not summarized.

3. I. Howard Marshall, "'Israel' and the Story of Salvation: One Theme in Two Parts," in *Jesus and the Heritage of Israel: Luke's Narrative Claim upon Israel's Legacy* (ed. David P. Moessner; Harrisburg.: Trinity Press, 1999), 340–57, 340. Cf. also his "Acts and the 'Former Treatise,'" in *The Book of Acts in Its Ancient Literary Setting (*ed. Bruce W. Winter and Andrew D. Clarke; *BIFCS* 1; Grand Rapids, Mich.: Eerdmans, 1993), 163–82.

4. See Michael F. Bird, "The Unity of Luke-Acts in Recent Discussion," in this volume, 3–22 (first published in *JSNT* 29/4 [2007]: 425–48). Subsequent references are to this essay as it appears in this volume. An example is Verheyden, *The Unity of Luke-Acts.* Most of the essays in that volume assume unity and proceed to develop conclusions based upon it.

5. See Bird, "The Unity," 13. He says that Parsons and Pervo deny "a literary unity between Luke and Acts." Our subject was *narrative* unity (45–82)—the question of narrative techniques. For our position on broad literary unity see *Rethinking,* 121–22.

6. Parsons and Pervo, *Rethinking,* 127. The final words (the last in the book) are a homage to Cadbury: "Superfluous *kai* in the Lord's Prayer and Elsewhere," *Munera Studiosa* (Festschrift for W. H. P. Hatch. Ed. Massey H. Shepherd and Sherman E. Johnson; Cambridge, Mass.: Episcopal Theological School, 1946), 41–47. Patrick E. Spencer's exegesis of this phrase is revelatory: "They [Parsons and Pervo] contend the 'hyphen' Cadbury inserted in 'Luke-Acts' should be removed" ("The Unity of Luke-Acts: A Four-Bolted Hermeneutical Hinge," *CBR* 5 [2007]: 342).

7. For example, Robert C. Tannehill, *The Narrative Unity of Luke-Acts: A Literary Interpretation* (2 vols.; Minneapolis: Fortress, 1986, 1990), and the Sacra Pagina commentaries of Luke Timothy Johnson: *The Gospel of Luke* and *The Acts of the Apostles* (Collegeville, Minn.: Liturgical Press 1991, 1992). Tannehill, after acknowledging differences in the narrative techniques of Luke and Acts, says that "Luke-Acts is a unified narrative because the chief human characters (John the Baptist, Jesus, the Apostles, Paul) share in a mission which expresses a single controlling purpose—the purpose of God" (1:ii). This is a very general understanding. Cf. also 2:5 6.

8. Henry J. Cadbury, *The Making of Luke-Acts* (New York: Macmillan, 1927).

9. Cf. David P. Moessner, *Lord of the Banquet: The Literary and Theological Significance of the Lukan Travel Narrative* (Minneapolis: Augsburg Fortress, 1989).

10. Literary critical methods have been prominent in the work of both Parsons and Pervo.

11. A pertinent example is Charles H. Talbert's *Literary Patterns, Theological Themes, and the Genre of Luke-Acts* (SBLMS 20; Missoula, Mont.: SBL and Scholars Press, 1974).

12. Parsons and Pervo, *Rethinking,* 84–114; 123–26.

13. So Patrick Spencer, "The Unity," 346: "Theological dissonance between Luke and Acts is the final area Parsons and Pervo cite as evidence against the unity of Luke-Acts. . . . Rather than an argument in favor of disunity, their discussion in this area is more of a complaint than a detailed case." His conclusion that "Jesus does not seem to have a particular saving relevance in Acts, in contrast with his salvific representation in Luke" (346) is a thorough misunderstanding. Cf. Verheyden's erroneous claim that Pervo distinguishes "between the 'popular' Acts and 'Luke's serious theological program,' which is supposedly found in the Gospel only" ("Unity," 48 n. 225).

14. Despite occasional claims to the contrary (for example, Christoph W. Stenschke, "The Need for Salvation," in *Witness to the Gospel: The Theology of Acts* [ed. I. Howard Marshall and David Peterson; Grand Rapids, Mich.: Eerdmans, 1998], 125–44, 128; and Verheyden, "The Unity," 7 n. 16), *Rethinking* did not attempt to distinguish the anthropology of Acts from that of Luke, nor did it attempt a complete sketch of Lukan anthropology.

15. Parsons and Pervo, *Rethinking,* 113.

16. Ibid., 126.

17. Daniel Marguerat once told Pervo, "Acts was not a good book for Calvin to write a commentary on." This was not because Calvin rejected the notion of a divine plan.

18. For example, Jacob Jervell, *The Theology of Acts* (New Testament Theology; Cambridge: Cambridge University Press, 1996), and I. Howard Marshall and David Peterson, eds., *Witness to the Gospel: The Theology of the Acts of the Apostles* (Grand Rapids, Mich.: Eerdmans, 1998). For a review of research see Marshall, "How Does One Write on the Theology of Acts?" in the same volume, 316. Studies of Lukan theology in general also continue, such as Petr Pokorný, *Theologie der lukanischen Schriften* (FRLANT 174; Göttingen: Vandenhoeck & Ruprecht, 1998), and the new edition of François Bovon's *Luke the Theologian* (2d ed.; Waco, Tex.: Baylor University Press, 2006).

19. Marshall, "'Israel,'" 347–57.

20. Parsons and Pervo, *Rethinking,* 86. The distinction comes from Rudolph Bultmann, *Theology of the New Testament* (trans. K. Grobel; 2 vols.; New York: Charles Scribner's Sons, 1951, 1955), 1:33–37.

21. Marshall, "'Israel,'" 348–49.

22. Ibid., 349–51.

23. The two occurrences of *send* in Acts apply to Paul (22:21; 26:17).

24. Marshall, "'Israel,'" 351–53.

25. Ibid., 353–54.

26. Acts 9:25 evidently speaks of disciples of Paul. Cf. also the *v.l.* at 14:20.

27. Marshall, "'Israel,'" 355–57.

28. Eschatology and ethics are among the more prominent of these. On the latter see Thomas E. Phillips, ed., *Acts and Ethics* (NTMon 9; Sheffield: Sheffield Phoenix Press, 2005).

29. Jacques Dupont, "La conclusion des Actes et son rapport à l'ensemble de l'ouvrage de Luc," in Jacob Kremer, ed., *Les Actes des Apôtres: Traditions, redaction, théologies* (BETL 43; Leuven: Leuven University Press 1979), 359–404.

30. Parsons and Pervo, *Rethinking,* 45–83; 120–23.

31. This chapter did not pretend to be complete, a fact overlooked by Martin Rese, who chastises the authors for not dealing with the term Ιουδαῖος ("Jew," "Judean") and invents a reason for this neglect, "The Jews in Luke-Acts: Some Second Thoughts," in Verheyden, *The Unity of Luke and Acts,* 185–201, 196–97. On *Ioudaios* in Acts see Richard I. Pervo, "Israel's Heritage and Claims Upon the Genre(s) of Luke and Acts: The Problems of a History," in *Jesus and the Heritage of Israel: Luke's Narrative Claim upon Israel's Legacy* (ed. David P. Moessner; Harrisburg: Trinity Press, 1999), 127–43, 137–38.

32. Martin Dibelius, *From Tradition to Gospel* (trans. B. Woolf; New York: Charles Scribner's Sons, 1935 [first published 1919]). Martin Dibelius, "Style Criticism of the Book of Acts," in *Studies in the Acts of the Apostles* (ed. H. Greeven; trans. M. Ling and P. Schubert; New York: Charles Scribner's Sons, 1956), 1–25.

33. For example, Luke 12.

34. This point—scarcely disputable—is misrepresented by Spencer, "The Unity," 343.

35. Bird, "The Unity," states, "I think that many of the apparent scriptural echoes and thematic connections identified between the two volumes are only evident to those who read Luke-Acts through a computerized search engine," 16. This is hyperbole, but not without value.

36. C. K. Barrett, "The Third Gospel as a Preface to Acts? Some Reflections," in *The Four Gospels 1992: Festschrift Frans Neirynck* (ed. F. van Segbroeck et al.; BETL 100; 3 vols.; Leuven: Leuven University Press, 1992), 2:1451–66, 1454–62.

37. The tentative nature of his findings is not always reflected in references to this work: for example, Verheyden, "The Unity," 17–18.

38. Gregory Sterling, "'Opening the Scriptures': The Legitimation of the Jewish Diaspora and the Early Christian Mission," in *Jesus and the Heritage of Israel: Luke's Narrative Claim upon Israel's Legacy* (ed. David P. Moessner; Harrisburg: Trinity Press, 1999), 199–225, 215, appeals to the *absence* of references to Gentile mission as an argument for the unity of Luke and Acts.

39. The author of Mark did not have a close understanding of Jewish practice. For retrojection of the Gentile mission into the life of Jesus see, for example, Mark 7:1–20; 12:1–12. On the question of the Gentile mission in Q see John S. Kloppenborg, *Excavating Q: The History and Setting of the Sayings Gospel* (Minneapolis: Fortress, 2000), 191–93. Cf. also John 12:20–26.

40. For a concise description of the meaning of "legitimating narrative" in relation to Luke and Acts see Pervo, "Israel's Heritage," 136–37.

41. Barrett, "Third Gospel," 1455.

42. Isa. 40:5 contains the nominalized adjective σωτήριον, which, as Jacques Dupont first, to my knowledge, observed ("La conclusion") recurs in Acts 28:28. This is one theme that links the beginning of Luke to the end of Acts, exhibiting both narrative continuity and, to a degree, discontinuity, as it now applies to Gentiles. This keen observation does not prove that the author planned it from the outset. It is equally possible that Luke took the opportunity at the end of Acts to make this cross-reference. It is not impossible that he was unaware of his earlier use.

43. Barrett, "Third Gospel," 1456.

44. On the subject see John Painter, *Just James: The Brother of Jesus in History and Tradition* (Columbia: University of South Carolina Press, 1997), 11–41.

45. It is absent from the *Gospel of Thomas* 64, which has its own thrust. Presuming a common source (Q) for Matthew and Luke, the Gentile mission theme may have already occurred in Q. See James M. Robinson, Paul Hoffmann, and John S. Kloppenborg, eds., *The Critical Edition of Q.* (Hermeneia; Minneapolis: Fortress, 2000), 432–49.

46. Barrett, "Third Gospel," 1459.

47. Barrett (ibid., 1460) points to the use of στηρίζω ("strengthen") in Luke 22:32 as a possible foreshadowing. One could apply this verb to the role of Peter in Acts. The verb, however, is used but once, and that of Paul (Acts 18:23). Peter's promise (Luke 22:33) that he is willing to follow Jesus to "confinement" (φυλακήν) and death is noteworthy. The assertion looks forward both to events recorded in Acts, that is, imprisonments, and an event outside of Acts: martyrdom. This is a foreshadowing (cf. also John 13:37) of events that were probably familiar to the implied reader of Luke, certainly to the author. Those who read Acts and then (re)turned to Luke would view it as prophetic. The promise does not prove that the author already planned to write a second volume.

48. Barrett, "Third Gospel," 1460–61.

49. Ibid., 1454.

50. Acts 2:46 speaks of the community's daily presence in the temple, but does not relate this to the cult. In the light of 2:43a and 5:12 instruction was the evident object of their visits. Acts 3:1 states that Peter and John went to the temple at the hour of prayer at 3 P.M. "Prayer" was the apparent object of this visit, an object that was, in any case, not fulfilled.

51. Parsons and Pervo, *Rethinking,* 88.

52. Barrett, "Third Gospel," 1460.

53. Ibid., 1461.

54. Cf. Mikeal C. Parsons, *The Departure of Jesus in Luke-Acts The Ascension Narratives in Context* (JSNTS 21; Sheffield: Sheffield Academic Press, 1987).

55. Cf. the once popular notion that much of Acts 1:1–11 was composed after the separation of the two scrolls. For literature see Étienne Trocmé, *Le livre des Actes et l'histoire* (Paris: Presses Universitaires de France, 1957), 30–4; Gerhard Schneider, *Die Apostelgeschichte* (2 vols; HTK 5; Freiburg: Herder & Herder, 1980–82), 1:77 n. 7; and *Rethinking,* 9–11.

56. The quotation formulae in 11:16 and 20:35 refer, as Barrett notes, to Acts 1:5 in the first instance and to no source found in Luke for the second ("Third Gospel," 1461–62).

57. Spencer claims that Luke's use of material from Mark and Q in Acts shows that the author refrained from using them in the Gospel in order to reserve them for Acts ("The Unity," 352–53). He cites only examples from Mark (on which see Richard I. Pervo, *Dating Acts: Between the Evangelists and the Apologists* [Santa Rosa, Calif.: Polebridge, 2006], 35–47). This explanation is possible, but it is far from the most likely solution.

58. See Bird, "The Unity," 3–22.

59. For a review of the various options and arguments see Verheyden, "The Unity," 14–16.

60. Loveday C. A. Alexander, *Acts in Its Ancient Literary Context: A Classicist Looks at the Acts of the Apostles* (Library of New Testament Studies 298; London: T & T Clark, 2005), 27.

61. Barrett, "Third Gospel," 1453. Barrett's own tentative solution is not based upon an argument for unity. He proposed, first in "Third Gospel," 1462–66, and later in "The

First New Testament?" *NovT* 38 (1996): 94–104, that Luke and Acts are a two-part "new testament."

62. Pervo, *Dating Acts,* 11–12. The question of whether canonical Luke is the original edition of that Gospel continues to arise. Joseph B. Tyson has recently revived the hypothesis that canonical Luke is subsequent to the edition known to Marcion. See Joseph B. Tyson: *Marcion and Luke-Acts: A Defining Struggle* (Columbia: University of South Carolina Press, 2006). If this hypothesis is correct, the author who produced canonical Luke probably wrote Acts as a companion piece. The hypothesis cannot be demonstrated (saving the discovery of a manuscript), but it is not easily refuted.

63. Cadbury, *The Making of Luke-Acts,* 127. His still valuable attempts at classification (127–39) are governed by his presupposition of unity. Cadbury emphasizes the "popular" character of Luke's writing, an observation that launched Pervo on what became a career-long focus.

64. See these surveys: Richard I. Pervo, "Must Luke and Acts Belong to the Same Genre?" (ed. D. J. Lull; SBLSP 1989; Atlanta: Scholars, 1989), 309–16; Parsons and Pervo, *Rethinking,* 20–44; A. J. M. Wedderburn, "Zur Frage der Gattung der Apostelgeschichte," in *Geschichte, Tradition, Reflexion: Festschrift für Martin Hengel zum 70* (ed. Hubert Cancik, Hermann Lichtenberger, and Peter Schäfer; Tübingen: Mohr Siebeck, 1996), 303–22; and Thomas J. Phillips, "The Genre of Acts: Moving Towards a Consensus?" *CBR* 4 (2006): 365–96. Note also Alexander, *Literary Context,* 133–63, and Todd C. Penner, "Madness in the Method? The Acts of the Apostles in Current Study," *Currents in Biblical Research* 2/2 (2004): 223–93.

65. David E. Aune, *The New Testament in its Literary Environment* (LEC 8; Philadelphia: Westminster, 1987), 80.

66. Parsons and Pervo, *Rethinking,* 20. Note also 13–16.

67. Ibid., 43.

68. Richard I. Pervo, *Profit with Delight: The Literary Genre of the Acts of the Apostles* (Philadelphia: Fortress, 1987). Spencer, for example, who begs the question by speaking of "the genre of Luke and Acts" ("The Unity," 343), incorrectly says that Parsons and Pervo relate Luke to biography and Acts to the ancient novel (344). He also misrepresents (34) the conclusions of Richard I. Pervo, "Direct Speech in Acts and the Question of Genre," 28/3 (2006): 285–307. In his remarks upon genre Verheyden ("The Unity," 45–48) says: "Still others have invented a genus mixtum such as 'historical novel'" (47). "Historical novel" is, however, a well-known phenomenon, scarcely the invention of Robert Karris or Richard Pervo. Thomas E. Phillips is among the few who recognize how tentative Pervo's identification of Acts as an ancient historical novel was ("The Genre," 368).

69. Pervo would not reject any of these classifications: "Israel's Heritage," 135. Note also *Profit with Delight,* 137. For Pervo the issue is whether classification seeks to exclude the presence of some fictional material.

70. Comparison is often made between Luke/Acts and Josephus's *Against Apion,* which is not a specimen of historiography but an apology. Contrast is also in order. At *Ag. Ap.* 1.320 the narrator announces that the book is long enough and that he will move on to a second. Luke does not do this. The project announced in *Ag. Ap.* 2.2 is a continuation of what has preceded: refutation of opponents. 2.296 announces a full closure to both books. Acts lacks such a statement—and is much the better for it.

71. Parsons and Pervo, *Rethinking,* 42–43.

72. The earliest known explanation for the separation of Luke and Acts is that of Chrysostom: "And why did he not make one book of it. . . . For clearness, and to give the brother [Theophilus] a pause for rest. Besides, the two treatises are distinct in their subject matter" (*Hom. 1;* trans. J. Walker et al.; NPF 11: *Saint Chrysostom: Homilies on the Acts of the Apostles and the Epistle to the Romans* [1889; repr. Grand Rapids, Mich.: Eerdmans, 1979], 4).

73. See Parsons and Pervo, *Rethinking* 21–22, 42–43, 118, and 126, which states that the term *sequel* "most accurately describes the reception and reading of the book from earliest times."

74. Andrew F. Gregory, *The Reception of Luke and Acts in the Period before Irenaeus: Looking for Luke in the Second Century* (WUNT 2/169; Tübingen: Mohr Siebeck, 2003). See also C. Kavin Rowe, "History, Hermeneutics, and the Unity of Luke-Acts," in this volume, 43–65 (first published in *JSNT* 28/2 [2005]: 131–57; subsequent references are to this essay as it appears in this volume); Rowe, "Literary Unity and Reception History: Reading Luke-Acts as Luke and Acts," in this volume, 74–81 (first published *JSNT* 29/4 [2007]: 449–58); Markus Bockmuehl, "Why Not Let Acts Be Acts? In Conversation with C. Kavin Rowe," in this volume, 70–73 (first published *JSNT* 28/2 [2005]: 163–66; subsequent references are to this essay as it appears in this volume); Luke Timothy Johnson, "Literary Criticism of Luke-Acts: Is Reception-History Pertinent?" in this volume, 66–69 (first published *JSNT* 28/2 [2005]: 159–62; subsequent references are to this essay as it appears in this volume); Andrew F. Gregory, "The Reception of Luke and Acts and the Unity of Luke-Acts," in this volume, 82–93 (first published *JSNT* 29/4 [2007]: 459–72); and Gregory, "Looking for Luke in the Second Century: A Dialogue with François Bovon," in *Reading Luke: Interpretation, Reflection, Formation* (ed. Craig Bartholomew, Joel B. Green, and Anthony C. Thiselton; Scripture and Hermeneutics; Carlisle, U.K.: Paternoster, 2005), 401–13.

75. See Bockmuehl, "Why Not Let Acts Be Acts?" 70. The essays of Rowe and Bockmuehl are quite penetrating.

76. I believe that the Muratorian Fragment should play at most a limited role in the discussion. The objections of Albert C. Sundberg, Jr., "Canon Muratori: A Fourth-century List," *HTR* 66/1 (1973): 1–41, and Geoffrey M. Hahneman, *The Muratorian Fragment and the Development of the Canon* (Oxford: Clarendon Press, 1992), cannot be ignored or dismissed. The counter arguments of Joseph Verheyden, "The Canon Muratori: A Matter of Dispute," in *The Biblical Canons* (ed. Jean-Marie Auwers and Henk Jan de Jonge; BETL 163; Leuven: Peeters, 2003), 487–556, are detailed but not decisive. Muratori clearly identifies the same person, Luke, as the author of both books, while affiliating the Gospel of Luke with the other Gospels (*l.*2). The comments on Acts, however, follow those on the four Gospels. The assertion that "the acts of all apostles are written in one book" (*ll.*34–35) intimates knowledge of other acts and is not correct. Lines 38–40 report, after noting that Acts did not relate the death of Peter, Paul's journey from Rome to Spain. This reflects the view of the *Acts of Peter* (Verc.) 1–3. These chapters are a later addition to the late-second-century text (Gérard Poupon, "Les 'Actes de Pierre' et leur remaniement," *ANRW* II.25.6 [1988]: 4363–83, 4367–74). The Muratorian Fragment may contain late-second-century material, but it appears to be a mélange of various sources, often unreliable, and translated (evidently) from

Greek to Latin by a person whose knowledge of the latter, if not of the former, was highly deficient.

77. Johnson, "Literary Criticism," 66.

78. Pervo, *Dating Acts,* 25.

79. P. Vielhauer, "On the 'Paulinism' of Acts," in *Studies in Luke-Acts; Essays Presented in Honor of Paul Schubert* (ed. Leander E. Keck and J. Louis Martyn; Nashville: Abingdon, 1966), 33–51.

80. Dibelius, "Style Criticism," 88.

81. See Julian Hills, "The Acts of the Apostles in the *Acts of Paul,*" (*SBLSP* 33; ed. E. Lovering; Atlanta: Scholars, 1994), 24–54.

82. Johnson, "Literary Criticism," 67, says: "It is this gap that traditional historical-critical exegesis has tried to fill."

83. The problem of the text of Acts cannot be discussed within the scope of this article. I refer readers to my *Acts: A Commentary* (Hermeneia; Minneapolis: Fortress, 2008), 1–5 et passim, for details.

84. Pervo, *Dating Acts.*

85. See Willy Rordorf, "Actes de Paul," in *Écrits apocryphes chrétiens 1* (ed. François Bovon and Pierre Geoltrain; Paris: Gallimard, 1997), 1115–77: 1122. Spencer, "The Unity," 359, incorrectly states that Pervo suggested that the *Acts of Paul* is a sequel to Acts. See Richard I. Pervo, "A Hard Act to Follow: *The Acts of Paul* and the Canonical Acts," *Journal of Higher Criticism* 2/2 (1995): 3–32. The honor for advocacy of that view belongs to Richard Bauckham, "The Acts of Paul as a Sequel to Acts," in *The Book of Acts in Its Ancient Literary Setting* (ed. Bruce W. Winter and Andrew D. Clarke; *BIFCS* 1; Grand Rapids, Mich.: Eerdmans, 1993), 105–52. On 344 Spencer says that Pervo labeled the *Acts of Paul* as a "replacement" for Acts. That is closer to Pervo's thesis, which is that it is a rival to canonical Acts.

86. Pervo is willing to concede that Polycarp, *Phil.* 1.2 may derive from Acts (*Dating Acts,* 17–20). This would be the earliest indicator of usage, but it is not attributed to a source.

87. For a somewhat less brief survey see Richard I. Pervo, "Israel's Heritage," 139–42.

88. For one view of the process see Christine M. Thomas, *The* Acts of Peter, *Gospel Literature, and the Ancient Novel: Rewriting the Past* (New York: Oxford University Press, 2003).

89. For arguments that the canonical Acts served as their model see G. del Cerro, "Los hechos apócrifos de los Apósteles. Su género literario," *EstBíb* 51 (1993): 207–32. The title πράξεις ἀποστόλων ("Acts of the Apostles"), which is not original (the work's central figure was not, technically, an apostle), may have been inspired by the title of the *Acts of Paul.*

90. F. Stanley Jones, "A Jewish Christian Reads Luke's Acts of the Apostles: The Use of the Canonical Acts in the Ancient Jewish Christian Source behind Pseudo-Clementine *Recognitions* 1.27–71," *SBLSP* 34 (Atlanta: Scholars, 1995): 617–35. Cf. also his *An Ancient Jewish Christian Source on the History of Christianity: Pseudo-Clementine Recognitions 1.21–71* (SBLTT 37; Atlanta: Scholars, 1995).

91. Helmut Koester, *Ancient Christian Gospels: Their History and Development* (Philadelphia: Trinity Press International, 1990), 349–430. (The essay on Tatian, 403–30, was contributed by William L. Peterson.)

92. Spencer's summary of Pervo's view of the *Protevangelium Jacobi* ("The Unity," 344) is erroneous.

93. Parsons and Pervo, *Rethinking,* 118. This view is developed with considerable detail and nuance by Gregory in *Reception.* It should also be noted that in *A. H.* 3.1.1 Irenaeus says that, after empowerment by the Spirit, the apostles set out to evangelize the world. Acts does not record this mission. Irenaeus may have got this view from Justin (*1 Apol.* 39.3), or from common lore. It is akin to the legend of the "Apostolic Lottery" found, for example, at the beginning of the *Acts of Thomas.*

94. See Rowe, "History, Hermeneutics," 44–45, who refers to Hans F. von. Campenhausen.

95. Henry J. Cadbury (*The Book of Acts in History* [London: A & C Black, 1955] 139), acknowledged this: "Fortunately our author had the judgment or foresight to make each of his two volumes somewhat self-sufficient, though in doing so he has perhaps prevented some modern readers from recognizing their fundamental unity." Johnson acknowledges that the two can be read independently or in conjunction with other works ("Literary Criticism," 66–69). Spencer calls this "an argument from silence." It is, in fact, an argument from the completeness of the text of each book ("The Unity," 355).

96. See my note 70.

97. Spencer, "The Unity."

98. Daniel Marguerat, "Luc-Actes: une unité à construire," in *The Unity of Luke-Acts,* 57–81, (ed. Joseph Verheyden; Leuven: Leuven University Press: Peeters, 1999); see also Marguerat, *The First Christian Historian: Writing the "Acts of the Apostles"* (SNTSMS 121; Cambridge: Cambridge University Press, 2002), 43–64, 80–81.

99. This is already apparent in Cadbury's discussion of literary form (n. 63).

PART TWO

HISTORY, HERMENEUTICS, AND THE UNITY OF LUKE-ACTS

C. Kavin Rowe

This essay does not dispute the notion that Luke-Acts can be read as a literary unity.[1] Nor does it take up the much debated question of genre.[2] Instead the essay centers upon a historical difficulty that impinges upon our guild's almost unquestioned assumption that to read Luke-Acts together is to interpret this literary unity historically.[3] The argument receives its shape from the thesis that the history of reception presents us with a problem to which we ought to give serious thought. In order to get at this problem the essay will sketch briefly the reception history relevant to our question, draw out the hermeneutical consequences thereof, and finally suggest further lines to follow in our reflection upon a first-rate difficulty in New Testament interpretation.

RECEPTION HISTORY

Even for prophets the future can be rather hazy. Hananiah after all was presumably at least somewhat sincere. Yet—with no claim to the prophetic gift—I will hazard a prediction: reception history of the texts of the New Testament will come to constitute a greater and greater portion of the scholarly work in the field, partly because of the seeming eternal return of the same in the exegetical debates and partly because of the ability of the text's forward history to shed substantial light on substantive issues of interpretation.[4] A case in point is Andrew F. Gregory's recent study, a comprehensive and meticulous treatment entitled *The Reception of Luke and Acts in the Period before Irenaeus.*[5] It is Gregory's study, in fact, that provides the departure point for the problem with which we have to deal.

In a sense Gregory's title gives the game away, even as it also acts as a provocateur to the typical New Testament scholar. Why not *The Reception of* Luke-Acts *in the Period before Irenaeus*? Why the bothersome little "and," *Luke and Acts*? Far from a careless or reckless run into academic obstacles, this *and* is purposively employed, for it points us implicitly to the results of the investigation.[6]

After a virtually exhaustive (not to say exhausting) tour through the many candidates for testimony to the reception of Luke and/or Acts prior to and including Irenaeus, Gregory concludes that, with only two exceptions, there is "no evidence . . . to demonstrate that Luke and Acts were read as two volumes of one work."[7] The first exception is Irenaeus himself, who, so contends Gregory, "explicitly treats Luke-Acts as a two volume work, and he reads each volume in light of the other."[8] Gregory's evidence for this interpretation of Irenaeus is essentially twofold: Irenaeus's knowledge of the common authorship of Luke and Acts, and the particular use of Luke and Acts in Irenaeus's argument in the opening section of *Against Heresies* 3.

Taking the latter first we may note that *A.H.* 3.1.1 indubitably reflects Irenaeus's knowledge of the end of Luke and the beginning of Acts[9]:

> For it is not permitted to assert that [the apostles] preached before they possessed "perfect knowledge," as some have the audacity to affirm, glorying in themselves as correctors [*emendatores*] of the apostles. After our Lord rose from the dead, [the apostles] were invested with Power from on high [cf. Luke 24:49; Acts 1:8a] when the Holy Spirit came down [cf. Acts 1:8a], were filled with all gifts, and had perfect knowledge. They departed to the ends of the earth [cf. Acts 1:8b], preaching the glad tidings of the good things sent from God to us, and proclaiming the peace of heaven to those who have—all equally and each one in particular—the Gospel of God. *Matthew* produced a written gospel . . . *Mark* handed down to us in writing what had been preached by Peter. So, too, *Luke* recorded in a book the Gospel preached by [Paul]. Then *John* . . . published a gospel during his residence in Ephesus.[10]

With respect to this passage Gregory notes that "the unity of Luke-Acts plays an important part in Irenaeus's anti-Gnostic polemic, for it allows him to argue that there was no time when the apostles were without perfect knowledge, for they had such perfect knowledge from the moment they received power from on high after Jesus had risen from the dead."[11]

Gregory is to be commended for his sophistication in attempting to uncover the hermeneutical presupposition that underlies Irenaeus's argumentation. Yet to construe *Haer.* 3.1.1 as evidence for the claim that Irenaeus "explicitly treats Luke-Acts as a two volume work, and he reads each volume in light of the other" is, at best, to exaggerate its significance.

It is certainly true that in making his argument Irenaeus coordinates the end of Luke with the beginning of Acts and, hence, uses what we would call the literary unity of Luke and Acts. Thus Irenaeus perceives—probably reflecting an awareness of the "chain-link interlock" described by Lucian[12]—that Luke and Acts go together narratively, that is, that the beginning of Acts overlaps with the end of Luke in order to pick up the Gospel story and carry it forward.

However, Irenaeus's sequential coordination and perception of the "chain-link" bear little similarity to a literary-critical reading practice that self-consciously separates Luke from the other gospels to read with Acts as one work. Indeed, precisely what we do not see in Irenaeus is any kind of sustained reading of one "volume in light of the other," that is, a reading of *Luke-Acts.* In point of fact, in the worthiest candidate for consideration, the passage cited just above, Irenaeus observes the connection between the story of Luke and Acts not in order to claim legitimacy for a unified reading of Luke-Acts, but in the service of a "historical" argument for the authority of the *Tetraevangelium:* the fact that the apostles had perfect knowledge proves, contra the "correctors," that Matthew, Mark, Luke, and John need no correction—they are the Gospel of God (cf. esp. the coordination of the four *Evangelia* with the single *Evangelium* in *Haer.* 3.11.9).[13] Irenaeus does not, then, ask how the ending of Luke and beginning of Acts go together, what Luke's larger point was in unifying the stories, what in the Gospel prefigures the mission to the end of the earth, or any other questions that would presuppose a unified literary reading. Instead he simply takes the joint material in Luke 24 and Acts 1 as historical *facta* and argues on that basis.

Yet there is an important way in which Irenaeus does actually exhibit considerable reflection upon the fact that Luke and Acts must be taken together, that of their common authorship. As Hans von Campenhausen put it, "Luke, the author of Acts, is above all else the author of the Gospel of Luke . . . the authority of Acts . . . depends on the authority of the Gospel."[14] Gregory is thus correct to note that "Irenaeus . . . argues those (unnamed) opponents who receive Luke's (Pauline) Gospel must accept also what Luke says concerning Paul in Acts: those who accept what Luke wrote in his former volume must accept also what he wrote in his second."[15]

But recognizing Irenaeus's acknowledgment of the common authorship of Luke and Acts is still not the same thing as evidence of a particular reading practice that separates Luke from the fourfold gospel to read alone with Acts.[16] Indeed the use to which Irenaeus puts his knowledge is that Acts should be read not along with Luke in particular but along with the fourfold gospel. In this respect Acts is, as Campenhausen rightly saw, Irenaeus's "second text"—the *Tetraevangelium* as a whole being his first.[17]

Irenaeus may well accept the Lukan authorship of both Luke and Acts[18] and make use of Luke's literary coordination of the beginning of Acts with the end of the Gospel, but Irenaeus does not evidence a sustained reading of the two volumes together as a single work in a way formally similar to our literary-critical focus on one unified story. In terms of his actual reading practice and strategy, Acts is read in connection to four gospels, not one.

Gregory's second exception is the Muratorian Fragment. Even if we retain a traditional dating, which seems the best option,[19] it is again far from clear that the Muratorian Fragment supports the supposition that the two volumes of Luke and Acts were read as a single literary whole. Gregory's evidence for this claim is tied not to an indication of a literarily unified interpretation, but rather, once more, to the issue of common authorship: "the association of the name of Luke with the third Gospel may be explained solely on the conjecture that he wrote Acts, and the observation that similarities between these two volumes, not least their respective dedications to Theophilus, require that they be read as a literary whole."[20]

In fact, however, the only "similarity" that the fragment mentions is that of authorship.[21] That the writer of this fragmentary piece recognizes the common authorship of Luke and Acts is beyond dispute: "the acts of all [*omnium*] the apostles are written in one book. For the 'most excellent Theophilus' Luke summarizes the several things that in his own presence have come to pass."[22] But acknowledgment of common authorship, as we noted above, is still well removed from an explicit requirement to read the work Luke-Acts as a single, literary whole, and the two should neither be confused nor conflated. One should infer, moreover, from the phrase "third book of the Gospel" that the author of the fragment reads Luke not with Acts as *Luke-Acts* but, as did Irenaeus, with the other three Gospels.[23] Indeed John is called the author of the *quartum evangeliorum,* the *fourth* of the Gospels.[24] In any case, that the author of the Muratorian Fragment reads Luke and Acts together as a single, literary work similar to the way (post-) modern New Testament exegetes do is highly doubtful, if not wholly wrong.

While the second-century evidence is not in itself valid for the end of the first century—we must always be wary of anachronism and arguments from silence—it is still worth our consideration.[25] Indeed, where it is not contradicted by earlier material, later evidence may help to shape our perception of the phenomenon in question, perhaps especially when the weight of the evidence is so entirely one-sided.

In this light we may return to the preface in Acts. Though Acts 1:1–2 provides a clear and purposive link to Luke's Gospel,[26] it can nonetheless be read simultaneously as presupposing a separation between the two volumes that fits well with the situation noted by Gregory, in two interconnected respects in particular.

First the address to Theophilus in Acts 1:1 can easily be interpreted to imply that he (they) has (have)[27] already read, and presumably understood, the Gospel. Brief reference is made to its contents, and Luke speaks of the first book he has "made" (ἐποιησάμην). Even for the author, then, reading the story of the Gospel would not depend definitively upon Acts. Literarily Luke's Gospel is more than "somewhat self-sufficient";[28] it is intelligible on its own.

Second Acts 1:1–2 also seems to presuppose at least some chronological space between the two volumes,[29] space which might allow the Gospel at least some time to become associated with other narratives focused explicitly on the life of Jesus (for example, Mark) and which would thus make good sense as a sort of

Ausgangspunkt for the different treatment of Luke and Acts in the second century.[30] The Gospel, in other words, could well have been treated as a Gospel (though of course the word might not have been used[31]) prior to the "publication," or at least distribution, of Acts. In such an early association or grouping, Acts would not really even have had the chance to become inseparably attached to Luke.

In addition, even if we accept an early date for Acts (late first rather than second century),[32] the widespread assumption in modern scholarship of an early *division* of Luke from Acts is actually without an indisputably solid foundation.[33] The only existing evidence that can be adduced in favor of this assumption is the preface in Acts, if this preface is taken to establish an original historical, chronological unity. Yet as we have discussed above, the preface might as easily be interpreted as implying that "Theophilus" has already read Luke's first λόγος and that Acts came later. And if Loveday C. A. Alexander is correct, such a preface would not be anomalous in the ancient world:

> Our study of recapitulations in scientific treatises makes it less clear that the two [Luke and Acts] are necessarily so closely linked. Things seem to have been looser in practice than logic might demand. Not all multi-volumed works have recapitulations; and conversely, not all recapitulations signal a close literary unity of the type presupposed in current study of Luke-Acts. The critic who finds a unitary conception in the texts themselves may indeed find confirmation for this unity in the two prefaces. But . . . the critic who finds that the two works . . . are none the less very different in conception, need not find the prefaces a stumbling-block. The connection between two successive works of a corpus linked by recapitulations is not always as tight as we might expect.[34]

Moreover, as far as we know, though Luke was on occasion in the fourth position among the four Gospels—thus giving the opportunity for Acts to follow—Luke and Acts were never placed beside each other in any ancient manuscript.[35] Of course the composition of Luke and Acts, even if we accept a relatively late date,[36] came well before our existing manuscripts, but it is surely more than an unlikely coincidence that the (alleged) separation left no trace of an original unity at any point in the pre-Irenaean evidence or in subsequent, highly varied manuscripts.[37] In fact the mention of common authorship of the two volumes in Irenaeus and in the Muratorian Fragment might point, if indirectly, to the fact that Acts was not universally known or acknowledged to have been written by Luke, despite the historically correct orthodox assumption.[38]

Stanton's proposal that "the acceptance of Luke into the fourfold Gospel led to its early separation from Acts"[39] may thus make more sense the other way around: Luke and Acts were not divided because they were not really read together in the first place. By itself Luke was rather naturally grouped with other gospels and found its way unhindered into the fourfold gospel rather early on.[40] Interestingly, with this view the unsettled history of Acts then becomes somewhat easier to understand. Its various placement in the canonical lists,[41] rejection by Marcion if he knew it[42] and other heretical groups who accepted Luke,[43] the discussion regarding its authority in Irenaeus et al. vis-à-vis such rejection, and so on are difficult to account for in light of an original historical unity.[44] Yet if the two volumes were not read as one, much of the difficulty disappears: Luke came within the gravitational pull of the other Gospels, and Acts was left to float about, as indeed it seemed to do.

Had Luke first written the Gospel amid, or sent it to, a particular community and then quickly followed it with Acts, and had this community existed without Mark, Matthew, John, or Q or any other sources, or at least been willing to set them aside (perhaps in accordance with Luke's intention in the Gospel προοίμιον) so that they would not read such sources in harmony with Luke's Gospel, then there might have been a chance that Luke and Acts would have been read together as a literary whole. But over the distribution and circulation process—in short, the ins and outs of a community's reading practices—Luke himself would have had little to no control (particularly if Theophilus was his patron),[45] and an identifiable Lukan community has been notoriously hard, if not outright impossible, to find.[46]

We may thus not only draw attention to the importance of Gregory's study in general,[47] but may as well even strengthen the overall impression it gives. If the two sole exceptions to Gregory's findings on Irenaeus and the Muratorian Fragment are not really exceptions at all but, indeed, also count against the idea that Luke and Acts were read as Luke-Acts, and if my additional remarks point in the right direction, then our current interpretive practice certainly appears in a rather different light.

CONSEQUENCES FOR INTERPRETATION

> "From the first generations Acts is little mentioned. We infer what happened largely by still later evidence rather than by contemporary knowledge. . . . The book itself tells much of its own history up to the time it was written. After that we are in the dark, as in a tunnel, and emerge only late and partially."[48]

The implication of the history of reception of Luke and Acts for our interpretation comes at the juncture between the course of history as we can detect it and our decision to work hermeneutically on a particular level in relation to this history. In reading Luke-Acts as a unity we have often proceeded on the assumption that this hermeneutical choice is more historical than, for example, the canonical choice that was eventually made to place John between Luke and Acts.[49] In one way this hermeneutical claim to historical accuracy is indisputably true. Even if he thought he was composing Scripture,[50] Luke almost certainly did not write the *Doppelwerk* with the idea of a New Testament canon in mind, least of all one in which John would be situated between his own two volumes, even if he knew a form of John's Gospel.[51]

Yet, in a different way, the hermeneutical choice to read Luke-Acts together may in an important sense be less historical than we have thought, especially if we mean here by "history" something like the course of the actual reading of Luke and Acts. If Gregory's study and our supplementations are near the mark, then we are virtually forced to ask whether Luke-Acts was *ever* routinely read as Luke-Acts in the earliest period. If the answer is, as Gregory's work suggests, a fairly clear *no,* then we will have to face the possibility that our interpretations of Luke-Acts as a unity may be at best as it was intended but not as it was: that is, our interpretations of Luke-Acts may not reflect the practice of the earliest readers after all.

We may thus ask: When speaking of what the ancient Christians may have made of *Luke-Acts,* are we, to state it candidly, simply engaging in an interpretive trick, a hermeneutical fudge that results in an easy welding of the ancient world together with our own? More precisely, do we not confuse literary unity with historical unity, at least insofar as how the text(s) would have been heard? A perfectly satisfying answer is hard to come by, but an important part of any attempt involves the relation between the course of history and our hermeneutical decisions.

At this point it may help to clarify the situation if we take a concrete example from the scholarly literature as a way toward a discussion of our problem. The explicit, sophisticated commitment to a unified interpretation of Luke-Acts makes Luke Timothy Johnson's commentaries in the Sacra Pagina series an ideal place from which to gain some illustrative clarity.

In the introduction to his commentary on the Gospel, Johnson articulates clearly the hermeneutical commitment to literary unity that informs his work in both commentaries: "The decision to read these separate texts as a single literary work means deliberately to adopt a literary critical approach to the New Testament, and to rely upon a contemporary literary designation in preference to a traditional perception of the texts or even their canonical placement. Although formal acknowledgement of Luke-Acts' literary unity is today almost universally given, few commentaries (if any) have yet taken that decision seriously in their treatment of the respective volumes. The present commentary intends systematically to exploit the implications of the designation 'Luke-Acts.'"[52] This commitment is consistently carried forward into his commentary on Acts. In the introduction to the second commentary he simply refers the reader—in good Lukan fashion—back to the previous volume where "the framework for reading both volumes as a single story was established."[53]

The literary-critical enterprise that reads Luke-Acts together is one that I fully support. It is in fact, as Johnson writes elsewhere, "magnificently rewarded by the results."[54] Yet precisely here where we may be wooed by "results," the historical evidence for the reception of Luke and Acts points up hermeneutical slippage, or maybe even confusion, insofar as we endeavor on literary-critical grounds to tie our interpretation to the ancient world.

That study of the ancient world provides substantial insight into Luke's literary style, technique, sophistication, and the like is hardly debatable, and it is not here that our problem is located. The problem, rather, arises when from literary-critical assumptions about the unity of Luke-Acts we draw conclusions about the meaning of Luke-Acts for the early Christians who would have heard the texts. Johnson's remarks at the end of his Acts commentary illustrate the predicament: "For the final time, therefore, Paul announces a turn to the Gentiles with a ringing affirmation: the salvation from God has been sent to them, and they will listen! Luke's readers recognize this as the prophecy that has indeed taken place 'among us' (Luke 1:1), and which has generated the question that made the writing of this narrative necessary in the first place: how did the good news reach the Gentiles, and did the rejection of it by the Jews mean that God failed in his fidelity to them? Luke's answer is contained in the entire narrative up to this point."[55] Leaving aside the actual exegetical proposals, Johnson here moves from a unified literary-critical reading to what "Luke's readers" may have recognized (cf. "us"). Moreover, he implies that to answer the question "how did the good news . . . ?" the readers will have had to read Luke-Acts together: "Luke's answer is contained in the entire narrative up to this point." But to make this move is to confuse literary results with historical evidence.

Here then is the hermeneutical problem: the interpretation that Johnson claims the ancient Christian readers would have understood is predicated upon reading Luke and Acts together as a unified narrative, but the evidence from reception history makes it doubtful that early Christian readers would have read the two volumes together in this way. Johnson's interpretation, while literarily ingenious, thus appears to be historically implausible inasmuch as it depends on readers' perception of *Luke-Acts.* By extension, we may rightfully wonder about the historical viability of interpretations that claim a connection to an ancient Christian audience but depend in principle for their intelligibility upon the entirety of Luke-Acts as a single work. Thus, for example, when Gary Gilbert concludes a 2003 essay, "By echoing and repackaging various forms of Roman propaganda, Luke-Acts provides Christians with their source of legitimization and bolsters the nascent self-identification of the Christian community in the first and second centuries,"[56] we may point out that his interpretation presupposes the existence of Christian communities in the first and second centuries who would have read Luke-Acts together and, moreover, in such a way that this one work would have contributed substantially to the construction of their identity as Christians. Or when John T. Carroll states that his article "will develop a picture [of God] that would result from repeated reading, or hearing, of the narrative over a period of time—the sort of engagement that might have occurred in an early Christian community that treasured Luke's two books 'to Theophilus,'"[57] we may ask, But where are such Christians?[58] And, indeed, where is Luke-Acts?

In other words it is doubtlessly true on a literary level that Luke-Acts *can* "be read as a *single* story."[59] The problem is that historically it hardly ever—if ever—was.

AN OPEN QUESTION

To raise bedeviling hermeneutical and historical questions without offering clear, constructive answers is somewhat like dumping a puzzle onto the table without attempting to put the pieces together—one can easily see that there are various pieces to the puzzle but not necessarily how they should be arranged to form a coherent picture. We must do more than simply dump the puzzle out, but to say that we can at this point put all the pieces together may be to move too fast.

The dilemma we face is how to relate interpretations based on literary unity to the course of history which evidences separation—or perhaps, to borrow from Raymond E. Brown in another context, how to relate "what most likely was meant by the first-century author" to what was "most likely understood by the first- [and second-] century audience."[60] It would seem that when we read Luke-Acts together as a single work we have made the hermeneutical choice to focus upon Luke's intention (for traditional, "old-fashioned" hermeneuts), or the effect generated from reading two volumes together (for those of a more modish outlook) and given up claim to an understanding of the perception of the text by its early auditors. The necessary basis for literary-critical interpretation to claim historical insight into the early Christian reading of the Lukan writings has so far not been provided: an actual person or community that reads Luke and Acts together as the single story Luke-Acts, and, furthermore, to the exclusion of a sort of canonical current that allows Acts to be heard with Luke but not Luke with other Gospels. Yet literary-critical interpretation of Luke-Acts divines something of Luke's overall purpose, plan, and theology and is in this way historically closer to the genesis of the work and the person who wrote it (or at least the implied author) than a so-called historical interpretation that would attempt to trace more closely the actual reading of the work in two separate parts.

Conversely it would seem that when we seek to read Luke and Acts as they were read and understood early on, we have made the hermeneutical choice to focus upon the course of history and of historical plausibility in relation to ancient Christian readers'/auditors' perceptions and given up our right to draw historical conclusions on the basis of interpretations that presume literary unity. Yet in this respect we become somewhat further removed from Luke's intention and estranged from the literary dynamics of the two volumes. *The Trial of the Gospel,* Alexandru Neagoe's 2002 study of the "trial narratives" in Luke-Acts, can serve as a final example to illustrate the problem.[61]

Neagoe argues persuasively that not only are the various trial scenes in Acts (Peter, Stephen, Paul, and so on) related to each other but they are also related literarily to the trial of Jesus in the Gospel (which itself has "narrative precedents" in the Gospel narrative). When the two volumes are read as Luke-Acts, the trial of Jesus thus helps by virtue of its reappearance in "retrospective references" to fund the interpretation of the trial scenes in Acts. When the scenes in Acts and in the Gospel of Luke are related to one another, it becomes clear—so Neagoe—that Luke's intention therewith was to display the defense of "the gospel" (*apologia pro evangelio*). The trial scenes, that is, are part of an overall literary project within Luke-Acts and in their connectedness reveal something basic to the Lukan project: the intention to defend the gospel via a two-volume literary work.

Even if one is disinclined to accept the claim that Luke's overall purpose in writing was to defend the gospel (*apologia pro evangelio* in the broadest sense), it can hardly be doubted that in relating the trials to one another Neagoe has drawn our attention to a salient literary feature of Luke-Acts. In so doing, he has, in my judgment, also opened a window onto something of Luke's intention. That is to say, through the elucidation of a particular literary dynamic of Luke-Acts, we have moved closer to Luke's intention in linking the scenes together and perhaps even to his larger compositional purpose. Neagoe's study is thus a literary one and, to its credit, does not really push to say that the early Christians would have made the connections between Jesus' trial in the Gospel of Luke and the trials of Paul and so on in Acts. Perhaps the early Christians would have heard in Paul's trials echoes of Jesus' own trial, but to restrict such echoes to the Gospel of Luke is to make a literary decision about Luke's intentional narrative stitching, not—insofar as we now know—a historical one about the reading of the texts.

To make a historical determination about how the trials in Acts would have been heard in early Christian communities is to admit the serious likelihood that Acts was not heard as part of a work Luke-Acts but with several other writings. But to allow this separation of Luke from Acts is to lose contact with the literary dynamic of Luke-Acts in which the trials of Acts reach back to and are meaningfully informed by the trial of Jesus in Luke. Neagoe's study, that is, would lose its ability to be specific—and thus its tie to the Gospel of Luke in particular—as it would need to forfeit the possibility of reading a specifically Lukan trial of Jesus into the trials of Acts. The study could then hardly be said to be a study of *Luke-Acts.* Is there a way to relate these choices to one another in a coherent manner, or are our readings of Luke-Acts by necessity bifurcated into literary (Luke-Acts) and historical (Luke and Acts) interpretation?

Fully satisfying answers remain in the distance. Yet some differentiation may nonetheless help to move forward the discussion about the interpretation of Luke's work in light of its early reception, at least with respect to the issues involved. To suggest that historical interpretation may require us to read the volumes separately is not to say that a return to the present canonical shape of the material is the most accurate way of pursuing a connection to a *precanonical* audience's perception of the texts. Strictly speaking a *canonical* interpretation is one that attempts to read Luke after Matthew and Mark but before John, and Acts after the four Gospels and before the *corpus Paulinum.*[62] Acts' well-known, checkered canonization history—it was quite differently placed[63]—is alone sufficient reason to doubt the canonical route as a sufficiently historical one for the attempt to get at the earliest Christians' perception of the texts under discussion. Canonical interpretation is thus to be distinguished hermeneutically from questions of reception history and literary-critical interpretation of Luke-Acts. Yet how we might inquire historically after the potential impact of the Gospel and Acts upon their earliest Christian readers/auditors is not sufficiently clear.

It is probably both logical and, in light of what we know, academically sound to assume that we could know something of the impact of Luke's Gospel upon its early Mediterranean audience(s), even if this something is rather general in nature;[64] yet when speaking about Christian communities we must bear in mind that the Gospel's preface might well—though it is not strictly necessary—assume "Theophilus's" knowledge of other gospel-like writings. Whether Luke was then read by itself, against, or with these other accounts would depend on the community's reading practices, a point that I touched on above and about which we know practically nothing. But in theory at least Luke's Gospel could have been read by itself, and it seems a legitimate undertaking to wonder about how it might have been heard.

The case is not necessarily the same with Acts, which, insofar as we can discern, was neither meant to be nor read alone but always in conjunction with another early Christian writing or writings. But to assume that this other Christian writing was Luke's Gospel by itself is precisely what the reception history of the texts calls into question. It is of course possible to think of certain scenes or vignettes in Acts as having a particular impact on this or that audience. It is conceivable, for example, that various auditors in the ancient world could glean in a rather general sense from Paul's trials that the gospel is being defended (*apologia pro evangelio*), even if they were unable to perceive the literary and material connections of such trials to Jesus' trial in Luke's Gospel.[65] But this possibility of the impact of particular scenes hardly settles the larger question about Acts as a whole.

Would not the perception of Acts by the early Christians vary considerably depending upon the other writings with which Acts was (or was not) read? To return to Johnson's proposal regarding the ending of Acts, can we really say, with reference to concrete Christian communities, how this ending would have been heard apart from the other texts with which it would have (and have not) been read? Would it not make a substantial difference, to take only the most obvious example, to hear the ending of Acts *before* rather than *after* the Pauline corpus if the issue at stake is anything like the theological question involved in Paul's mission to the Gentiles?

One hesitates to end an essay without making some "new" proposal that will solve all difficulties and send us off to hermeneutically confident and exegetically fruitful work. But the topic is, as the puzzling reader has now realized, seriously perplexing and invites further reflection from and conversation with others. It seems then that the problem of history and hermeneutics in relation to Luke-Acts leaves us—at this point—with an open question. We are left with the need to think more clearly about the relation of literary-critical interpretation to the actual course of history and, conversely, about the relation of historical interpretation to Luke's intention and literary design. Perhaps in short what we are forced to do is to consider anew the actual course of history of reading *Luke and Acts* (reception history) in relation to Luke's intention and plan in *Luke-Acts* (literary interpretation). For Luke, it would seem, set out to write a two-volume work, even if he knew volume one would be read first, but the church as a whole did not take his point. Theologically this turned out for the best,[66] but historically and for literary-critical interpretation it presents an open question.

To conclude, I shall simply summarize the main arguments of the essay in the form of some theses and questions:

1. Insofar as Luke intended Acts to go with Luke as two volumes of a connected work, and insofar as they exhibit literary connectedness, it is clearly legitimate and valuable to study the two works as the literary unity Luke-Acts. Since, however, we have virtually no evidence that the early Christians actually treated the two volumes as a literary unity, such studies cannot claim to be recovering or reproducing the ways in which the early Christians read/heard Luke and Acts.

2. Since the two works were not read as a unity by the early Christians, there is certainly no reason why modern studies *must* treat the two as a connected unity in every dimension of the interpretive enterprise;[67] indeed the claim that a unified reading is historically rooted—in the sense of grounded in actual reading practices—is, as far as we can ascertain, at best seriously disputable and perhaps even false. In the case of Luke's Gospel, this means that readings and studies of the Gospel itself, as with Matthew, Mark, or John, are entirely appropriate.[68] Further,

the evidence of early Christian readings would press us more toward studies of Luke in the context of other Gospel traditions than toward studies of Luke-Acts.

3. There is probably a wide variety of ways in which Acts can legitimately and valuably be read, depending on whether the legitimacy of a reading strategy is connected with the author's intention and/or literary character of the work—both of which would validate reading Acts with Luke—or with the evidence for Acts' early reception and its textual and canonical history—which would validate reading Acts in a variety of relationships and canonical connections: as a sequel to the fourfold gospel tradition, as a prelude or sequel to the Pauline letters, and so on.

4. In relation to the preceding theses we might, however, pose the question: Do we not forfeit an understanding of the literary dynamics of Luke-Acts if we separate Luke from Acts and/or join them together with other writings?[69] Is it possible to retain the depth of understanding of both Luke and Acts gained by reading them together if we read them apart?[70]

5. Finally, to put the larger issue as simply as possible: What are the current interpretive options if we take seriously the possibility that Acts was intended to go with Luke but that they were not actually read together?

NOTES

1. Luke Timothy Johnson *The Gospel of Luke* (SacPag 3; Collegeville, Minn.: Liturgical Press, 1991), 1, puts it well: "In addition to the prologues, the volumes are joined by an intricate skein of stylistic, structural, and thematic elements which demonstrate convincingly that the same literary imagination was at work in both."

2. Whether Luke and Acts belong in the same genre is still hotly contested. See, for example, the recent and extensive essay of Talbert and Stepp (Charles H. Talbert and Perry Stepp, "Succession in Luke-Acts and in the Lukan Milieu," in *Reading Luke-Acts in its Mediterranean Milieu* [NovTSup 107; Leiden: Brill, 2003], 19–55), which is used (in part) to buttress his widely known arguments in favor of a unified biographical genre.

3. For an exception to this assumption, see Mikeal C. Parsons and Richard I. Pervo, *Rethinking the Unity of Luke and Acts* (Minneapolis: Fortress, 1993). Parsons and Pervo mention five different kinds of unity, the last three of which they discuss in detail and dispute in at least some way: (1) authorial (2) canonical (3) generic (4) narrative, and (5) theological. Unlike Parsons and Pervo, I do not think the narrative or theological unity of Luke-Acts can be called into question (and authorial unity is now a given). As they recognize, the question of genre remains debated, but even if Luke and Acts turn out not to belong in the same genre, this would not preclude their literary unity. The five and a half pages on canonical unity (a rather unclear designation) contain several interesting observations, particularly with respect to the differing textual traditions, but such observations are not developed any further. As will become clear, it is precisely these more tangible, historical matters that raise the greatest questions about the unity of Luke-Acts. On the various facets to the "almost

complete consensus" regarding the unity of Luke-Acts, see the *Forschungsbericht* of Verheyden (Joseph Verheyden, "The Unity of Luke-Acts: What Are We Up To?" in *The Unity of Luke-Acts* [ed. Joseph Verheyden; BETL 142; Leuven: University Press, 1999], 3–56). On the different meanings of *unity* used in the scholarly literature see I. Howard Marshall, "Acts and the 'Former Treatise,'" in *The Book of Acts in Its First Century Setting* (ed. Bruce W. Winter and Andrew D. Clarke; Carlisle: Paternoster, 1993), 163–82; esp. 164–72.

4. See, for example, for Matthew's Gospel, Wolf-Dietrich Köhler, *Die Rezeption des Matthäusevangeliums in der Zeit vor Irenäus* (WUNT 2/24; Tübingen: Mohr Siebeck, 1987), and for John's, Titus Nagel, *Die Rezeption des Johannesevangeliums im 2. Jahrhundert: Studien zur vorirenäischen Aneignung und Auslegung des vierten Evangeliums in christlicher und christlich-gnostischer Literatur* (ABG 2; Leipzig: Evangelische Verlagsanstalt, 2000). For the Johannine corpus see Charles E. Hill, *The Johannine Corpus in the Early Church* (Oxford: Oxford University Press, 2004). In terms of New Testament commentaries that display a concern with reception history, Ulrich Luz's Goliath on Matthew stands above the rest (*Matthew 1–7: A Commentary* [Hermeneia; Minnneapolis: Fortress, 2007]).

5. Andrew F. Gregory, *The Reception of Luke and Acts in the Period before Irenaeus: Looking for Luke in the Second Century* (WUNT 2/169; Tübingen: Mohr Siebeck, 2003). This work is a revised version of the author's Oxford Ph.D. dissertation and, to date, is the only extensive investigation of Lukan reception history. Cf. the brief piece of Arthur J. Bellinzoni, "The Gospel of Luke in the Second Century CE," in *Literary Studies in Luke-Acts: Essays in Honor of Joseph B. Tyson* (ed. Richard P. Thompson and Thomas E. Phillips; Macon, Ga.: Mercer University Press, 1998), 59–76. Bellinzoni notes that his essay is a condensed version of a longer paper that he hopes to publish. At present, as far as I am aware, the longer paper has not been published, although Bellinzoni does return to this subject in "The Gospel of Luke in the Apostolic Fathers," in *Trajectories through the New Testament and the Apostolic Fathers* (ed. Andrew F. Gregory and Christopher M. Tuckett; Oxford: Oxford University Press, 2005), 45–68. See also François Bovon, "The Reception and Use of the Gospel of Luke in the Second Century," in *Reading Luke: Interpretation, Reflection, Formation* (ed. Craig Bartholomew et al.; Grand Rapids: Zondervan, 2005), 379–400 (with a response from Gregory). Interestingly, matters of reception history receive only a (rather vague) footnote in Veryheyden's thorough survey of virtually every other significant area that pertains to the question of "unity" (*The Unity of Luke-Acts,* 6 n. 13).

6. Cf. the suggestion of Parsons and Pervo (*Rethinking,* 127) regarding the appropriateness of the conjunction *and.*

7. Gregory, *Reception,* 352.

8. Ibid., 39. This statement stands in some tension with his later remark that in the work of Irenaeus "Acts is not used separately from either the Gospels or from Paul but in close association with both" (301).

9. For our purposes it is sufficient to note the allusions to Luke 24:49 and Acts 1:8, but it should be said that for Irenaeus the entire beginning of Acts seems to be in mind. Whether or not Irenaeus actually needs Luke 24:49 for his argument to work is a fascinating question (see n. 11 below), but the point that he used this text remains (suggesting that Irenaeus, at least, thought Luke 24:49 necessary).

10. Irenaeus, *A. H.* 3.1.1. I use here the text printed in F. Sagnard, *Contre les hérésies, Livre III. Sources Chrétiennes* (vol. 34, critical text and translation of *Against Heresies;* Paris: Éditions du Cerf, 1952).

11. Gregory, *Reception,* 39–40. Gregory's reading of Irenaeus here is nuanced and remarkably perceptive. In light of contemporary Lukan scholarship, as well as the text of Luke-Acts itself, our initial, reasonable assumption may be that Irenaeus is speaking about the gift of the Holy Spirit at Pentecost in Acts 2. As odd as it may seem to us, however, Irenaeus's actual argument is rather different. His point here at the opening of Book 3 (whose purpose, Irenaeus tells us, is to deal with the heretics' treatment of the Scriptures) is that the apostles had received the Holy Spirit—and hence had "perfect knowledge"—*before* they departed to the ends of the earth to preach the gospel (Acts 1:8b). Irenaeus thus reads Luke 24:49 together with Acts 1:8a in order to say that the apostles had received the Power from on high before they departed to preach, and he reads Acts 1:8b to announce their departure. The preaching of the apostles is thus from a point of perfect knowledge, and their testimony, that is, the Scriptures, therefore needs no correction. Exactly what text of Luke and Acts Irenaeus is reading or quoting from memory is a complex question and cannot be addressed here. On Irenaeus's biblical text see William Sanday and Cuthbert H. Turner, *Novum Testamentum Sancti Irenaei Episcopi Lugdunensis* (Oxford: Clarendon Press, 1923). John Lawson suggests that the notion that the apostles had "perfect knowledge" is based upon John 14:26 and 16:13 (*The Biblical Theology of Saint Irenaeus* [London: Epworth, 1948], 88 n. 1). As a background influence for the idea of "perfect knowledge" in this passage, Lawson's suggestion is plausible, and it illustrates well the complexity in attempting to identify biblical influence upon Irenaeus. But the Johannine texts are not in the foreground here in *A.H.* 3.1.1 as are the Lukan.

12. See Lucian, *Historia* 55. For a discussion of this narrative device in relation to the New Testament see Bruce Longenecker "Lukan Aversion to Humps and Hollows: The Case of Acts 11.27–12.25," *NTS* 50/2 (2004): 185–204.

13. Given the character of this "historical" argument, it is probably not too much to suggest that the fact that Luke in particular is the Gospel that contains the information necessary to the argument is really of no importance to Irenaeus. Especially given the absence of a sustained reading of Luke-Acts, one can easily imagine that if Matthew had been the Gospel with the relevant information, Irenaeus would have used it. This is obviously an exercise in imagination, but it helps to illustrate that what *A.H.* 3.1.1 reflects in terms of Irenaeus's treatment of Luke's two volumes is Irenaeus's knowledge of the contents of each. It is not Irenaeus but modern critics who formulate such knowledge in the categories of literary unity and hermeneutical consequence. It is imperative that we not conflate modern formulations with ancient reading practice.

14. Hans von Campenhausen, *The Formation of the Christian Bible* (trans. J. A. Baker; Philadelphia: Fortress, 1972), 201–202. Gregory makes reference to Campenhausen as illustrating "Irenaeus' use of the unity of Luke-Acts to link Acts both with the fourfold Gospel and Paul," but fails to mention that the emphasis of Campenhausen's own account falls on the issue of authorship (*Reception,* 39 n. 58).

15. Gregory, *Reception,* 39.

16. One may also wonder about Irenaeus's argumentative tactics: if he were to separate Luke from the other Gospels to be read alone with Acts, would he not thereby undermine his basic argument regarding the theological necessity of the *Tetraevangelium* and play directly into the hands of his opponents who denied the necessity of the "four" (specifically the variously striped Marcionites known for their reading of "Luke" without the other Gospels; cf. *A.H.* 3.14.3–4)? On this point see especially his polemic in *A.H.* 3.11.9.

17. Campenhausen, *Formation,* 201. Note, too, that Irenaeus not only grants primary unity to Luke as part of the "fourfold" gospel but also grounds its fourfold character in the created order (four zones of the world, four winds, and so on) and in the activity of God, who has bound the four together "by one Spirit" (*A.H.* 3.11.8). Thus is the fourfold gospel theologically necessary in the strict sense (cf. Graham N. Stanton, "The Fourfold Gospel," *NTS* 43/3 [1997]: 319–21, 342–43). The theological necessity of the "four" does not preclude, of course, Irenaeus's freedom to relate particular material from within the individual Gospels to Acts, but it does mean that, in terms of his overall hermeneutical practice, Acts is not isolated to read in relation to Luke alone but is instead taken with the fourfold gospel as a whole.

18. Though in fact his focus is more on the authority of Acts than upon authorship per se. Authorship is a derivative issue in the sense that it serves the purpose of establishing the authority and trustworthiness of Acts (in contrast to the position of his opponents).

19. Cf. convincingly, Stanton, "The Fourfold Gospel," 322–25, and Bruce M. Metzger, *The Canon of the New Testament: Its Origin, Development and Significance* (Oxford: Clarendon, 1997), 193–94, against A. Sundberg et al.

20. Gregory, *Reception,* 41. Gregory's prose both here in the sentence quoted above (missing a word?) and in this larger section is somewhat opaque and his actual argument difficult to discern. "The reference to Luke as a physician is additional to any information that we are given by Irenaeus, but it could come from Colossians 4, so that Luke's name, his profession, and his status as companion of Paul may each rest on existing tradition, and these may then provide the grounds for the conjecture that Luke was the companion of Paul whose presence is to be detected in the we-passages of Acts. Here therefore is clear evidence that the association of the name of Luke with the third Gospel may be explained solely on the conjecture that he wrote Acts, and the observation that similarities between these two volumes, not least their respective dedications to Theophilus, require that they be read as a literary whole."

21. For example, contrary to what Gregory seems to suggest with "their respective dedications" (in the quoted sentence above), the Muratorian Fragment does not actually mention the dedication to Theophilus in relation to the preface to Luke's Gospel but only in relation to the preface to Acts; yet Gregory himself knows this well, as he indicates explicitly: "silence on the preface to Luke" (*Reception,* 42).

22. Lines 34–35. "Apostolic" authorship is of course part of what appears to be at issue. Cf. line 80: The *Shepherd of Hermas* is not to be read publicly with the "apostles," for, among other things, "it is after their time." Of course the lacuna at the beginning of the fragment and the "wretched state of the [existing] Latin text" (Metzger, *The Canon,* 305) are well known and make perilous any guess as to the document's specific purpose.

23. Line 2. Since, however, the beginning of the text is missing there is no way to know for sure. But see Stanton, "The Fourfold Gospel," 322–25.

24. Line 14. Noted also by Stanton, "The Fourfold Gospel," 333. Significantly Stanton remarks that the Muratorian Fragment explicitly mentions, as did Irenaeus, the Spirit as that which holds the Gospels together (324).

25. The relationship of the second century evidence to Luke-Acts is not necessarily dependent upon the date of their composition, but neither is it unaffected by the date. In fact the later one dates Luke and Acts the more direct the relationship of our other second-century sources to them could be.

26. Cf. Stanton, "The Fourfold Gospel," 334, who notes that "the short preface to Acts with its rededication to Theophilus was a conventional way of introducing the second roll of a single work" (cf. Longenecker, "Lukan Aversion," 188, with reference to "the seam between the two Lukan volumes"). The emphasis on literary unity is well placed, but specificity such as the "second scroll of a single work" may be problematical (see, for example, Loveday C. A. Alexander, *The Preface to Luke's Gospel: Literary Convention and Social Context in Luke 1.1–4 and Acts 1.1* [SNTSMS 78; Cambridge: Cambridge University Press, 1993], 145–46.

27. Alexander is right to note that the address to Theophilus in no way means that Luke and/or Acts were written for private readership (esp., for example, *The Preface to Luke's Gospel*, 188). If one grants that Theophilus is not a fictive addressee (and this can be contested), it seems impossible to decide for sure whether or not he was Luke's *patronus.*

28. Henry J. Cadbury, *The Book of Acts in History* (New York: Harper & Brothers, 1955), 139. Cadbury's remark here is significant because it is part of his explanation of how Luke was separated from Acts. It is interesting to note that even Cadbury mentions that the volumes were at least self-sufficient enough "to have prevented some modern readers from recognizing their unity" (139). Cadbury also implies that Luke almost foresaw the possibility or even likelihood of separation: "Fortunately our author had the judgment or foresight to make each of his two volumes somewhat self-sufficient" (139).

29. How much time elapsed between the writing of Luke and Acts is of course impossible to know. It has been common at least since Kenyon's suggestion to assume that the reason Luke and Acts were separated is precisely because of the limitation of scroll length (for example, Cadbury, *The Book of Acts in History*, 138): Luke would fit on one scroll and Acts on a second. The preface to Acts would then be seen as the short introduction to the second scroll. Yet, even if this were the case, we do not necessarily have to assume that he sent both scrolls together at once (see Gregory, *Reception,* 300–01). In any case, at the very least they were physically separate volumes. There also seems now to be the possibility that Luke used a codex or codices for his work (see Gregory, *Reception,* 300–01 n. 9), which would raise the question of the absence of a unified reading even more acutely given that Luke could have written Luke-Acts together on one codex. The likelihood of the possibility of a codex would, it seems, increase in proportion to a late dating of the Lukan material. Yet see Harry Y. Gamble, *Books and Readers in the Early Church: A History of Early Christian Texts* [New Haven: Yale University Press, 1995], 63, who, despite the rapid and expansive adoption of the codex in early Christianity, argues that it is unlikely that a Gospel would have first been written on a codex due to the former's narrative character. Again it is important at this point to emphasize that we are dealing with probability and hypotheses, not firm knowledge. As Gregory notes, "We cannot say with certainty that Acts circulated independently before Irenaeus as we do not know how (or if) it circulated at all" (*Reception,* 301).

30. There are of course some who date Acts quite late (Knox, O'Neill, Koester, and so on). We should also note Gregory's finding—though remembering, too, his use of Koester's rigorous redaction criterion—that there exists no evidence of external attestation for Luke until mid-second century and Acts slightly later (Gregory, *Reception,* 5 n. 11). Yet as Gregory later notes regarding the absence of attestation, the "lack of evidence for the reception of Luke-Acts [sic] before the middle of the second century does not mean that these texts were not used, let alone not written" (353).

31. For a recent study of εὐαγγέλιον see James A. Kelhoffer, "'How Soon a Book' Revisited ΕΥΑΓΓΕΛΙΟΝ as a Reference to 'Gospel' Materials in the First Half of the Second Century," *ZNW* 95/12 (2004): 134, who argues that εὐαγγελίον as a literary designation predates Marcion, *2 Clem.,* and even the *Didache.* Kelhoffer places the terminus a quo after the writing of the Synoptics, arguing that their authors did not use the word to designate a writing, and thus sees the time frame in which the designation emerged as chronologically rather narrow (between the composition of Matthew and the *Didache*).

32. Thus opening the space between the composition and attestation of Acts as wide as possible.

33. See Helmut Koester, *Ancient Christian Gospels: Their History and Development* (Harrisburg: Trinity Press, 1990), 332, for example, whose statement is remarkably confident: Luke and Acts "were originally two volumes of *one* work . . . Luke's work has not been preserved in the form in which it was published by its author" (emphasis original). François Bovon, *Luke 1. A Commentary on the Gospel of Luke 1:1–9:50* (Hermeneia; Minneapolis: Fortress, 2002), 1, is no less confident: the acceptance of Luke and Acts into the canon "led to the division of the two volumes . . . presumably against Luke's intentions. From that point on, the Gospel of Luke and the book of Acts ceased to be two volumes of a single work circulating at the book markets." Cf. also, for example, Cadbury, *The Book of Acts in History,* 139; Brevard S. Childs, *The New Testament as Canon: An Introduction* (Philadelphia: Fortress, 1984), 239; Stanton, "The Fourfold Gospel," 334–35. See, however, W. A. Strange, *The Problem of the Text of Acts* (SNTSMS 71; Cambridge: Cambridge University Press, 1992), 181: "There is no strong evidence to suppose that the two works were issued or ever circulated together" (cf. also Parsons and Pervo, *Rethinking,* 117–18 n. 6). Gregory is careful to say that we do not know that Luke and Acts circulated independently (*Reception,* 301–02). He is correct that absence of evidence is not the same as negative evidence (not knowing if something is the case is quite different from knowing it to be or not to be the case). Yet the somewhat strange reluctance to acknowledge separation on the basis of the prologue in Acts is unnecessary. It is also possible to understand the Muratorian Fragment to distinguish between the time at which Luke wrote the Gospel (while with Paul, lines 4–6) and Acts (later when recollecting the things that transpired in his presence; lines 34–39).

34. Alexander, *The Preface to Luke's Gospel,* 145–46: "Scientific" for Alexander is of course not used "in the limited sense operating in the British educational system, where 'Science' is distinguished from 'Arts' or 'Humanities,' but in a sense closer to that of the French, or of the German *wissenschaftlich*" (21).

35. Speculation about P^{53} (P. Mich. Inv. 6652, third century) as an exception cannot be more than speculation due to the incompleteness of the manuscript (two leaves: Matt. 26:29–40; Acts 9:33–10:1) and debate over whether or not the fragments are part of the same

codex (see Stanton, "The Fourfold Gospel," 326 n. 32 and 334 n. 60). For Luke as the fourth gospel see Metzger, *The Canon of the New Testament,* 230–31 [and 231 n. 5], 296–97, 310). (Gregory's study may increase the likelihood that Luke and Acts were not together in the case of P[53], since if he is correct there would be no precedent in the second century for this joining.)

36. Thus closing the space as much as possible between the composition and manuscript evidence of Acts.

37. See Gregory, *Reception,* 27–32, for a concise and careful discussion of P[75], P[4], and the reliability of manuscript evidence for a pre-Irenaean text of Luke.

38. See Cadbury, *The Book of Acts in History,* 146.

39. Stanton, "The Fourfold Gospel," 335.

40. This reversal of Stanton's suggestion might actually contribute to his overall argument of an early fourfold gospel (though it is strictly speaking a separate issue): in terms of historical order the fourfold gospel did not separate Luke from Acts, but the fact that Luke and Acts were separate made it easier to get the fourfold gospel together. Though he opts for an original historical unity, Cadbury also notes that "it was natural that the Gospel of Luke should be associated with other Gospels" (*The Book of Acts in History,* 139).

41. See, for example, the lists in Alexander Souter, *The Text and Canon of the New Testament* (New York: Charles Scribner's Sons, 1920), 211–12, or appendices II and IV in Metzger, *The Canon of the New Testament.*

42. If Marcion did not know Acts, as for example Cadbury inter alia maintained (*The Book of Acts in History,* 145), this would only strengthen the idea that Luke and Acts circulated independently. C. K. Barrett ("Acts and Christian Consensus," in *Context: Essays in Honour of Peder Johan Borgen* [ed. Peter W. Bøckman and Roald E. Kristiansen; Trondheim: Tapir Press, 1987], 19–33, and "The Third Gospel as a Preface to Acts? Some Reflections," in *The Four Gospels 1992: Festschrift Frans Neirynck* [ed. Frans Van Segbroeck et al.; BETL 100; 3 vols; Leuven: Leuven University Press, 1992], 2.1451–66), following the suggestion of Harnack that Luke was the first Gospel to arrive in Pontus (explaining, at least in part, its high esteem), conjectured that Luke-Acts was in fact seen as a sort of first "New Testament" by Marcion. Marcion "based his own New Testament upon it, editing the gospel, and substituting for Acts . . . the Antitheses and the Pauline letters" (*The Four Gospels,* 2.1466).

43. See Adolf von Harnack, *The Origin of the New Testament and the Most Important Consequences of the New Creation* (London: Williams & Northgate, 1925), 66.

44. Harnack's statement may be overdone but is nevertheless worth recalling: "The placing of this book in the growing Canon shows evidence of reflection, of conscious purpose, of a strong hand acting with authority" (*The Origin of the New Testament,* 67). In replying to Strange's thesis in *The Problem of the Text of Acts* that Luke died with Acts in draft form (hence its late publication, by a Western and non-Western editor, in textually different forms), Stanton remarks that "neither Irenaeus nor the Muratorian Fragment presses a case for accepting Acts" ("The Fourfold Gospel," 335). Perhaps it depends upon what Stanton means by "presses," as in fact just a few lines earlier he wrote—correctly reading Irenaeus in my view—that Irenaeus "insists that if his opponents accepted Luke's Gospel, they should also accept Acts" (335). Irenaeus certainly takes it that Acts is ancient, but he nonetheless notes the need for its acceptance.

45. Cf. Gregory (*Reception,* 2), who notes in passing, "Once Luke released each volume he would have had no control over its circulation and copying."

46. Popular guesses both modern and ancient have included locations as diverse as Rome, Caesarea, the whole of Achaia, and more (for a brief list see, for example, Joseph A. Fitzmyer, *The Gospel According to Luke I–IX* [Garden City: Doubleday, 1981], 1.57). Even if one is still inclined to argue, as would Philip Esler and David Sim, for example, that the Gospels reflect specific communities to which they were addressed, the ability to pin precisely Luke or Acts on a map of the Mediterranean world is seriously lacking (Philip F. Esler, "Community and Gospel in Early Christianity: A Response to Richard Bauckham's *The Gospels for All Christians,*" *SJT* 51 [1998]: 235–48; David C. Sim, "The Gospels for All Christians? A Response to Richard Bauckham," *JSNT* 24/2 [2001]: 3–27). For the issue of Gospel communities in general, see, for example, the concise remarks of Stephen C. Barton ("Can We Identify the Gospel Audiences?" in *The Gospels for All Christians: Rethinking the Gospel Audiences* [ed. Richard Bauckham; Grand Rapids, Mich.: Eerdmans, 1998], 173–94, esp. 186–88). It is important at this point to note with Stanton ("The Fourfold Gospel," 336) that "the older view that the individual gospels circulated only in limited geographical areas is no longer tenable: the papyri . . . indicate clearly that there was a great deal of contact between different regions around the Mediterranean." See, for example, the essay of Michael B. Thompson ("The Holy Internet: Communication Between Churches in the First Christian Generation," in *The Gospels for All Christians,* 49–70). We may also think in particular of the now classic studies of Abraham Malherbe, *Social Aspects of Early Christianity* (Philadelphia: Fortress, 1983), and Wayne Meeks, *The First Urban Christians* (New Haven: Yale University Press, 1983), as well as that of Peter Lampe, *From Paul to Valentinus: Christians at Rome in the First Two Centuries* (Minneapolis: Fortress, 2003), that have shown the importance of the travel between and interconnectedness among the early (usually Pauline) Christian communities. With respect to the circulation of texts in the ancient world, Loveday C. A. Alexander is willing to speak of "interweaving networks" ("Ancient Book Production and the Circulation of the Gospels," in *The Gospels for All Christians,* 104). In a general sense while they by no means prove its impossibility, such studies decrease the likelihood of a specifically Lukan community that would have read Luke's writings in isolation.

47. Gregory's study will surely also spark debate, perhaps especially over his application of Koester's redaction criterion to determine the reception of the texts. It may be, as Gregory recognizes, that Koester's criterion affords the best (only?) way we can know for sure that, say, Lukan rather than Lukan-like texts were directly received, but it may also filter out more than is necessary.

48. Cadbury, *The Book of Acts in History,* 137.

49. Cf., among many possible examples, Gilmore's statement over fifty years ago: "While Mark and Matthew are complete in themselves, Luke is the first volume of a two-volume work. The fundamental unity of Luke-Acts has . . . been obscured in part by an accident of manuscript transmission whereby Luke has included in the 'Gospel' section of the canon and Acts in the 'Apostle' section. The canonical separation by the Gospel of John is an unfortunate divorce" (S. McL. Gilmore, "The Gospel According to St. Luke" in *The Interpreter's Bible* [New York: Abingdon, 1952]: 8.15–16)

50. See N. A. Dahl, "The Story of Abraham in Luke-Acts," in *Studies in Luke-Acts* (ed. Leander E. Keck and J. Louis Martyn; Nashville: Abingdon, 1966), 139–58, esp. 153; and D. Moody Smith's presidential address to the Society of Biblical Literature ("When Did the Gospels Become Scripture?" *JBL* 119/1 [2000]: 3–20).

51. Gregory has a judicious discussion of the most important recent work on this problem and concludes that at present the *status quaestionis* is that of "a continuing debate" (*Reception,* 56–69).

52. Johnson, *The Gospel of Luke,* 1.

53. Luke Timothy Johnson, *The Acts of the Apostles* (SacPag 5; Collegeville, Minn.: Liturgical Press, 1992), 2. Johnson continues: "Everything said there about the identity of the author, the circumstances of composition, the genre and purpose of the work, and the literary methods used by the author, need not be repeated in detail" (2). We may—perhaps a bit mischievously—wonder here about a fuller analogy with Luke-Acts: Johnson's commentaries are meant to be read together as a single whole with two parts. Yet there was never a historical, chronological unity to the commentaries since they were written and published apart. Moreover, at least in the Divinity School library of Duke University, Johnson's commentaries do not sit next to each other on the shelf. Luke is with the other Luke volumes and Acts with its companions (this is also true within the Sacra Pagina series itself). The library grouping obviously reflects the later "canonical" arrangements, but such an order is intelligible on reception historical grounds.

54. Luke Timothy Johnson, "The Christology of Luke-Acts," in *Who Do You Say That I Am? Essays on Christology* (ed. Mark Allan Powell and David R. Bauer; Louisville: Westminster John Knox, 1999), 51. This is actually Johnson's response to his own observation (cued by Parsons and Pervo) that "the early separation of the Gospel and Acts in the process of canonization would argue for their separate treatment" (51).

55. Johnson, *The Acts of the Apostles,* 476 (emphasis removed).

56. Gary Gilbert, "Roman Propaganda and Christian Identity in the Worldview of Luke-Acts," in *Contextualizing Acts: Lukan Narrative and Greco-Roman Discourse* (ed. Todd C. Penner and Caroline Vander Stichele; SBJSS 20; Atlanta: Society of Biblical Literature, 2003), 256.

57. John T. Carroll, "The God of Israel and the Salvation of the Nations," in *The Forgotten God: Perspectives in Biblical Theology: Essays in Honor of Paul J. Achtemeier on the Occasion of his Seventy-fifth Birthday* (ed. A. Andrew Das and Frank J. Matera; Louisville: Westminster John Knox Press, 2002), 91. Cf., for example, F. Gerald Downing (*Doing Things with Words in the First Christian Century* [JSNTSup 200; Sheffield: Sheffield Academic Press, 2000], 198–217), who presupposes a single, first reading of Luke-Acts in his chapter on Theophilus's "first hearing of Luke-Acts." See in this connection Pieter J. J. Botha ("Community and Conviction in Luke-Acts," *Neotestamentica* 29/2 [1995]: 145–65), whose article assumes a unified reading of Luke and Acts in the attempt to specify "the occasion for the presentation of Luke-Acts" in analogy to the readings and performances that "were a common feature of the symposia and dinner parties" in the Graeco-Roman world (150–51).

58. Cf. the widely recognized work of Philip F. Esler (*Community and Gospel in Luke-Acts: The Social and Political Motivations of Lucan Theology* [SNTSMS 57; Cambridge:

Cambridge University Press, 1987]), which concludes that "Luke's two volumes may be described as an exercise in the legitimation of a sectarian movement, as a sophisticated attempt to explain and justify Christianity to the members of his community at a time when they were exposed to social and political pressure" (222). Esler's general point, that Luke himself "theologized" in relation to a concrete community, may be correct (though it is debatable, as the controversy surrounding Bauckham's proposals regarding Gospel audience have illustrated), but it does not ipso facto follow that this community would have read Luke-Acts together in a way analogous to modern critical practice, or even that Luke wrote Luke and Acts close together (for example, his Gospel could have gotten out and around, as it were, before he wrote Acts). In other words monographs such as Esler's that read community out of Luke-Acts are arguably much more about Luke's overall sociotheological concerns, at least methodologically speaking, than they are about an actual community that reads Luke and Acts together as Luke-Acts. Barrett's hypothesis (see note 42 above) that Marcion knew of Luke-Acts does actually attempt to provide a distinct group within a particular locale (Pontus) that would have known of an original unity of Luke's two volumes (though obviously Marcion did not read them together). Yet Barrett's primary piece of evidence—a statement from the Mesopotamian bishop Marutha of Maipherkat (ca. A.D. 400; Barrett, "Acts and Christian Consensus," 31)—is hardly a suitable basis for such a conjecture, and we may also note that Barrett's hypothesis probably rests on the prior assumption of just the type of unity that is in question. Moreover, as intimated earlier, it seems prima facie to make better sense out of the situation to assume either that Marcion did not really know Acts (though this runs against the testimony—albeit polemical—of the early church fathers) or that he came to know Acts only after he knew Luke (thus making sense of the totality of the rejection of Acts).

59. Johnson, *The Gospel of Luke,* 4: Luke-Acts "must be read as a *single* story" (emphasis original).

60. Raymond E. Brown, *An Introduction to the Gospel of John* (ed. Francis J. Moloney; New York: Doubleday, 2003), 111. Brown is speaking here about the purpose of a commentary.

61. Alexandru Neagoe, *The Trial of the Gospel: An Apologetic Reading of Luke's Trial Narratives* (SNTSMS 116; Cambridge: Cambridge University Press, 2002).

62. Of modern scholars Robert W. Wall's commentary in the *New Interpreter's Bible* series is an excellent example of a canonical interpretation of Acts, of what it might mean to read Acts after the four gospels and before Paul's letters. Cf., however, the intriguing discussion of Brevard S. Childs (*The New Testament as Canon,* esp. 239–40), in which he argues that "the canonical function of Acts was not determined by the order of its placement within the New Testament collection. . . . The canonical significance of Acts lies elsewhere, regardless of its order within the New Testament collection" (239). Yet Childs's canonical understanding does in fact take Acts as the framework for the interpretation of Paul, but perhaps in a way that is (somewhat?) independent of their actual order. In light of Childs's nuanced discussion, perhaps we should be even more specific within canonical criticism itself and term Wall's type of interpretation literary-canonical in the sense of reading the present canonical material literarily in order.

63. For example, after John, after Mark, after the Pauline Epistles, and so on.

64. See, for example, the still important essay of Charles H. Talbert, "Prophecies of Future Greatness: The Contributions of Greco-Roman Biographies to an Understanding of Luke 1:5–4:1," in *Reading Luke-Acts in its Mediterranean Milieu,* 65–77. Cf. Talbert's careful remarks on "authorial audience" as "larger cultural milieu" in the lead essay, "On Reading Luke and Acts," 1–18, esp. 17–18, of the same collection. As I read him, Talbert does not presuppose an actual early Christian community for his interpretations, but rather in a technically sophisticated way construes the meaning of Luke's text primarily through the lens of larger Graeco-Roman culture (specifically, relevant aspects of its "presupposition pool").

65. If Acts came after the Pauline letters, for example, the auditor's ability to connect the trial scenes in Acts to the Gospel of Luke would probably be greatly diminished. So, too, to take another example, in a canonical ordering where John precedes Acts, it is worth noting the serious differences in the narration of Jesus' trial before the Sanhedrin between John and Luke. Would hearing John's version not have an impact on the way in which one would hear the trials in Acts?

66. So, rightly, Stanton, "The Fourfold Gospel," 341–46.

67. The claim that scholars *must* treat Luke and Acts together is of course widespread in modern research. See, for example, W. Ward Gasque, *A History of the Criticism of the Acts of the Apostles* (BGBE 17; Tübingen: J.C.B. Mohr Siebeck, 1975), 309, who concludes his learned monograph thus: "The primary gain of the recent criticism of Luke-Acts has been the recognition that the Gospel according to Luke and the Book of Acts are really two volumes of one work which must be considered together."

68. Contra, for example, the critical remarks of Martin Rese, "Das Lukas-Evangelium. Ein Forschungsbericht," *ANRW* II.25.3 (1985): 2298 n. 162): "Es war . . . sicher keine gute Entscheidung, in der Reihe 'Wege der Forschung' einen Band allein für das LkEv zu bestimmen." Rese's note comes at the conclusion of his report on the research of the first half of the twentieth century. The point at which the scholarly discussion advanced, argues Rese, was the apprehension of the unity of Luke-Acts. To return to a separate treatment of Luke and/or Acts is to forfeit understanding: "LkEv und Apg sind als ein einheitliches Werk anzusehen, und man wird keinem der beiden Einzelteile dieses Werks gerecht, wenn man es je für sich allein betrachtet . . . Ohne diese Einsicht ist der jetzt noch zu behandelnde Abschnitt der Arbeit am LkEv nicht zu verstehen, und hinter diese Einsicht sollte keine Auslegung des LkEv mehr zurückfallen" (2298).

69. Cf. Alexander's comments ("Formal Elements and Genre," 11) on the preface of Acts: "Acts is 'Volume II': readers who begin here have missed a lot of essential information, very little of which will be directly explained for their benefit. . . . For the reader of Acts, in other words, the opening sentence makes it evident that the two volumes have to be read in sequence."

70. Cf. Barrett ("Third Gospel," 2.1451–66): "It is clear that the gospel . . . can be, and very often has been, read independently, and taken on its own makes the same good sense as Matthew, Mark, and John. But this does not in itself mean that it was not intended to serve the additional purpose of introducing a second volume which from the beginning was part of the author's plan" (1453).

LITERARY CRITICISM OF LUKE-ACTS

Is Reception History Pertinent?

Luke Timothy Johnson

I agree with C. Kavin Rowe in "History, Hermeneutics, and the Unity of Luke-Acts" that the history of reception is important. Indeed I am willing to argue that biblical scholars in the future will probably find the examination of the world that the New Testament creates more fruitful than the study of the world that created the New Testament. But in his attempt to use the evidence of the late second century, mainly Irenaeus and the Muratorian Fragment, to warn against drawing historical conclusions from the reading of Luke-Acts as a historical unity, Rowe may fall into the same error against which he warns. The fact that there is no evidence that Luke-Acts was received or read as a literary unity in late-second-century compositions does not answer the question of how the first readers might have read and understood Luke's writing.

In the first place one could find little evidence that any New Testament writings were read in the late second century—or for much of the patristic period—as "literary compositions." It is well known that patristic writers seldom advert to the distinctive literary characteristics of a Gospel or Epistle. That Luke-Acts was not read in the late second century as a literary unity is no more surprising than that no other New Testament writing was read that way.

In the second place the second-century writers to whom Rowe refers were already approaching the New Testament compositions precisely as parts of a New Testament, that is, as a collection of writings that were to be read in the church, in distinction from other writings that were not to be read in church. They were, furthermore, making arguments or statements precisely about matters of inclusion and exclusion for a church considered as universal rather than simply local. In contrast no original hearers of Paul's letters or of the Gospels could possibly have heard them as part of a collection. And even if we assert a wider audience for the Gospels than a single community, we must admit that the first hearers of Luke-Acts (or, if one insists, of Luke and Acts) would have heard the composition not as part of a scriptural collection written in the past, but as a single, discrete, literary composition addressed to them—and possibly others—in the present.

In short there is a gap between the authors cited by Rowe and the first readers of Luke-Acts, a gap not only of time, but also of circumstance and therefore of perspective. It is this gap that traditional historical-critical exegesis has tried to fill. Since we cannot supply the first readers of New Testament compositions, we try as best we can to imagine how they might have read. Literary criticism is very much like historical exegesis in this respect. Literary critics though, at least of the sort I try to be, think that historical critics pay too little attention to the rhetoric of the compositions and too much attention to the putative reconstruction of their historical situation—often at the expense of compositional integrity.

Literary critics seek to redress that imbalance by focusing on the composition's own rhetorical intentionality, but they do not thereby abandon historical imagination. To put it simply, the way the composition itself is put together suggests readers with certain characteristics and capabilities. Analysis of the composition's rhetorical or narrative logic also reveals not only the writing's argument but also something about the direction in which that argument wishes to turn its intended readers. A delicate sensibility is required in such reading. As I argued some thirty years ago, it is certainly wrongheaded to construct a "Lukan Community" from the narrative of Luke-Acts.[1] But this does not mean that some historical judgments cannot be made about the readers. Scholars can, for example, argue over the ethnic identity of author and readers, for the composition allows distinct conclusions to be reached. The composition does not allow the conclusion, however, that the readers were not intended to be intensely and existentially interested in the destiny of Jews and Gentiles in the unfolding of God's plan. To reach such a conclusion would mean to go against the composition's internal logic and to indict the author as rhetorically incompetent.

The same desire for balance accounts for the way literary critics speak of "intended readers" or "ideal readers" or "imagined readers." They do not want to make historical claims about actual readers. But they want to respect the nature of writing as communication, and point to the kinds of characteristics and competencies required to make full sense of the author's work. Such language points to the nature of the composition more than it does to the situation of the readers. And it is in this chastened and modest sense that I employed the phrase "Luke's readers recognize," in my commentary on Acts cited by Rowe.[2]

Rowe also tries to get some historical leverage from the prologue to Acts: the second volume may have been composed at a time substantially later than Luke and therefore could not have been read as "one work" even by its earliest readers. But the leverage is simply not there. Nothing in the second prologue suggests the passage of time between the composition of the two volumes. Indeed the very briefness of the prologue to Acts suggests the opposite, namely that the author could assume substantial knowledge of what the first volume contains.

On this point Rowe has some good-natured fun with my own two-volume commentary on Luke-Acts, noting that it was published separately and shelved in two different sections of the Duke Divinity library, even though I explicitly communicated to my readers that I wanted the volumes to be read together. Let me grant the point and push it further. I have no doubt that my books are used in a variety of ways. Some readers look in them for cross-references, others for a bit of historical data or lexical information, others for my opinion of a single verse or passage. Some readers of one volume may in fact be unaware that I have written the other volume.

But if we are to ask about the "intended" readers or "ideal" readers of my commentary, the ones who are most competent to follow my argument concerning Luke-Acts as a whole and therefore best understand what I wanted to communicate in my commentary, we would have to think of those readers who have, despite the vagaries of book cataloguing, read them as one. No one would suggest, furthermore, that those who read one without reference to the other are reading "Johnson's commentary" in a superior fashion, even if we were to show statistically that nearly all of my readers did read that way. I can state, finally, that although the commentary volumes were published in 1991 and 1992, both volumes could have been read together in sequence by my first "ideal reader," who was Daniel Harrington, S.J., the editor of the Sacra Pagina commentary series.

I make two final points quickly. First, as I think Rowe recognizes, I regard the literary-critical reading of Luke-Acts as a unity to be a genuine reading choice. By no means do I think it has exclusive value. It is perfectly legitimate to read Acts together with Paul's letters, and Luke together with the other Gospels. It is appropriate to read the Gospel as a source for historical knowledge about Jesus, and Acts as a source for historical knowledge about early Christianity. It is also appropriate to employ the various reading perspectives offered by source-history, tradition-history, form-criticism, and redaction-criticism. But I do claim that the sort of literary-critical reading I have done of Luke's entire narrative is best for one purpose, namely understanding his literary and theological voice. Second, as important as reception-history is, it cannot be prescriptive for all interpretation. Would Rowe seriously propose that the reading of Romans by Origen, Cyril of Alexandria, and Augustine should preclude the efforts to hear Romans fresh—within the frame of first-century social realities and rhetoric—by readers such as Stendahl, Sanders, and Stowers? Surely not. I hope he would agree that all of these ways of reading ought to be part of a vigorous and wide-ranging conversation about the meaning of the texts.

NOTES

1. Luke Timothy Johnson, "On Finding the Lukan Community: A Cautious Cautionary Essay," in *1979 Seminar Papers* (ed. Paul J. Achtemeier; SBL; Missoula, Mont.: Scholars Press, 1979), 87–100.

2. Luke Timothy Johnson, *The Acts of the Apostles* (SacPag 5; Collegeville, Minn.: Liturgical Press, 1992).

WHY NOT LET ACTS BE ACTS?

In Conversation with C. Kavin Rowe

Markus Bockmuehl

C. Kavin Rowe's article "History, Hermeneutics, and the Unity of Luke-Acts" is a welcome stimulus for the rekindling of a common and open conversation about the interpretation of Luke and Acts. As is appropriate for a "think piece," he offers more questions than answers; and most readers will, like this respondent, find their eyebrows ascending and descending at various points in the argument. That, of course, is all to the good; and the value of Rowe's contribution is that it requires not our assent but merely our participation in order to make its point.

To place my response in context I must let the cat out of the bag from the start and declare myself in substantial agreement with the overall argument, which in my case was pushing on open doors. The questions that follow therefore should be read as counterpoint rather than dissonance, encouraging Rowe to develop his case further along the lines he has already proposed.

Simply put, he suggests that the scholarly study of Luke and Acts needs to confront the implications of Andrew F. Gregory's recent work: the critical construct that sees these two biblical works as an indissoluble literary integrity runs up against the historical reality that no known ancient readers copied, read, or interpreted them together. The evangelist may have intended his two-volume work to be read as one, but the consistent practice of all known ancient readers was to read the first volume as integral to the fourfold gospel and the second as the story of the apostolic church—that is, as [τὸ εὐαγγέλιον] κατὰ Λουκᾶν and Πράξεις Ἀποστόλων, respectively, an early-second-century gospel designation, if Hengel is right.[1] Readers too pressed for time to read Gregory's book may find a brief look at Nestle-Aland's Appendix I revealing: in manuscripts where Acts keeps any company at all, it introduces the *Apostolos* (that is, the Catholic Epistles) or occasionally the Pauline corpus, but it never appears with Luke alone and very rarely with the Gospels alone (though in the third century P[45] has portions of Acts following all four Gospels, while P[53] contains Matt. 26:29–40 with Acts 9:33–10:1). Patristic evidence corroborates this view: both volumes were known to be Luke's, but each was read separately and for a different purpose. There is no evidence that Acts *ever* became "separated" from the Gospel, as is often assumed. In other words the unanimous practice of Luke's ancient readers clashes with the nearly unanimous verdict of modern literary criticism.

For purposes of the present discussion four questions may be worth pressing further.

1. The first concerns *Luke's purpose.* Rowe astutely highlights the tensions between Lukan literary-critical analysis and the actual historical footprint of his worksand between authorial intent and actual use. But might we benefit from further discussion of whether the Luke of history, as distinct from the implied author of literary criticism, did in fact "set out to write a two-volume work"? How obvious is it either that the evangelist designed the two volumes as an integral whole from the start, or that he meant them to be read as a single work even by the time he wrote Acts? True, the Gospel prologue more than hints at a continued Christian existence, and Acts 1:1 and later allusions to the story and teaching of Jesus presume at least some knowledge of what was in the Gospel (though passages such as Acts 6:13 or 20:35 suggest that Luke was less precise about that correlation than he is often supposed to be). In contrast most of the Gospel's literary and prophetic predictions have close Synoptic parallels or refer to a time beyond the end of Acts, or both. Deliberate pointers *forward* to Acts, if any, are at the level of generalities. Except as a purely *literary* (and ahistorical) judgment, then, there may be little justification for commentators' claims that only the reader who already has Acts in hand can do justice to what Luke intends in the Gospel. The much discussed narrative ruptures in the chain-link between Luke 24:45–53 and Acts 1–2 should suffice to give pause here, just as Rowe's quotation from Loveday C. A. Alexander rightly cautions against overinterpreting the recapitulation in Acts 1:1–2.[2] I wonder if the article here cedes unnecessary ground to the standard historical-critical construct it seems to want to question.

2. Second, might the earliest *reception history* actually be more relevant to the question of intention than Rowe allows? In the quotation from Raymond E. Brown, Rowe envisages quite a wide gap between "what was meant by the author" and "what was understood by the first readers."[3] He is of course right to do so, and twentieth-century hermeneutics has taught us to be wary about relating the two naïvely—quite apart from the chronological gap between the authors and what we know about their readers (though Justin and even Papias arguably narrow that gap to perhaps half a century or less). Nevertheless is it not also the case that consistency of reception serves, more often than not, as a useful rule of thumb about the drift of ancient texts and their range of plausible meanings? It points not perhaps to the intention of the author, into whose head we cannot enter, but certainly to the sense of what Umberto Eco calls the intention of the

work, the *intentio operis.* It would be unrealistic to expect precision here, but I wonder if being a little more explicit about the text's footprint and aftermath would allow our discussion of the potential hermeneutical "paydirt" of *Wirkungsgeschichte* to advance beyond what has too often been seemingly eclectic and arbitrary study in the service of ulterior concerns.

3. Third, a word about the question of the much-disputed "Lukan community" and its reading of Luke's two volumes. I am of two minds about this, although again in substantial agreement with Rowe. If it is a way of denoting Luke's first readers, that question seems in principle valid and worth asking. Historically defensible answers are, however, fewer than contemporary mirror-readers like to think. I personally suspect that Luke envisaged his readers to be Roman in polity and at least mental geography; but even that, if true, would not tell us much about a "community." The readers we actually know about did not take Luke and Acts as one, even if they knew both; indeed, like Marcion or Tertullian who rebuts him, they read Luke rather more often than Acts. Beyond that it may be relevant that communities in Rome and elsewhere appear not to have read *either* Luke or Acts all that much, certainly as compared with Matthew or John. "Where is Luke-Acts?" Rowe rightly asks. We can say a little more about where Luke and Acts were *individually,* though not a great deal more: of the extant single or multiple Gospel manuscripts before 300, 53 percent contain at least parts of the Gospel of John, while 40 percent have Matthew. Mark is invisible except in P45 (3 percent), but even Luke appears in only 23 percent of these texts. Thus if there ever was a "community" whose Gospel was Luke alone, conjoint with Acts, it has left no trace.

4. Finally, however, in relation to Rowe's questions 4 and 5, is not the answer in each case almost certainly *dialectical*? To understand the literary mind of the historical Luke we may indeed benefit from reading Luke and Acts in light of each other and perhaps especially the latter in light of the former. To understand the historical and canonical footprint of these works as heard by their early readers, however, it matters that the Gospel is self-identified in 1:1 as one διήγησις of the Gospel events among "many," which very soon became one among four. By the same token Acts introduces the *Apostolos:* looking back on the completed πρῶτος λόγος about what Jesus did and taught (1:1–2), it now embarks on a new chronicle concerning the postresurrection charge to his Spirit-filled apostolic witnesses (1:3–8). Scholarly investigation of Acts may be enriched by affirming both the literary and the historical insight, each in its place.

NOTES

1. Martin Hengel, *The Four Gospels and the One Gospel of Jesus Christ: An Investigation of the Collection and Origin of the Canonical Gospels* (trans. John Bowden; London: SCM, 2000), 48–56.

2. Loveday C. A. Alexander, *The Preface to Luke's Gospel: Literary Convention and Social Context in Luke 1.1–4 and Acts 1.1* (SNTSMS 78; Cambridge: Cambridge University Press, 1993), as quoted in C. Kavin Rowe, "History, Hermeneutics and the Unity of Luke Acts," in this volume, 43–65 (first published in *JSNT* 28/2 [2005]).

3. Raymond E. Brown, *An Introduction to the Gospel of John* (ed. Francis J. Moloney; New York: Doubleday, 2003), as quoted in Rowe, "History, Hermeneutics," 51.

LITERARY UNITY AND RECEPTION HISTORY

Reading Luke-Acts as Luke and Acts

C. Kavin Rowe

Every New Testament scholar knows that to speak correctly of Luke and Acts, we should talk of Luke-Acts. Or such is the conventional wisdom. Yet a consideration of the issues raised by the reception history of these texts problematizes our linguistic habits by forcing us to rethink some fundamental assumptions that shape our interpretation of the Lukan writings. In this respect Andrew F. Gregory's[1] remarkably thorough spadework uncovered central historical and hermeneutical problems with which New Testament scholars must deal—problems which I subsequently sought to press upon the field in my article "History, Hermeneutics and the Unity of Luke-Acts."[2] The present essay continues this conversation.

THE PRESENT SITUATION, *IN NUCE*

If we look first at the evidence "external" to Luke-Acts—ancient readers, copyists, and so on—we find no evidence of any interpretive practice that depends for its intelligibility upon the hermeneutical strategy of taking Luke-Acts as a single, unified literary whole. Furthermore, though the common authorship of Luke and Acts was discussed in antiquity, there exist no arguments to the effect that Luke and Acts should actually be read together as Luke-Acts. This is obviously not to say that Luke and Acts were unknown prior to Irenaeus. It is, rather, to say that insofar as it can be discerned there is no indisputable indication that Luke and Acts were read as the literary unity we call Luke-Acts. Since Gregory's dissertation there have been a few minor articles that touch upon this topic,[3] but not one of them presents evidence that could qualify substantially this conclusion. With respect to the available data, we may thus say that Luke-Acts was not received as Luke-Acts.

There are of course debatable passages—chiefly in my view Justin Martyr's *First Apology* 50.12 and the opening of Book 3 of Irenaeus's *Against Heresies.* But I would submit that at best what these passages demonstrate is, on the one hand, knowledge of the contents of Luke and Acts taken primarily as historical facts (Justin and Irenaeus) and, on the other, knowledge of the Lukan *authorship* of Acts (Irenaeus alone). What such passages almost certainly do *not* demonstrate is any kind of larger or sustained reading of Luke and Acts together as Luke-Acts, a hermeneutical approach, in other words, that depends for its coherence upon an actual reading practice that treats literarily Luke's two volumes as one, unified work.[4]

From the perspective of reception history, we may thus summarize the situation as follows: no ancient author exhibits a hermeneutical practice that is founded upon the reading of Luke-Acts as one work in two volumes; no ancient author argues that Luke and Acts should be read together as one work in two volumes; and there is not a single New Testament manuscript that contains the unity Luke-Acts or even hints at this unity by placing Acts directly next to the Gospel of Luke.[5]

If we look, second, at the evidence internal to Luke-Acts we find an absence of any concrete indication that Luke and Acts were issued together as one work. There is every reason to think that the two volumes are unified structurally, thematically, and theologically—which is to say literarily in a rather full sense—but it does not follow that the volumes had to be, or were intended to be, issued together as one work. To those who would invoke the preface of Acts as evidence to the contrary, it should be pointed out that (1) the admittedly ambiguous preface can easily be read to presuppose a chronological gap between the composition of Acts and the πρῶτος λόγος; (2) within Luke's literary milieu "recapitulatory" prefaces did not necessarily imply chronologically close composition;[6] and (3) Luke's Gospel is narratively intelligible on its own, apart from Acts. (Even Cadbury was quick to recognize this point; indeed, he offered it as a reason for their subsequent separation.[7]) To be sure, for those who have ears to hear there are various items in the Gospel that receive their completion, as it were, in Acts (for example, Simeon's prophecy in Luke 2:32 that Jesus will be a φῶς εἰς ἀποκάλυψιν ἐθνῶν points through Luke 7:1–10 toward the second volume). But such connections only show Luke's literary deftness as a writer. They do not say anything one way or another about the reception of the works; they do not render the Gospel unintelligible by itself; and they do not show that Acts must have been bound together with Luke from the start.

LITERARY UNITY AND RECEPTION HISTORY

In light of the foregoing sketch, we may make two important distinctions. (1) In contrast to Parsons and Pervo I do not question the literary, theological, or "architectonic" unity of Luke-Acts. Indeed I think it demonstrable that the author of the Gospel did write Acts as a sequel to Luke. However, what unity in this sense tells us has to do with Luke's literary achievement, his talent as an author; it does not—and this point bears repeating—tell us how the texts were actually read. Luke's narrative artistry, his ability to write a richly textured, two-volume work is emphatically not the same thing as what other people did with his writings: the intention and success of Luke the author should not be confused or conflated with the reception of Luke and Acts.

This simple distinction is actually far-reaching in two senses: (a) further demonstration of the literary unity of Luke-Acts as a response to my earlier article, to Gregory,[8] or to Bockmuehl,[9] misses the point of the argument from reception history. To take but one example, questions of whether the preface to Luke's Gospel refers to both volumes or to the Gospel alone (see Bird in this volume) really do nothing whatever to alter the force of the reception historical argument, which is, I think, that we have no evidence that the two volumes were read together as Luke-Acts. Irenaean nuance aside, this is a historical fact that cannot be altered by additional attention to Luke's literary skill. To defeat Parsons and Pervo on "literary unity" is not yet even to grapple seriously with reception history. (b) To affirm the literary unity of Luke-Acts while questioning its actual reception as Luke-Acts suggests that we should speak both of Luke-Acts (when thinking in terms of Lukan theology, christology, politics, and so on) and of Luke and Acts (when inquiring after what the texts' early auditors would have heard). Thus I agree with Luke Timothy Johnson that "a literary-critical reading . . . of Luke's entire narrative is best . . . for understanding his literary and theological voice"[10] but disagree that we can move assuredly from Luke's "voice" as displayed through both volumes to what ancient readers would have heard. In the case of the Lukan writings reconstructing the latter on the basis of the former is exactly what is made difficult by the evidence from reception history. Despite the confidence of modern New Testament scholarship, the hermeneutical difference between the two modes of reading cannot so easily be collapsed into one interpretive process.

(2) Hence we come second to the division among scholars of reception history that results from the absence of first-century evidence. On one side there are those who think that the literary unity of Luke-Acts supplies sufficient ground for us to suppose that the writings were read together as Luke-Acts prior to their separation:[11] ideal readers must be translated into a group of real readers. On the other there are those who think that we have no evidence for such a smooth translation and that what later evidence we do possess points uniformly in the opposite direction:[12] ideal readers may not so easily be translated into real readers (literary unity does not offer us the concrete, requisite community of interpreters). With respect to the late-first or early-second century (assuming the more or less traditional dating of Luke and Acts), perhaps we are simply at a stalemate. Yet, each view de facto presupposes an earlier state of affairs that allegedly renders intelligible the later evidence: the former view, that "somehow" Luke and

Acts became separated in the history of transmission; the latter, that Luke and Acts may well have been read separately from the start. We thus arrive at the question of a historically plausible *Ausgangspunkt* for the subsequent history of the texts.

THE SEARCH FOR AN *AUSGANGSPUNKT*

To search behind our extant evidence for a plausible *Ausgangspunkt* is of course to deal with probabilities rather than with knowledge. Yet it is hardly unreasonable to ask whether there might be a situation that could explain well the subsequent developments. If we examine the common hypothesis that Luke and Acts were *separated* at some point after their initial, joint publication, we find that it has less to commend it than we may have thought (cf. Bockmuehl: "There is no evidence that Acts *ever* became 'separated' from the Gospel, as is often assumed"[13]). To the absence of literary indications that a joint publication was necessary, we may add that if Luke and Acts were originally designed to fit almost exactly on one scroll each, as has long been suggested (Kenyon et al.), then it becomes much harder—rather than easier—to think of their mutual publication and interpretation. If on two separate scrolls, Luke and Acts were in a physically important sense primed or ready for different treatment, particularly if whoever received these scrolls already knew a gospel-like writing that would bear substantial similarity to Luke (say, the Gospel of Mark). Interestingly, in the preface to his Gospel, Luke mentions other such writings (πολλοί!), and for all practical purposes invites Theophilus to contrast Luke's account with the others. Whether the recipients of Luke's Gospel actually did compare or contrast different writings we cannot know. But we may surely observe that it would be natural for Luke's readers to associate the Gospel with these other gospels or gospel-like writings.[14]

Moreover there are the issues of the two different forms of the text of Acts (the "Western" text is almost ten per cent longer) and the varying placement of Acts in the canonical "lists" and New Testament manuscripts. With respect to the former we may take notice of the important fact that it is more difficult to account for the messiness of Acts' textual situation with the supposition of a neat, joint publication with Luke—*Luke-Acts*—than it is to suppose that Acts' textual situation is at least in some way intrinsically related to the manner in which it actually began to circulate. Though hardly an attempt at a text-critical solution, to tie Acts' textual anomalies to its originating circumstances is to account better for (1) the fact that it is cited as authoritative in various forms without discrimination (for example, Tertullian and Cyprian read the Western text; Clement of Alexandria, Origen, and Athanasius cite the Alexandrian; and Eusebius of Caesarea evinces a mixture of Western and non-Western readings) and (2) to account better for the dramatic difference between the textual problems in Acts and those of the other New Testament writings—especially the Gospel of Luke.

With respect to the placement of Acts in "lists" and New Testament manuscripts, it is well known that Acts often introduces the Catholic Epistles (for example, Athanasius's Easter letter of 367 and P[74]). To stay at this level of generality, however, is to obscure the considerable diversity of Acts' particular placement. It also seems to conclude the Catholic Epistles (for example, "Pope Innocent to Exsuperius of Toulouse," ca. 400), as well as the *Tetraevangelium* (for example, Eusebius, *Hist. Eccl.* 3.25.1 and P[45]), which of course varied as to its order. It both introduces and follows the *corpus Paulinum* (for example, the canon of Gregory of Nazianzus and the Cheltenham canon, respectively). And at least in one fragmentary papyrus from the third century a small portion of Acts is found with Matthew alone (P[53]). More strikingly, in Codex Claromontanus (ca. sixth century)—where Luke is the fourth of the four Gospels—Acts occurs near the end of the list, between Revelation (which itself follows the Epistle of Barnabus) and the *Shepherd of Hermas.* How frequent or rare was such an odd positioning of Acts may be impossible to know, but it is probably not without significance that the final canon in the *Apostolic Constitutions* (Can. 85, ca. late fourth century) positions Acts thus: "Our sacred books are . . . the four Gospels . . . fourteen Epistles of Paul; two Epistles of Peter; three of John; one of James; one of Jude; two Epistles of Clement; and the Constitutions dedicated to you, the bishops, by me, Clement, in eight books . . . ; and the Acts of us, the Apostles."[15]

Such variation prohibits our ability to trace a clear line of reception. If, however, we take the picture in a more holistic manner, Acts' unsettled canonical history is more readily comprehensible with the hypothesis that it circulated ab initio independently from the Gospel of Luke than with the idea that in the face of an ecclesial tradition of reading Luke-Acts, the two volumes were nonetheless later separated—but left *no trace whatever* of their original unity. At the very least it is beyond doubt that in strong contrast to the Gospel of Luke, the role of Acts in the scriptural parameters of the church was far from clear. Indeed, perhaps this is the historical reality that underlies the surprising remarks of John Chrysostom in 401: "to many persons [Acts] is so little known, both it and its author, that they are not even aware there is such a book in existence."[16]

Given the physical (scrolls), textual (Western/non-Western), and canonical (various placement) picture—as well as the knowledge of the preexistence of other gospel-like writings with which Luke (but not Acts) could have easily and perhaps immediately been associated—does not a separate publication of Luke and Acts serve as a better point of departure for the separate treatment of these works we find in the second century and beyond? If the standard view requires a theory to explain Luke's separation from Acts (typically, the fogging "somehow"), the alternative view that would allow for separate publication and circulation, by contrast, has considerable explanatory power. Its solution is elegant and simple:

Luke and Acts were not treated as Luke-Acts because they were not issued as one work in the first place; separate publication and circulation amounted to separate treatment. Of course, in terms of our actual data, this puts the matter in reverse. The lack of joint publication and circulation is what might make the best sense in light of the absence of evidence that the two works were read as a unified literary whole.[17]

CONCLUDING REFLECTIONS

I conclude with two observations that should merit further discussion and elaboration. First, in the study of the reception history of the New Testament documents, the differences between the various New Testament writings should not be overlooked or minimized. Indeed they should be given careful attention.[18] Thus, for example, when Luke Timothy Johnson questions the usefulness of the reception history of Luke and Acts for the historical-critical imagination by drawing on Paul's Epistle to the Romans, he obscures the central problem.[19] The point of my earlier article was not to object to the historical-critical method as such but rather to note the way in which the reception history of Luke and Acts *in particular* creates hermeneutical problems for the assumptions that undergird standard scholarly practice.

Johnson's conflation between Paul's writings and Luke's leads nicely to the second observation, which pertains to the importance of reception history for traditional New Testament studies. Because there are no "laws" or "principles" that govern the history of textual reception, the usefulness of a text's forward history to traditional historical-critical exegesis cannot be determined in general but instead only through specific investigation. To stay with Romans and Luke-Acts: the reception history of Romans does not render problematic the historically imaginative attempt of contemporary scholars to read this letter "within the frame of first-century social realities and rhetoric,"[20] for such history—as much as it illuminates important aspects of Romans—clearly does not undermine hermeneutically the presuppositions that support the modern reading strategy. The case is simply otherwise with Luke-Acts, where—at the very least—the study of reception history presents a complex and significant challenge to the dominant historical-critical practice.

NOTES

1. Andrew F. Gregory, *The Reception of Luke and Acts in the Period before Irenaeus: Looking for Luke in the Second Century* (WUNT 2/169; Tübingen: Mohr Siebeck, 2003).

2. C. Kavin Rowe, "History, Hermeneutics, and the Unity of Luke-Acts," in this volume, 43–65 (first published in *JSNT* 28/2 [2005]: 131–57). Subsequent references are to this essay as it appears in this volume.

3. Ibid., 56 n. 5.

4. My point here with respect to *Against Heresies* 3.1 is that while Irenaeus may well perceive an essential connection between the end of Luke and beginning of Acts (so Gregory), this says more about Luke's literary ability that it does about Irenaeus's reading practice. When asking about the latter—that is, does Irenaeus actually read a two-volume work as one (Luke-Acts)?—the answer is that he manifestly does not. In terms of hermeneutical strategy and practice Irenaeus reads the *Tetraevangelium* together with Acts. With respect to Justin the situation is even more complex: it is arguable that 50.12 reflects the plotline of Luke-Acts, but it is also possible (as Gregory pointed out in private conversation) that 50.12 derives from Justin's knowledge of the end of Luke and Matthew (esp. 28:19–20). Of course it has also been argued that Justin did not know Acts at all.

5. This despite the fact that Luke could assume the fourth position in the *Tetraevangelium* (for example, Codex Claromontanus, the Cheltenham canon, the Curetonian Syriac Gospels, Theophilus of Antioch, and New Testament ms. 888).

6. Contra Luke Timothy Johnson, "Literary Criticism of Luke-Acts: Is Reception-History Pertinent?" in this volume, 66–69 (first published in *JSNT* 28/2 [2005]: 159–62; subsequent references are to this essay as it appears in this volume); see Loveday C. A. Alexander, *The Preface to Luke's Gospel: Literary Convention and Social Context in Luke 1.14 and Acts 1.1* (SNTSMS 78; Cambridge: Cambridge University Press, 1993).

7. Henry J. Cadbury, *The Book of Acts in History* (New York: Harper & Brothers, 1955), 139.

8. Gregory, *Reception.*

9. Markus Bockmuehl, "Why Not Let Acts be Acts? In Conversation with C. Kavin Rowe," in this volume, 70–73 (first published in *JSNT* 28/2 [2005]: 163–66). Subsequent references are to this essay as it appears in this volume.

10. Johnson, "Literary Criticism," 68.

11. See Andrew F. Gregory, "The Reception of Luke and Acts and the Unity of Luke-Acts," in this volume, 82–93 (first published in *JSNT* 29/4 [2007]) and Johnson, "Literary Criticism of Luke-Acts."

12. Rowe, "History, Hermeneutics, and the Unity of Luke-Acts"; Bockmuehl, "Why Not Let Acts be Acts?"

13. Bockmuehl, "Why Not Let Acts be Acts?" 71 (italics in the original).

14. The mention of πολλοί in the preface also renders difficult the possibility of reconstructing a community that would know of only Luke's Gospel. Moreover, for all its differences from the Synoptics, even John—simply because of the intensity of focus upon Jesus—is prima facie more like these Gospels than Acts is like the Gospels.

15. Trans. Bruce M. Metzger, *The Canon of the New Testament: Its Origin, Development, and Significance* (Oxford: Clarendon, 1997), 313. Metzger's work is of course indispensable to this entire paragraph, as are the "selected documents" in Alexander Souter, *The Text and Canon of the New Testament* (New York: Charles Scribner's Sons, 1920), 205–37.

16. Cited also in Mikeal C. Parsons and Richard I. Pervo, *Rethinking the Unity of Luke and Acts* (Minneapolis: Fortress, 1993), 1.

17. The language of "publication and circulation" in this section derives primarily from Harry Gamble's chapter of that title in his seminal study *Books and Readers in the Early*

Church: A History of Early Christian Texts (New Haven: Yale University Press, 1995). I use it here as a way of raising an issue for further research (cf. Gregory, *Reception,* 300–302). Gamble has taught us much about the publication and dissemination of ancient Christian and non-Christian texts, but he does not address comprehensively the question of publication and circulation as it relates to two- or multi-volume works. Were the evidence to permit it, our ability to be more precise about questions of "publication" in relation to Luke-Acts would be greatly aided by a thorough study of the publication and distribution of two- and multi-volume works.

18. One instance of this is that the Johannine Epistles do not have a uniform reception history.

19. Johnson, "Literary Criticism," 68.

20. Ibid.

THE RECEPTION OF LUKE AND ACTS AND THE UNITY OF LUKE-ACTS

Andrew F. Gregory

What consequences should the largely separate reception history of Luke and Acts have for the overwhelming majority of contemporary scholars for whom the literary unity of Luke-Acts is a given?[1] This is the hermeneutical question raised by C. Kavin Rowe, who takes as his starting point my conclusion that there is no evidence prior to that of Irenaeus and the Muratorian Fragment (which I take to be second-century) to demonstrate that Luke and Acts were read as two volumes of one work.[2] My book is entirely historical in its focus. In it I make no attempt to draw hermeneutical conclusions about its implications for the interpretation of the modern construct "Luke-Acts," but address myself entirely to the very limited question of which ancient authors or texts make demonstrable use of either Luke or Acts or both. I found no external evidence to suggest that these two texts ever circulated together as a two-volume book, but did not conclude (as does Rowe) that this need call into question contemporary assumptions about the unity of Luke-Acts. Thus I am grateful not only to Rowe for his carefully considered critique of my work, but also for this opportunity both to present my own views on the wider hermeneutical issues that he raises and to respond to some challenges that he raises against my claim that Irenaeus and the author of the Muratorian Fragment each read Luke and Acts as two parts of one literary whole. I shall begin with these disputed points of historical detail before moving on to the wider hermeneutical issues that these matters raise.

EXTERNAL EVIDENCE FOR THE RECEPTION OF "LUKE-ACTS"

Rowe identifies two debatable passages that might indicate that Luke and Acts were received together, although he argues that neither does.[3] The first is Justin Martyr's *First Apology* 50.12, a passage that Ernst Haenchen identified as the earliest external evidence for the use of Acts.[4] I find here no convincing evidence for the use of Acts. I agree with Rowe that it contains knowledge of something that Acts recounts (that is, the ascension of Jesus), but I see no reason why it should depend on Acts for this information. Belief in the ascension was widespread by the time of Justin,[5] and there is nothing in this passage that cannot be accounted for as a conflation of the endings of Matthew and Luke. Justin frequently conflates Matthew and Luke, so it is much easier to view this passage as yet another instance of Justin's conflation of these two texts than as the single instance of his use of Acts (and therefore, by extension, of Luke-Acts).[6]

The second passage that Rowe concedes may indicate some evidence for the reception of Luke and Acts as two volumes of one unified whole is the opening of Book 3 of Irenaeus's *Against Heresies.*[7] He suggests that I exaggerate the significance of the fact that Irenaeus coordinates the end of Luke with the beginning of Acts when I take this as evidence that Irenaeus "explicitly treats Luke-Acts as a two-volume work, and he reads each volume in the light of the other."[8] I take Rowe's point that the way in which Irenaeus coordinates the ending of Luke with the beginning of Acts is not evidence that he linked Acts exclusively with Luke, so I do not deny that he treated Acts as a continuation of all four elements of his fourfold gospel, not just the Gospel according to Luke. On this point (as on many others) Rowe and I are in full agreement. Where we differ is on the question of whether it follows from Irenaeus's use of Acts alongside the various components of the fourfold gospel that Irenaeus was not aware of the literary unity of Luke-Acts, even if he read Luke primarily as part of the fourfold gospel, and Acts primarily as a bridge passage that stood between and connected different parts of the collection of authoritative Christian texts that he used. If recognizing the unity of Luke-Acts means reading those texts *only* in the light of each other and not in connection with other apostolic writings (which is certainly what many contemporary scholars seem to take it to mean) then *of course* Irenaeus did not recognize the literary unity of Luke-Acts. My contention, however, is that this modern dichotomy is unfortunate and that there is no good reason why readers (ancient or modern) who recognize the literary unity of Luke-Acts need preclude themselves from choosing to read either book apart from the other.[9] Thus one reader may read Luke in two different ways—sometimes as part of the fourfold gospel and sometimes as part of Luke-Acts. Similarly there may be some contexts in which the same reader reads Acts as part of Luke-Acts and others in which she reads it as part of a wider body of apostolic writings. Thus there is no necessary reason why Irenaeus's use of Acts as part of his fourfold gospel and his use of Acts alongside texts other than Luke means that he could not have been cognizant of the literary unity of these two texts.

Further, two additional points about the opening of *Against Heresies* 3 may also be made. The first is that Irenaeus does not only coordinate Acts 1 with Luke 24;[10] he links it also with Luke 10:16, which is the first scriptural authority that he cites in Book 3.This might suggest an awareness on Irenaeus's part of distinctively Lukan concerns, but the fact that Luke 10:16 is single tradition means that the point cannot be pressed too far. Irenaeus's use of Luke 10:16 is certainly suggestive, but it is possible that Irenaeus employs it here simply because it was the single most apposite saying of Jesus that he could draw from any part of his fourfold gospel, not because he wished to draw on Luke rather than on any other Gospel. Second, to describe the way in which Irenaeus uses Luke 24 and Acts 1 as "coordinating" them may be to underplay the significance of what he does. Irenaeus conflates Luke 24:49 with Acts 1:8 in such a way that it seems difficult not to conclude that he reads these two texts together in the way that Luke appears to have invited his readers to do. Neither of these observations makes a watertight case that Irenaeus recognized the literary unity rather than simply the common authorship and narrative continuity of Luke and Acts, but each may contribute to a cumulative case that he did.

Also of significance for this case is the way in which Irenaeus may refer to Acts in *Against Heresies* 3.14[11]. Here Irenaeus is arguing against those who claim that Paul alone knew the truth, for he was the sole recipient of revelation that was not given to others (3.13.1). This is not true, says Irenaeus, for Paul's teaching is consistent with Luke's teaching about the testimony of the other apostles, and in Acts Luke has faithfully recorded the story of Paul and the early church just as eyewitnesses and ministers of the word delivered it to Luke (3.14.2). This is the immediate context in which Irenaeus goes on to note a great deal of single tradition from the Third Gospel and to argue that those who accept part of what Luke has written must be prepared to accept it all. Here it is very tempting to find the strongest evidence yet for Irenaeus reading Luke and Acts as two parts of a literary whole, but it is actually very difficult to be certain exactly what he means. It is not long since Irenaeus has read Acts through the lens of Luke 1:2, but at this particular point (3.14.3) Irenaeus turns to castigate Marcion and Valentinus for using only certain parts of Luke's Gospel and not others. This is the immediate context in which Irenaeus states that these men must either receive the rest of Luke's narrative or reject the parts that they already accept. ("Necesse est igitur et reliqua quae ab eo dicta sunt recipere eos aut et his renuntiare," 3.14.4).

Irenaeus's use of both Luke and Acts in Book 3 of his *Against Heresies* makes it tempting to suppose that his reference to the other things that Luke has said[12] includes his second volume as well as his first, for Irenaeus has no doubt that both are from Luke's hand. In contrast, when he refers to the selective way in which he accuses Marcion and Valentinus of using Luke, he refers only to the use that they make of Luke's Gospel. Neither here in Book 3, nor in Book 1 where Irenaeus first refers to each of their selective uses of Luke, does Irenaeus make any explicit reference to their knowledge or use of Acts.[13] Therefore although the general tenor of Irenaeus's argument may make it more likely than not that he calls on his opponents to read the Third Gospel not only in its entirety but also in its entirety as part of a two-volume work, the immediate context in which his statement occurs is too ambiguous to allow any firm conclusion to rest upon it.

Elsewhere Irenaeus certainly notes the common authorship and probably also the literary unity of Luke-Acts. Here, however, just when we might like him—and perhaps even expect him—to make more of the connection and its consequences, Irenaeus does not do so. Thus although a good case can be made that Irenaeus did associate Luke with Acts in such a way as to suggest that he saw each of them as part of one literary whole, that case cannot be described as compelling.

Something similar may be said of the Muratorian Fragment. This text refers to Luke as one of four books of the Gospel and to Acts as a separate one-volume work, yet its author is aware that each is the work of the same author. But the case for the fragment's author reading Luke and Acts together does not rest solely on his knowledge of their common authorship,[14] but also on the fact that he (perhaps unconsciously) draws on the preface to Luke when, in reference to Acts, he states that Luke summarizes for the most excellent Theophilus things that have happened in his presence. The author of the fragment not only introduces an implicit contrast between Luke's participation in events in Acts (as implied by the we-passages) and his nonparticipation in events in Luke (as stated in the preface) but also introduces to his comments on Acts the honorific address (*optimo Theophilo*) that Luke uses only in the preface to his first book and not in his second. Again this may fall short of being compelling evidence that this author read Luke and Acts as two parts of a whole, but it is very suggestive. At the very least it requires us to note that the author's awareness of the separate transmission of Luke (as part of the fourfold gospel) and of Acts does not prevent him from making links between the two books.

INTERNAL EVIDENCE FOR THE RECEPTION OF "LUKE-ACTS"

In what I have said above I have drawn on two extant texts that are each later than the composition of Luke and Acts, and I have argued that their authors read each of these two texts together even if they did not receive them in the physical form of two parts of one literary whole. Now I want to argue that the internal evidence of the text of Luke-Acts may allow us to infer, although certainly not to demonstrate, that there may have been a much earlier period when the two volumes were received as two parts of one literary whole. The fact that I can call on no external evidence to support my position means that by its very nature it is speculative, but the absence of any external evidence to substantiate this hypothesis is neither surprising nor necessarily detrimental to the case that I wish to make. Further, I am not convinced that there is any external evidence that favors the alternative case that Rowe presents.

According to Rowe it may be better to argue that there was never a time when Luke and Acts circulated together than to conclude that the two were separated at an early point in their transmission history. The fact that there is no indisputable evidence that they were ever read together may be better explained on the basis that they never circulated together than on the basis that they came to be separated. This is a coherent hypothesis, but it is important to note that it works only if we can assume that each of Luke's two volumes was sent to Theophilus under separate cover.[15] If Luke dispatched both volumes at once, then they would have been received together by Theophilus,[16] even if neither he nor anyone else were ever again to circulate them together.[17] Thus the two volumes would have circulated as two elements of one literary whole at the earliest stage of their reception history, even if no external evidence of such transmission survives. Theophilus would have received these two volumes as part of one literary whole even if he were the only person ever to have done so.

But what if the two volumes were presented to Theophilus at different times? As Rowe acknowledges, the greater the time that elapsed between the time when Theophilus (or anyone else) encountered Luke's first book and the time when he encountered his second, the more plausible it is that volume one might have become associated with other texts like itself (for example, Mark, or any of those written by the πολλοί of Luke 1:1) so that it would be difficult for Acts (a text which might not be associated with Luke as easily as another biographical account of Jesus might be, especially if such texts were already circulating together) to be associated with Luke. How long a gap between the "publication" of Luke and the "publication" of Acts would such a scenario require? We can hardly answer this question with reference to clearly defined periods of time, but if readers of Luke were already familiar with Mark, they would need at least long enough to decide that Luke's apparent wish to distinguish his narrative from other accounts of Jesus (Luke 1:1–3) did not mean that those who read Luke's work could not associate it with other texts of a similar nature. Such an association may have arisen very quickly, not least if some of Luke's early audience were more positive about the work of his predecessors than Luke himself may have been.

Rowe's hypothesis that there may never have been a time when Luke and Acts circulated together because even Theophilus already thought of Luke as one kind of book (a "Gospel," even if he did not call it that) and therefore thought of Acts as something else—even though he knew that it too came from Luke's pen—is simple and elegant. It, like the alternative "traditional" hypothesis I have outlined above, is also not falsifiable on the basis of the evidence that we have, although that should not be held against it. Historians do not work in laboratory conditions. If correct, Rowe's hypothesis would imply that at least two Gospels circulated together at a very early stage, certainly prior to the composition of Acts, and might therefore contribute to the case for a very early origin of the fourfold gospel. But the fact that there is no early evidence for Luke and Acts circulating together may be explained just as easily on the basis that they were separated at such an early time that they left no traces of their prior joint circulation as on the basis that at no point did they circulate together. Either hypothesis offers a plausible

Ausgangspunkt for the subsequent history of Luke and Acts, or at least as much of that history as the evidence allows us to trace. From the perspective of the later evidence, such as the earliest extant papyri and the varying canonical placements of Acts, the difference between these hypotheses is actually very slight. Whereas Rowe suggests that the later evidence may be explained most economically by the argument that there was never a time when Luke and Acts circulated together, I suggest that it may be explained just as easily by suggesting that this evidence emerges from a time in which there was no awareness or memory that Luke and Acts had ever circulated together. This does not mean that they did ever circulate in this way, but it shows how the later evidence may be read in a way that is consonant with the possibility that they did.

What then may we conclude from the internal evidence of Luke and Acts, two volumes of remarkably similar length that are widely recognized as being of such similarity in style and content that they are almost certainly the work of one author? All that we can demonstrate from the internal evidence of Luke-Acts is that there are so many close connections between the two volumes[18] that it seems very likely that Luke planned and wrote his two volumes as part of one project, however great or small a period of time may have lapsed between a copy of each book leaving his possession. An ideal Theophilus and other ideal readers would have recognized this, but whether either the real Theophilus or other early readers of Luke and Acts did so is a question to which we should forego any confident answer. Certainly ideal readers do not have to be translated into real readers, but neither is there any a priori reason why they may not be translated in this way.[19]

HERMENEUTICAL REFLECTIONS

Up to this point I have focused on particular historical evidence for the reception of Luke and Acts and have argued that there may be times when Luke and Acts circulated and/or were read in the light of each other. In what follows I turn to consider more general issues that arise from the comparison of the generally separate reception history of each of these texts with the modern scholarly reception of these texts as Luke-Acts[20]. The argument that I want to make, albeit briefly, is that reception history tells us only how different people have approached Luke and Acts. It does not tell us how we should read them, nor does it tell us anything about how Luke may have intended his readers and hearers to approach his two books. In my view only a close reading of his text can do that. Therefore I agree with Luke Timothy Johnson and with Rowe that "a literary-critical reading . . . of Luke's entire narrative is best . . . for understanding his literary and theological voice."[21] However, I acknowledge that this is not how most readers have read Luke and Acts. The modern scholarly approach to Luke-Acts, which reads each volume in the light of the other and consciously excludes reference to other texts, is therefore something of a novelty in the reception of Luke and Acts.

Yet to acknowledge that most readers and hearers of Luke and Acts have not read them consciously and critically as Luke-Acts need not call into question the scholarly consensus that this is how they should be read, at least in certain contexts and for certain purposes. Thus I believe that a close reading of Luke's two volumes demonstrates that they are two parts of one continuous text, each written by the same author. I also believe that the pattern of correspondences between the two volumes and the distribution of at least some of their content strongly suggest that the author already intended to write the second volume as he wrote the first. Therefore readers who read and interpret each volume in the light of the other volume will gain a fuller understanding of both.

I also believe that each volume can be read on its own without any knowledge of the other volume, and that readers who read the volumes in this way need have no awareness of any deficit in their appreciation of either volume. Readers who have access to Luke but not to Acts have no reason to believe that they are missing anything, just as they have no reason to be any less satisfied at the end of Luke than they are at the end of Matthew, John, or one of the longer versions of Mark. Readers of Acts who have no access to the former volume to which the beginning of Acts draws attention are made aware that they are picking up a text that follows an earlier work, yet can read Acts as a text that is complete in itself.

Whether the author of these texts ever envisaged that many of his readers would read his two volumes largely in isolation from each other is unclear, although I think that there is evidence that this is not what Luke intended. This is not to say that I wish to argue that readers of texts need necessarily be constrained to read texts only in the way that their authors may be thought to have intended them to be read nor that the meaning of the text is restricted to what its author may have envisaged. Different readers may read the same texts from different perspectives and for different reasons. One reading strategy may not always be better than another. This is certainly true of two different reading strategies that may be discerned from even a brief and selective survey of the reception of Acts. The strategies are not absolute, and we may take other positions that fall somewhere between them, but I shall risk caricature in the hope of finding some clarity. Neither are the strategies startling or new, but I shall use them in the hope that they allow us to reflect on what they involve.

The first of these strategies, which for want of a better term I shall call the historico-literary critical approach, is the scholarly consensus that Luke and Acts were written as two parts of one whole. This is what most modern Lukan scholarship takes for granted. It also in some respects comes closer to what I think Luke intended his readers to do when he wrote his two volumes than does the second strand with which I shall compare it.

The second strategy is what may be referred to as the canonical approach to Acts.[22] This is the strategy that reads Acts as having some form of bridging function by virtue of its position in the canon. Thus it may be read either as looking back to all four Gospels and as looking forward either to the Letters of Paul or to other writings associated with apostles or to both. Different modern scholars advocate slightly different ways in which canonical readings may be pursued. With many premodern readers they divide what Luke brought together. Thus they read Luke's first volume as part of a fourfold gospel and his second as an important crossover text that relates not specifically to Luke's earlier narrative but to a range of texts concerned with the significance of Jesus of which the Gospel according to Luke is only one. In so doing they read Luke and Acts as part of a body of Scripture, not as a literary text to be read on its own terms. There are some respects in which this approach reflects more closely what I think Luke intended, but the cost may be giving less attention to the literary unity of these texts than Luke appears to have had in mind.

At the heart of the historical-critical approach to Luke-Acts is an emphasis on the literary unity of these two texts in the sense that they were written by one author. As Joseph Verheyden has observed, discussion on this matter is closed.[23] This need not mean, however, that hermeneutical questions following from agreement on common authorship are also closed. In addition to common authorship Mikeal C. Parsons and Richard I. Pervo note four headings under which the unity of Luke-Acts might be discussed.[24] Three of them—generic, narrative, and theological unity—are all in some sense debates about the extent to which the authorial unity of these two texts has resulted in consistency between the two volumes. In that sense they are debates about the text that depend on an assessment of what its author did.

The fourth heading, that of canonical unity, is quite different. It concerns decisions that were made not by the author of these texts but by their later readers. The subsequent canonization of Luke's two volumes as two distinct texts in two distinct parts of the canon, albeit with Acts functioning as a bridge between them, may be said to have taken place contrary to Luke's stated intentions insofar as they may be inferred from what he wrote. Parsons and Pervo ask what impediments were formed to understanding Luke's thoughts and the distinctive features of Luke and Acts when Cadbury made "Luke-Acts."[25] More pertinent, I suggest, is the question that they seek to challenge: what was lost or what was gained when Luke-Acts (which is what I think Luke wrote and expected at least his earliest readers to read) was split to become Luke and Acts as later enshrined in the canon? By no means, however, must we assume that this decision was either botched or lamentable.[26]

This question brings me back to Irenaeus. Rowe suggests that there is some tension between my acknowledgement that Irenaeus uses Acts in close association with both the fourfold gospel and Paul and my argument that he treats them as parts of a two-volume work.[27] But I wonder whether this might not be turned on its head. Might the way in which Irenaeus uses Luke and Acts together, as I have argued that he probably did, and yet uses them also as discrete texts with separate canonical functions, not provide an early example of someone who in different contexts employed something akin to each of the two reading strategies that I have sketched out above?

Here it may be pertinent to note Irenaeus's description of Luke as an instrument through whom God worked (*Against Heresies* 3.15.1; "operatus est Deus plurima Euangelii ostendi per Lucam" / "ἐνήργησεν ὁ Θεὸς τὰ πλείονα τοῦ εὐαγγελίου ἀναδειχθῆναι διὰ τοῦ Λουκα"[28]). For Irenaeus, Luke is less an author than a witness. Luke and Acts are less written texts than written testimonies to the God whose Spirit was at work in the prophets of Israel, in Jesus his son, and in the church on which Jesus lavished God's Spirit. This, I think, brings us to the heart of the distinction between canonical and historical-literary-critical approaches to the unity of Luke-Acts. Modern scholars who focus on the two-part textual or rhetorical unit that is Luke-Acts are often more interested in the text itself than in any external reality to which it might refer. If they are interested in the world behind and outside the text it is often in order to get insights into how the text functions as a product of the context in which it is written. Such approaches need not exclude theological interests, but they concern themselves more with the text and its workings than with claims or questions about God that the text might raise. This interest in the text that Luke wrote and what he may have intended it to convey makes it natural to adopt a reading strategy that reads Luke and Acts together, for that is what Luke's second authorial preface encourages us to do. Luke's resumptive preface at the beginning of Acts brings us back to his preface at the beginning of his first book. There we learn that Luke appears to have written an orderly account so that Theophilus might know the truth about the things in which he had been instructed, and that he did so because other accounts to which he had access were not satisfactory. Thus Luke's preface appears to suggest that he did not want his narrative to be read alongside those of his predecessors, for their work is defective. If so, it is almost inconceivable that Luke would have envisaged his first book being read alongside three other broadly similar accounts, not least if he included among his predecessors the author of what we call the Gospel according to Mark.

Luke wrote his two books to be read together, but for most of their history they have been read in their canonical context, as two discrete texts that relate to a range of others. This does not mean that Luke and Acts cannot or should not be read in this way. It simply acknowledges that many readers have privileged the way in which the canon suggests that these texts should be read over the way in which the author appears to have suggested that these texts should be read. Each reading strategy is appropriate for the community in which it has been followed (a community of believers, or a community of scholars) and many individuals will use one strategy or the other at different times. Some will also adopt a middle position between them, as Jaroslav Pelikan does in his recent theological commentary on Acts. There he notes that in his cross-references to the four Gospels he will "in the first instance cite the Gospel of Luke where possible, and the other three Gospels as appropriate."[29] Pelikan recognizes the authorial unity of Luke-Acts but does not feel excluded from noting how Acts may be related to other canonical Gospels besides Luke, just as he relates it also to other New Testament books.

Prior to Irenaeus, Luke and Acts appear to have been used as separate texts. Often Luke is used alongside other Gospels, but our early evidence for the reception of Acts is too scant to allow us to draw any generalizations. After Irenaeus they are read primarily as respective parts either of the Gospel or of the Apostolos, the two principal components of what becomes the New Testament.[30] Only in modern scholarship are Luke and Acts read primarily as Luke-Acts, even if that is what their author appears to have intended. One strategy is not better than the other. One strategy does not rule out the other. Each is appropriate to different circumstances and reflects different needs and interests on the part of those who employ it at any particular time.

NOTES

An earlier version of this essay was delivered as a paper at the British New Testament Conference in Sheffield in September 2006. I am grateful to copanellists C. Kavin Rowe and Michael F. Bird, and also to Loveday C. A. Alexander, for their comments on the paper.

1. Michael F. Bird, "The Unity of Luke-Acts in Recent Discussion," in this volume, 3–22 (first published in *JSNT* 29/4 [2007]: 425–48). Subsequent references are to this essay as it appears in this volume.

2. C. Kavin Rowe, "History, Hermeneutics, and the Unity of Luke-Acts," in the volume, 43–44 (first published in *JSNT* 28/2 [2005]: 133), citing Andrew F. Gregory, *The Reception of Luke and Acts in the Period before Irenaeus: Looking for Luke in the Second Century* (WUNT 2/169; Tübingen: Mohr Siebeck, 2003), 352. Subsequent references are to this essay as it appears in this volume.

3. C. Kavin Rowe, "Literary Unity and Reception History: Reading Luke-Acts as Luke and Acts," in this volume, 74–75 (first published in *JSNT* 29/4 [2007]: 450; subsequent references are to this essay as it appears in this volume); cf. Rowe, "History, Hermeneutics," 43–46.

4. Ernst Haenchen, *The Acts of the Apostles: A Commentary* (ed. and trans. R. McL. Wilson; Oxford: Basil Blackwell, 1971), 8.

5. John G. Davies, *He Ascended into Heaven* (London: Lutterworth Press, 1958), 45–46, 69–71; C. K. Barrett, *A Critical and Exegetical Commentary on the Acts of the Apostles,* Volume 1 (ICC; Edinburgh: T & T Clark, 1994), 42.

6. Cf. Gregory, *Reception,* 287–91, 317–21; Andrew F. Gregory, "Irenaeus and the Reception of Luke and Acts in the Second Century," in *Contemporary Studies in Acts* (ed. Thomas E. Phillips; Macon, Ga.: Mercer University Press, 2009), 47–66.

7. Rowe, "Literary Unity," 74–75; Rowe, "History, Hermeneutics," 43–45.

8. Rowe, "History, Hermeneutics," 43, citing Gregory, *The Reception of Luke and Acts,* 39.

9. See further below, pp. 87–91.

10. Rowe, "Literary Unity," 79 n. 2.

11. Here and in the following paragraph I draw on a fuller discussion of Irenaeus's use of Acts that was published in Thomas E. Phillips, ed., *Contemporary Studies in Acts* (Macon, Ga.: Mercer University Press, 2009), 47–66.

12. Is it significant that Irenaeus refers to what Luke has *said* rather than to what he has written?

13. Elaine Pagels suggests that at 3.12.6–7 Irenaeus is responding to Gnostic exegesis of Acts' account of Peter's vision. See her "Visions, Appearances and Apostolic Authority: Gnostic and Orthodox Tradition" in *Gnosis: Festschrift für Hans Jonas.* (ed. Barbara Aland; Göttingen: Vandenhoeck & Ruprecht, 1978), 423. However, I am unclear whether Irenaeus is responding to prior Valentinian use of Acts or introducing Acts as a weapon against Valentinian claims that are made quite apart from Acts.

14. Cf. Rowe, "History, Hermeneutics," 46.

15. I assume that Theophilus was a real person and that he would have known the identity of the author of Luke and Acts. In the discussion that follows I use Theophilus to stand for any reader(s)/hearer(s) to whom Luke sent copies of his work.

16. I assume that Luke wrote each book on a premanufactured scroll of similar length and that the need to fit each of his books on such a scroll will have affected the way in which Luke planned and composed his work. However, the possibility that he may have written each book on a codex should not be excluded altogether, although there is no evidence to suggest that it would have been a codex that could have accommodated the two volumes together. Had Luke used such a codex then the subsequent decision to separate his two volumes would have been much more significant than it would have been if they had once circulated as two companion volumes on separate scrolls (or codices).

17. Of course Luke might have sent his two volumes to others besides Theophilus, and may have tried to encourage their recipients to keep them together if, by the time he wrote Acts, he was aware that his former volume was already being used alongside other accounts of Jesus' ministry. But this is speculative in the extreme.

18. See Bird, "The Unity," 4–9, and the studies to which he refers.

19. Cf. Rowe, "Literary Unity," 76.

20. This designation goes back to Cadbury. For discussion and references, see Robert L. Maddox, *The Purpose of Luke-Acts* (SNTW; Edinburgh: T & T Clark, 1982), 3–6.

21. Luke Timothy Johnson, "Literary Criticism of Luke-Acts: Is Reception-History Pertinent?" in this volume, 68 (first published in *JSNT* 28/2 [2005]: 162), cited in Rowe, "Literary Unity," 76.

22. Brevard S. Childs, *The New Testament as Canon: An Introduction* (Philadelphia: Fortress, 1984); Robert W. Wall, "The Acts of the Apostles in Canonical Context" in *The New*

Testament as Canon (ed. Robert W. Wall and Eugene E. Lemcio; JSNTSup 76; Sheffield: JSOT Press, 1992), and "The Acts of the Apostles" in *New Interpreter's Bible* (ed. Leander E. Keck; 12 vols.; Nashville: Abingdon, 2002); and David E. Smith, *The Canonical Function of Acts: A Comparative Analysis* (Collegeville, Minn.: Liturgical Press, 2002).

23. Joseph Verheyden, "The Unity of Luke-Acts. What Are We Up To?" in *The Unity of Luke-Acts* (ed. Joseph Verheyden; BETL 142; Leuven: Leuven University Press, 1999), 6 n. 13.

24. Mikeal C. Parsons and Richard I. Pervo, *Rethinking the Unity of Luke and Acts* (Minneapolis: Fortress, 1993), 7.

25. Ibid., 13

26. Ibid., 12.

27. Rowe, "History, Hermeneutics," 44, citing Gregory, *Reception,* 39 and 301.

28. Latin text and Greek retroversion from Adelin Rousseau and Louis Doutreleau, *Irénée de Lyon Contre les Hérésies Livre III* (SC 211; Paris: Éditions du Cerf, 1974).

29. See Jaroslav Pelikan, *Acts* (Brazos Theological Commentary on the Bible; Grand Rapids, Mich.: Brazos Press, 2005), 31, where he presents this decision as a consequence of the common authorship of Luke and Acts as seen in the two prefaces and their repeated address to Theophilus.

30. On Acts see Henry J. Cadbury, *The Book of Acts in History* (London: A & C Black, 1955); Werner Bieder, *Die Apostelgeschichte in der Historie. Ein Beitrag zur Auslegungsgeschichte des Missionsbuches der Kirche* (ThSt 61; Zurich: EVZ-Verlag, 1960); P. F. Stuehrenberg, "The Study of Acts before the Reformation: A Bibliographical Introduction," *NovT* 29/2 (1987): 100–36; François Bovon, *De Vocatione Gentium. Histoire de l'interprétation d'Act. 10, 1–11, 18 dans les six premiers siècles* (BGBE 8; Tübingen: Mohr Siebeck, 1967), and "The Reception of the Book of Acts in Antiquity" in *Contemporary Studies in Acts* (ed. Thomas E. Phillips; Macon, Ga.: Mercer University Press, 2009), 66–93.

PART THREE

LUKE AND ACTS—THE EARLY YEARS

Some Comments in the Margin of a Recent Monograph

Joseph Verheyden

Ancient Christian authors were slow in disciplining themselves (or being disciplined) into more or less carefully handling or citing the text of the written Gospels. Modern scholars likewise took a long time fully to address this issue and to sense its complexity. It has often been said that the second century—this crucial period which in so many respects "made things happen"—seems to stand as an unconquerable barrier that prevents us from getting any insight into what "happened" to the Gospels, and to oral tradition, in these first decades after the Gospels were written. By the time this century was drawing to an end, however, things seem to have been sorted out and to have become clear for us to see. I am well aware that this sketch of the state of affairs may perhaps look somewhat too simplistic, though it is not absolutely wrong. On the one hand we can recover bits of fairly useful evidence—unfortunately not as much as we would have wished—to give us some idea at least of what was going on, while on the other hand it is not true that all problems had been resolved by the time of Irenaeus and Tertullian. But it is fair to state that in those years it had become clear that "the text" had won the battle and that oral tradition was rapidly retreating at the horizon. At what cost did all this happen?

Over the past decades the fate of text and tradition in the second century has been studied in some detail for a number of documents. All these efforts resulted in impressive monographs and some fine essays. Paul, Matthew, and John had their share of glory and attention, and rightly so.[1] Mark, Luke, and Acts, however, have been lagging behind.[2] Evidence of the early reception history of the two latter writings has now been gathered and studied in a monograph by Andrew F. Gregory, *The Reception of Luke and Acts in the Period before Irenaeus.*[3]

Gregory's monograph has been hailed, not without reason, as a most welcome in-depth study of the matter, covering a significant lacuna.[4] Careful and cautious are the qualifications that first come to mind upon reading through the book. Yet these qualifications also need to be qualified in turn as I will try to demonstrate in the following. There is no need for commenting on all the many passages Gregory has studied. Rather I wish to share some observations I noted down while reading his work, address some issues I have been struggling with, and then illustrate one or another point I am making on the basis of Gregory's analysis of the relevant passages in Polycarp's *Letter to the Philippians.*

I

Gregory opens with an introduction that deals with methodology and previous research on reception history of the Gospels (1–21), and throughout the book this survey is filled out. What is said of the work of predecessors is essentially correct, but rather unfortunately the older, especially German literature is almost completely absent. I miss a reference, for example, to the likes of Adolf Hilgenfeld and Wilhelm Bousset for Justin.[5] There is also no mention of Eduard Zeller's 1848 essay that in a sense put the issue on the table for the generations to follow.[6] Now the less informed reader might have the impression that the whole issue of the reception history of the Gospels in the second century started with Helmut Koester and Eduard Massaux. The latter's dissertation, originally published in 1950, is here systematically referred to as "Massaux, 1990"—the date of the publication of the first volume of the English translation—a decision that is not really helpful for getting the perspective right. However, taking Massaux and Koester, who in postwar Germany had no access to his immediate predecessor's dissertation, as the starting point is not completely wrong either, as these two authors have developed and argued for positions that have dominated much of the discussion and research over the past sixty years. But it might have been helpful if their work had been put in a somewhat broader context.

II

Method is at the heart of the whole enterprise and constitutes an issue of itself. Anyone who has ever looked into the early reception history of the Gospels knows but all too well that it is a world haunted by "unknowns" and huge methodological difficulties. The few certainties there are, moreover, immediately raise new questions and problems and lead to new uncertainties. For one, the presence of features that are characteristic of a particular evangelist's style and redaction can by definition be regarded as "certain evidence" that his Gospel has been used. However, there is no general consensus on what counts as "characteristic," nor whether the criterion can be used indiscriminately to explain the same phenomenon. Further, it stands beyond doubt that the situation is complex and that several factors should be taken into account or reckoned with in assessing the evidence. But again it is disputed how many such factors there are, how they may have influenced or interfered in the evidence, and which ones did what and where. Literary dependence on the Gospels is one factor, but so is oral tradition, or a combination of both, not to mention theories of intermediate, hypothetical, or additional sources, of (harmonizing) revisions of the Gospels, or of the unstable or chaotic state of the textual tradition in general in these first decades. Third, and specifically with regard to Luke and Acts, there is solid evidence that the Gospel and, to a far lesser degree, Acts were known and used by a number of second-century authors before the days of Irenaeus. Or to put it from the latter's perspective, there is no reason for thinking that Irenaeus was somehow "reinventing" or recovering Luke and Acts from a distant and long-forgotten past.[7] The way Irenaeus writes about Luke very much gives the impression that he was well familiar with the text and expected his readers to be so as well.[8] The possible objection that admitting to the opposite would have weakened his position is not altogether true, for Irenaeus could also easily have made a case out of it, claiming that he had finally brought his readers back to the old, original, and "true" tradition against the novelties of the heretics. But then it remains to be explained why there apparently is after all relatively little of such material and much more that is, at best, ambiguous, at worst, utterly useless for our goal. Much depends, so it would seem, on how the criterion of style and redaction is defined and applied, and above all for what purpose; on how the several factors are played out along and against each other; and on how the "solid evidence" is handled and given a place and role in an overall picture.

Basically this whole issue of the earliest reception of the Gospels has been approached in what could be described as a maximalist and a minimalist way. Each of these has its assets and its shortcomings. It is true that scholars who have taken the former approach—Massaux can be cited as a classic example—may perhaps not have been sufficiently careful formally to define what they understand by "undisputed evidence." This may at times have created an impression of shakiness in matters of methodology, but it would not be fair nor correct to say that it constitutes a certain path toward total randomness. Massaux did not consider all of the evidence that could possibly point to the use of the written Gospels indiscriminately to be of the same rank and status. One should just take a look at the great variation and the use of modal verbs he uses in formulating his conclusions.[9] This position also opens the door for a more "pragmatic," or indeed also more "realistic" approach on the assumption that there may well be various degrees of certainty in such matters, because there are various ways in which an author can make use of a text. In such an approach the "undisputed evidence" for dependence on a written Gospel that can be identified in a particular author can then be used, in an inclusive way, also to argue that other, less "solid evidence" should perhaps best be explained in the same line. In the alternative (opposite) approach, as exemplified by Koester, much care is given rigorously to define and apply an "unequivocal" criterion.[10] This is indisputably a positive element. But then it appears that de facto the criterion can also be used, in an exclusive way, primarily to argue that it is extremely difficult, some will say even virtually impossible, to identify evidence that formally meets the criterion. As a result the criterion itself threatens to become an impediment for reaching any positive results.

If the one is sometimes driving perhaps a bit too dangerously, the other is almost constantly driving with the brakes on, and one knows that both of these can be risky and cause damage to car and driver alike. Or to put it perhaps somewhat more bluntly, one could say that if the one side proposes to reason and argue along the line that "if A ['solid evidence' that allows us to conclude that there is literary dependence], then possibly/plausibly also B ['less solid evidence' that in itself does not allow for such a conclusion]," the other side basically wants to hold that "A does not equal B," or still, that "A = A, and B = B," and the two shall not meet.

There should be no doubt on which side Gregory stands. He repeatedly notes that there is after all some good evidence for concluding that some authors of the latter half of the second century at least were familiar with Luke (Acts) and indeed used it. Thus he writes in his conclusion to the part of his book that deals with Luke, "That *Luke* was known, at least to the authors of *2 Clement, Thomas,* and the *Gospel of the Ebionites* as well as to Marcion, Justin, Tatian, at least some Valentinians, and the author of the *Protevangelium of James* is not in doubt, and some readers will conclude that the evidence is sufficient to make likely the case for its use elsewhere as well."[11] This is all good and well of course. But Gregory's first and main interest, it would seem, is in calling attention, time and again, to the complexity of the situation—with its so many "unknowns"—which should prevent one from opting too readily for the "dependence" solution. Closely linked to this, and almost as a consequence, is his utmost critical application of the style/redaction criterion. Or as Gregory formulates it, "The importance of Koester's criterion must be noted, but it is important to emphasise that he has not spoken the last word on the question of how literary dependence is best established."[12] It looks as if Gregory is rather more interested in pointing out its limits and possible deficits than in positively applying it as a fairly reliable criterion.[13] Accordingly it is (too) often handled in such a way that at best it becomes a solution equal to, or in fact even less probable than its major contender—oral tradition. And consequently it is no surprise that "solid evidence" turns out to be minimal indeed—a sort of extravaganza in the steady flow of tradition(s)—and literary dependence on the Gospels very much looks like a "mere alternative" or even the kind of solution to which one accedes only if it is absolutely necessary.

Of course there is nothing wrong with constantly bearing in mind the weaknesses of any criterion and putting the finger on its limits, but the one is not exactly identical with the other, and all hangs on where the emphasis lays. It is true that what, on any source hypothesis, can reasonably be identified as characteristic for an author's pen, because also the source text is known, does not automatically have to be so in other instances in which the source can no longer be known, or is lost, or no longer attested to independently.[14] My major problem with such observations is that the same degree of critical attitude is apparently not required in handling the alternative, or that this alternative is in fact faced far more uncritically.

Oral tradition was around before the Gospels were put to writing, and it continued to exist after that and probably even may have influenced the newly born written tradition for some time. But it should be said with equal certainty that the Gospels were composed and redacted by authors who put in them also something of their own, whether they were (merely) relying on tradition or (also) on written sources. Yet in the latter instance strict criteria are requested to argue for it—and rightly so—but why then not also in the former instance, where it looks as if its mere existence excuses one from any further questioning of the contents and wording of those traditions? It is not because it may now be difficult to point to particular evidence in its favor that the hypothesis of oral tradition may be invoked without adequate argumentation. This hypothesis may certainly travel lightly, but it should not for that reason be allowed to enter each and every house without any notification. On this rule what in one instance can be taken for a trace of an author's hand (because the source is available) may have a different origin in another instance (where the possibility for checking is missing), or it may have the same origin. In such a case the two solutions should be handled on an equal basis. Or maybe not. Formally the two explanations seem to be equally valid. Strictly speaking, however, the literary dependence option has the additional merit of effectively having tried to argue for its position on the basis of positively described evidence. For that same reason I have difficulties with clauses of the type, "it may be A (redaction), but also B (oral tradition)," of which there are many in Gregory's book. It is important to realize that formally it may look as if it does not make any difference when the two elements of this clause are inverted, but rhetorically it does—a great deal. Also it is significant that one hardly will find an instance of the inverted type. All things equal, it seems that, according to Gregory, it is oral tradition that after all wins the hand.

An outsider looking into the matter might be sensible of the irony that lurks behind all this. One might have the impression that the two options here described oppose each other as gung-ho tactics against safety play. As a matter of fact, however, the "certainty" that seems to have been given up or lost in the first option might in the end well have helped to gain some plausibility, and this is probably the best that can be reached. And the "certainty" that is thought to be gained by taking the other option might well lead into a cloud of unknowing. For theoretically a maximalist application of the style-and-redaction criterion—using it to build a case for an hypothesis—might indeed yield a more correct result than a somewhat anxious hiding behind "certainty claims." All certainties can turn out to be delusive, which hurts, but would it not hurt more the one who has made (the aspiration for) "certainty" his ultimate paradigm than the one working with that of plausibility? Not much is gained, it would seem, in looking for "certainty" and then in settling for this one certainty, that "certainty" is beyond our reach. We are visiting an area of plausibility.

III

The problem and the discussion have not only to do with searching for valid criteria or for the role assigned to various explanatory factors, but also with the way the evidence is presented, searched, and studied in general. There are two aspects to this and they are interrelated. Gregory has studied the evidence for the use of Luke and Acts in separate parts. For Luke there are chapters dealing with the oldest manuscript evidence, narrative outlines of Jesus' life that may have been influenced by Luke (the Fourth Gospel, Ignatius's *Letter to the Smyrneans,* the *Ascension of Isaiah,* the Gospel of Basilides, the Valentinians, Theophilus's *ad Autolycum,* Longer Mark, the *Gospel of the Ebionites,* the *Protevangelium of James, Papyrus Egerton 2,* and the *Diatessaron*), collections of Jesus sayings as found in the *Didache,* the *Apocalypse of Peter, 1 Clement,* Polycarp's *Letter to the Philippians, 2 Clement,* the spare references to the teaching of the Naassenes and the Carpocratians, the *Gospel of Thomas* (and other texts from Nag Hammadi), Marcion, and Justin Martyr. In the part on Acts Gregory first discusses the earliest and "ambiguous" evidence (2 Timothy, Longer Mark, *1 Clement,* Polycarp's *Letter to the Philippians*), then the few possible references to Acts in Justin, and finally a number of narrative accounts that may contain traces of Acts (*Epistula Apostolorum, Letter from Lyons and Vienne, Pseudo-Clementine Recognitions,* Eusebius's account of the Montanists, and the oldest Apocryphal Acts). The combination of a chronological and a genre-based approach offers chances for pointing out differences, while also drawing attention, as far as the evidence allows it, to particular developments in the exegesis of the texts. Gregory has been touring widely in the second-century landscape, and he does not seem to have missed any place of some importance. In studying individual authors he as a rule arranges the material according to the order of the Gospel,[15] thereby, if appropriate and as a further subdivision, distinguishing between simple, double, and triple tradition material.[16] Gregory keeps to this arrangement, even to the point of jumping from one section to another in dealing with Justin.[17] The few exceptions to this basic rule are not always clearly singled out, but they can be explained more or less.[18] There is nothing revolutionary about this. As a matter of fact it is the traditional approach, the one followed by Massaux and Koester and by many others before and after them. It has as an important advantage its clarity of presentation. But cutting up the evidence in such a way also has some negative side effects. The evidence is atomized at the cost of losing sight of the broader picture, and there are instances where the loss may turn out to be greater than the gain.

Moreover, and this is the second aspect, scholars working in this field have concentrated above all—indeed almost exclusively—on the source texts (Paul, the Gospels, or Acts), making sure that the evidence that is being studied is truly "Lukan," or "Matthean," and so on. They have paid far less attention to tracing and identifying marks of the receiving author's redaction and characteristic style, or of his theological or other intent, that might explain why this author has been handling the text the way he does. Obviously this is of special interest for authors who are writing at a time in which the Gospel text had not yet gained the sacrosanct character, and the authority that goes with it, that it will later obtain. Of course this is not an easy exercise nor one that can be performed in each and every case, because the material is lacking. It surely will not explain all of the evidence, but it certainly constitutes a factor to be reckoned with, and maybe even a more important one than many have thought. But maybe some of what has just been said can best be illustrated with an example. In the following I look in some detail at the section on Polycarp's *Letter to the Philippians* (*Phil.*). It was picked for no particular reason, and so is a random choice.[19]

IV

Of the three passages in *Phil.* that are studied (2.3a.b; 12.3b) "none provides any decisive evidence for Polycarp's knowledge and use of Luke."[20] Yet, Gregory goes on, "too much weight should not be placed on the absence of firm evidence for the use of Luke."[21] It is best not to use this conclusion for dating certain parts of the letter, as Gregory rightly notes in the following table. But it could also be read as indicating that Polycarp may after all have used Luke a bit too freely in order fully to convince the more sceptical modern scholar. The case of *Phil.* is interesting, because it is one of the few cases on which both Massaux and Koester deviate from their "standard explanation."[22]

4.1. *Phil.* 2.3a

Phil. 2.3a	*1 Clem.* 13.2	Luke 6:31, 36–38	Matt. 5:7; 6:14; 7:1–2, 12
μνημονεύοντες δὲ ὧν εἶπεν ὁ κύριος διδάσκων·			
	ἐλεᾶτε, ἵνα ἐλεηθῆτε·	<6:36> γίνεσθε οἰκτίρμονες καθὼς καὶ ὁ πατὴρ ὑμῶν οἰκτίρμων ἐστίν.	<5:7> μακάριοι οἱ ἐλεήμονες, ὅτι αὐτοὶ ἐλεηθήσονται.

(b) ἀφίετε, καὶ ἀφεθήσεται ὑμῖν·	ἀφίετε, ἵνα ἀφεθῇ ὑμῖν·	<6:37c> ἀπολύετε, καὶ ἀπολυθήσεσθε	<6:14> ἐὰν γὰρ ἀφῆτε τοῖς ἀνθρώποις τὰ παραπτώματα αὐτῶν, ἀφήσει καὶ ὑμῖν ὁ πατὴρ ὑμῶν ὁ οὐράνιος·
(c) ἐλεᾶτε, ἵνα ἐλεηθῆτε·			
	ὡς ποιεῖτε, οὕτω ποιηθήσεται ὑμῖν·	<6:31> καὶ καθὼς θέλετε ἵνα ποιῶσιν ὑμῖν οἱ ἄνθρωποι ποιεῖτε αὐτοῖς ὁμοίως.	<7:12> Πάντα οὖν ὅσα ἐὰν θέλητε ἵνα ποιῶσιν ὑμῖν οἱ ἄνθρωποι, οὕτως και ὑμεῖς ποιεῖτε αὐτοῖς
	ὡς δίδοτε, οὕτως δοθήσεται ὑμῖν·	<6:38> δίδοτε, καὶ δοθήσεται ὑμῖν·	
(a) μὴ κρίνετε, ἵνα μὴ κριθῆτε	ὡς κρίνετε, οὕτως κριθήσεσθε·	<6:37a> Καὶ μὴ κρίνετε, καὶ οὐ μὴ κριθῆτε	<7:1> Μὴ κρίνετε, ἵνα μὴ κριθῆτε· <7:2> ἐν ᾧ γὰρ κρίματι κρίνετε κριθήσεσθε,
	ὡς χρηστεύεσθε, οὕτως χρηστευθήσεται ὑμῖν	<6:35c> ὅτι αὐτὸς χρηστός ἐστιν ἐπὶ τοὺς ἀχαρίστους καὶ πονηρούς.	
(d) ᾧ μέτρῳ μετρεῖτε,	ᾧ μέτρω μετρεῖτε, ἐν αὐτῷ μετρηθήσεται ὑμῖν.	<6:38c> ᾧ γὰρ μέτρῳ μετρεῖτε	καὶ ἐν ᾧ μέτρῳ μετρεῖτε
ἀντιμετρηθήσεται ὑμῖν.		ἀντιμετρηθήσεται ὑμῖν.	μετρηθήσεται ὑμῖν.

Table reprinted from Gregory, 132–33.

Massaux thinks the parallel in 2.3a is too weak to argue for literary dependence on either Matthew or Luke and settles for the "catechism hypothesis," not necessarily the same but rather a variant version of the one used in *1 Clem.* 13.2.[23] For Koester, however, the evidence in 2.3a is best explained on the hypothesis that Polycarp relied on *1 Clem.*, which he has emended in two instances with the help of the parallel passages in Matthew (the phrase on judging) and Luke (the compound ἀντιμετρηθήσεται).[24] Gregory makes little of this: he acknowledges the possible "cumulative effect" of citing evidence from Matthew and from Luke, but all in all "it comes down to Polycarp's use of a compound verb that is shared with Luke rather than the simple form of the verb that is found in *1 Clement.*"[25] The verdict: influence from Luke is possible, but hardly compelling.

That might be true, if one limits the evidence to the sole compound. Yet it should be noted that ἀντιμετρέομαι is not only a hapaxlegomenon in the New Testament and in the Apostolic Fathers, but is commonly seen as a mark of Luke's hand, as is the case with other such compounds with ἀντι-, two observations that Gregory passes over in silence.[26] It could be argued that the choice for the compound was somehow inspired by the fourfold ἀντί in the immediately preceding context in 2.2b, but there is possibly more to it. The first half of the ἀντί-phrase occurs literarily in 1 Pet. 3:9a (μὴ ἀποδιδόντες κακὸν ἀντὶ κακοῦ ἢ λοιδορίαν ἀντὶ λοιδορίας). That Polycarp most probably had in mind the text and context of 1 Peter can be shown from two further elements.[27]

4.1.a

The ἀντί- phrases of 2.2b are preceded in 2.2a by a list of five vices (of which the first one is of a more general character) that one should abstain from (ἀπεχόμενοι πάσης ἀδικίας, πλεονεξίας, φιλαργυρίας, καταλαλιᾶς, ψευδομαρτυρίας). In 1 Peter, verse 9 is preceded by a list of five virtues (the first of which again is perhaps a more general one): τὸ δὲ τέλος πάντες ὁμόφρονες, συμπαθεῖς, φιλάδελφοι, εὔσπλαγχνοι, ταπεινόφρονες. The vices and virtues in the two lists are not really each others' counterparts, but the structural similarity that results from combining such a list with a partially identical list of ἀντί-phrases is most remarkable, to say the least. The closely comparable list in *Phil.* 4.3 may be sufficient evidence for concluding that it reveals a particular interest of Polycarp.[28] It is further also worth noting that some of the wording in 2.2a bears a Lukan tone. Ἀπέχω is found in Paul (1 Thess. 4:3; 5:22) and 2 Peter (2:11), but twice also in Acts in warning to abstain from sacrificing to idols (15:20, 29), and several times more in *Phil.* (5.3; 6.1, 3). While four out of the five words in the list of 1 Pet. 3:8 are hapaxlegomena in the New Testament,[29] and three are hapaxes in the Apostolic Fathers (συμπαθής, ὁμόφρων, φιλαδέλφος), all five vices in the list of *Phil.* 2.2 occur in the New Testament (καταλαλία in 1 Pet. 2:1). The first one is a favorite of Luke (as part of a Hebrew genitive construction).[30]

The second occurs in Mark, Paul, 2 Peter, and once also in Luke (12:15, here with the variant form ὁρᾶτε καὶ φυλάσσεσθε). The adjectival form of the third one is a favorite of *Phil.* (4.1, 3; 6.1; also *2 Clem.* 6.4; *Did.* 3.5) and is found in the New Testament only in 2 Timothy (3:2) and in Luke (16:14).

4.1.b

In 1 Pet. 3:9b the two ἀντί-phrases are contrasted to what one should then do: τοὐναντίον δὲ εὐλογοῦντες ὅτι εἰς τοῦτο ἐκλήθητε ἵνα εὐλογίαν κληρονομήσητε. In *Phil.* they have been expanded with two more components: ἢ γρόνθον ἀντὶ γρόνθον ἢ κατάραν ἀντὶ κατάρας. The noun γρόνθος occurs only here in the Apostolic Fathers and nowhere in the New Testament. As for the second, 1 Pet. 3:9b has, rightly I think, been compared to Luke 6:28 with its explicit call to "bless those who curse you" (εὐλογεῖτε τοὺς καταρωμένους ὑμᾶς; no direct parallel in Matthew).[31] Should we then not say that it was 1 Peter that led Polycarp to Luke in *Phil.* 2.2? And Luke is where he stayed in 2.3a.b. It looks this way. And it would in any case explain not only the expansion with κατάρα, but also the presence right after in 2.3a of various phrases that are comparable to similar ones from the immediate context in Luke 6:37–38.

And so we are back to *Phil.* 2.3a, which now seems already to show a somewhat stronger link to Luke. In assessing the kind of multiply attested passages as in the case of 2.3a, much hangs, it would seem, on the way the evidence is presented. Gregory notes that "Polycarp may depend either on *1 Clement* or on his source."[32] From his analysis of *1 Clem.* 13.2 we know that this source is not one of the Synoptics, but a pre-Synoptic entity.[33] In this respect the formulation on page 132 is rather unfortunate, for it already excludes from the outset the possibility that Polycarp at least might (in part) depend on Luke and/or Matthew. Unfortunate is also the way the evidence is presented (see the table above). Indeed the text is cited in the order of *1 Clem.* 13.2 (as it was on page 127), which yields the impression that this was the source, or at least that *1 Clement* somehow kept to the original order of the source which Polycarp would then have changed. On this hypothesis Polycarp would have reduced *1 Clement*'s seven formulas to four, of which only two (the second and the last one) are kept in their original order:

1 Clem. 13.2	*Phil.* 2.3a
(e)	a. μὴ κρίνετε
a. ἐλεᾶτε	(c)
b. ἀφίετε	b. ἀφίετε
(a)	c. ἐλεᾶτε
c. ὡς ποιεῖτε	
d. ὡς δίδοτε	
e. ὡς κρίνετε	(a)

f. ὡς χρηστεύεσθε	
g. ᾧ μέτρῳ	d. ᾧ μέτρῳ

However, a rather different picture emerges if one takes Luke 6:37–38 as the leading text:

Luke 6:37–38	*Phil.* 2.3a
a. καὶ μὴ κρίνετε	a. μὴ κρίνετε
b. καὶ μὴ καταδικάζετε	
c. ἀπολύετε	b. ἀφίετε
	c. ἐλεᾶτε
d. δίδοτε	
e. ᾧ γὰρ μέτρῳ	d. ᾧ μέτρῳ

Now three out of the four segments have a parallel in Luke, and they are all in the order of Luke and are basically closer to the way Luke has formulated them (an imperative or prohibition, followed by ἵνα (μή) or καί and the future passive or imperative of the same verb; no instance of a ὡς . . . οὕτως construction of which there are four in *1 Clement*).

The first segment is formulated in identically the same way as in Matt. 7:1, though one should note the widespread and apparently very early attested (Marcion!) variant ἵνα μή for καὶ οὐ μή in Luke 6:37a. Luke's second segment is lacking. It could easily be regarded as too much of a synonym of καὶ μὴ κρίνετε, especially when the latter is taken negatively with the connotation of "judging to condemn."[34] As for Luke's third segment, ἀπολύω and ἀφίημι are semantically related. They can both have a neutral ("to leave behind") and a stronger meaning ("to forgive one's sins" or "to acquit," in a juridical context), though in this latter case ἀφίημι rather carries the first of these two meanings and ἀπολύω the other (see Mark 15:6, 9, 11, 15 par. Matt./Luke). The combination of ἀπολύω with κρίνω and καταδικάζω is then quite appropriate indeed (see also Acts 3:13 κρίναντος ἐκείνου ἀπολύειν). Luke 6:37c has been linked to Matt. 6:14–15,[35] but apparently Polycarp can also combine κρίσις and ἀφίημι on his own, as in 6.1–2.[36] Luke's fourth segment is again lacking, or one should rather say that it has been replaced by one that gives a good, perhaps even a better sense after ἀφίετε than the somewhat too general δίδοτε.[37] The phrase leads us beyond Luke and toward *1 Clement* (or the common source).[38] It cannot be explained from Luke 6:36.[39] The parallel with *1 Clem.* 13.2 cannot be ignored, but it might be worth noting that Polycarp shows an interest in the concept of "mercy." The noun ἔλεος occurs in the inscription in a formula that recalls the one in 1 and 2 Tim. 1:2, but it is given rather more emphasis, for Polycarp drops χάρις and makes ἔλεος the first word in a combination with εἰρήνη. But this segment perhaps also offers one more trace of some subsidiary influence also from Matthew, this time not from the parallel to Luke 6:37–38, but from a nearby one (Matt. 5:7), and one to which Polycarp will turn right after in 2.3b. If Polycarp's third segment is not directly borrowed from Matt. 5:7, it was at least appropriate to retain it (from *1 Clement* or the common source) in view of what was to follow in 2.3b.

Obviously *Phil.* 2.3a cannot fully be explained on the sole basis of Luke 6:37–38. But still, it seems that a place has also been reserved for Luke (with an additional pinch of Matthean salt), and this in a double way. Luke 6:37–38 offers the model, the basic structure, and some of the wording for a shorter form of a very similar series of phrases than the one that has been preserved in *1 Clem.* 13.2, which Polycarp has, so to speak, reduced to its bare structure, closer in any case to the one that is found in Luke, leaving out what looked redundant (καταδικάζω) and what breaks the formal structure (Luke 6:38b), and creating a stronger link between the various parts by exchanging or replacing a few segments (ἀφίημι for ἀπολύω and ἐλέεω for δίδωμι). It looks as if for Polycarp, Luke's was maybe not yet the "perfect" form, but at least it was closer to it than *1 Clement*'s long series is.[40]

4.2. *Phil.* 2.3b

If there seems to be some need also for Luke and for Matthew in explaining all of the particulars of the formulation in 2.3a, the combined influence of these same two Gospels may offer the best solution also to account for what follows in 2.3b. Here we are left with only Luke and Matthew as the closest known parallels.

Phil. 2.3b	Luke 6:20	Matt. 5:3	Matt. 5:10
μακάριοι οἱ πτωχοί	μακάριοι οἱ πτωχοί,	μακάριοι οἱ πτωχοὶ τῷ πνεύματί,	
καὶ οἱ διωκόμενοι ἕνεκεν δικαιοσύνης,			μακάριοι οἱ δεδιωγμένοι ἕνεκεν δικαιοσύνης,
ὅτι αὐτῶν ἐστιν ἡ βασιλεία τοῦ θεοῦ.	ὅτι ὑμετέρα ἐστιν ἡ βασιλεία τοῦ θεοῦ.	ὅτι αὐτῶν ἐστιν ἡ βασιλεία τῶν οὐρανῶν.	ὅτι αὐτῶν ἐστιν ἡ βασιλεία τῶν οὐρανῶν.

The agreement with Luke in reading plain οἱ πτωχοί against Matthew's οἱ πτωχοὶ τῷ πνεύματι is of course a kind of argument from silence. But not all such arguments are equally weak. Matthew's is a most remarkable and potentially highly useful formula, and the combination with that other macarism that is found only in Matthew adds force to the assumption that the change was well premeditated. If the dramatic financial situation of the community, which has been said to have caused Polycarp to write the letter, played a role, and this may well have been the case (see the repeated warnings against greed and love of money in 2.2b and 4.3),[41] Luke's alternative formula in 6:20 may naturally have come to his mind.[42] It would in any case not be the only parallel with Luke. Gregory seems to belittle the importance of the agreement with Luke on τοῦ θεοῦ against Matthew's τῶν οὐρανῶν, which Koester regarded as an important indication for Polycarp's dependence on Luke at this point.[43] The issue is not that ἡ βασιλεία τῶν οὐρανῶν is "too common a phrase,"[44] but rather that Polycarp changes a strikingly Matthean formula in a context in which he closely parallels a text that is also found in Luke.[45] But again this is perhaps not yet the whole picture. The choice for combining Matt. 5:3 with 5:10 is a rather obvious one, for these two macarisms share the same reward, ὅτι αὐτῶν ἐστιν ἡ βασιλεία τῶν οὐρανῶν.[46] However, it is not so obvious where Polycarp got the idea for this kind of "reduced format" of the list of macarisms. Again, as in the case of 2.3a, it may well have been Luke who offered the model. If Polycarp in 2.3a had access to a longer (*1 Clem.* 13.2 or the common source) as well as to a shorter form (Luke 6:37–38), he chose to follow the latter one, both for the basic structure and in part also for the wording. Luke 6:37–38 offered a helpful specimen of such a shorter series of more or less similarly composed phrases. It may have inspired Polycarp also to bring a comparably reduced form of the macarisms. And here again Luke had preceded him, for what else are the Lukan version of the macarisms and the Woe sayings in 6:24–26 but other specimens of such a procedure, at least for one who was familiar with both versions of the macarisms and was used to reading and comparing them with no particular source theory in mind, as would most probably have been the case with Polycarp?[47]

4.3. *Phil.* 12.3b

Matthew's and Luke's versions of the Sermon on the Mount/Plain prove to be a crucial factor for explaining both the content and the composition of *Phil.* 2.3 as a whole. And the same goes for 12.3b, the third passage that is discussed by Gregory.

Phil. 12.3b	Luke 6:27	Matt. 5:44, 48
Orate etiam pro regibus		<5:44> καὶ προσεύχεσθε
et potestatibus et princi-	<6:27> καλῶς	
pibus atque pro perse-	ποιεῖτε τοῖς	
quentibus et odientibus	μισοῦσιν	ὑπὲρ τῶν διωκόντων
vos et pro inimicis crucis,	ὑμᾶς,	ὑμᾶς,
ut fructus vester mani-		<5:48> ἔσεσθε οὖν ὑμεῖς
festus sit in omnibus, ut		τέλειοι ὡς ὁ πατὴρ ὑμῶν
sitis in illo perfecti.		ὁ οὐράνιος τέλειός ἐστιν.

Table reprinted from Gregory, 135.

Discussion of this passage is complicated by the fact that it has been preserved only in a Latin translation, and this should be kept in mind. Theoretically it is possible that the translator has assimilated or mixed up elements from both Gospels.[48] Gregory also points to the possibility that some of the sayings in the Sermon on the Mount may have circulated independently of the Gospels.[49] That is possible, and even most probable, of course, but in this particular case the author was apparently very well aware of the fact that the phrase "those who hate you" is the Lukan parallel to "those who persecute you" in Matthew's Gospel. Could this really just have been a lucky shot? Gregory does not mention the possibility that Polycarp (or the translator) may have relied on an already assimilated version of Matt. 5:44. The textual tradition offers good, but comparatively late, evidence for a reading in which Luke 6:28a, 27b (TR D W Θ Φ sy^p Eus) or just 6:27b (lat) are inserted between ἀγαπᾶτε τοὺς ἐχθροὺς ὑμῶν and καὶ προσεύχεσθε . . .[50] However, in *Phil.* 12.3b the insertion is found after ὑπὲρ τῶν διωκόντων ὑμᾶς. It might be a mere mistake, a secondary variant of the assimilation, an attempt at retaining the fragment on hating in an otherwise truncated citation of verse 44 (without verse 44a), or a conscious move once more to create a condensed form of a longer section from the Sermon on the Mount/Plain. *Phil.* 12.3b can indeed be read as a combination from elements of the opening and the closing segments of Luke 6:27–36 by an author who knows that verses 27 and 36 are paralleled in Matthew by verses 44 and 48. As he had done before in 2.3a (cf. the combination of Matt. 7:1a and Luke 6:37b), he keeps to the wording of Matthew in verse 44b, but adds an element from Luke's verse 27. As in 2.3 the author obviously has done more than merely conflate two passages. The command to pray is applied to several categories that cannot all be clearly distinguished and probably partially overlap, but nevertheless make for a nicely composed phrase (threefold "pro," with first three, then two, and then one group only; should something be made of the variation between "atque pro" and "et pro"?). The first lists a trio of earthly powers that may render an original ὑπὲρ βασιλέων καὶ ἐξουσίων καὶ ἄρχων, all of them commonly used in such combinations. The last two occur together in Eph. 3:10; 6:12; Col. 1:16; 2:10 (sg.); Tit. 3:1; and Luke 12:11. But only in Luke are they part of a threesome (τὰς συναγωγάς preceding), who in the parallel in 21:12 offers a combination with βασιλεῖς (ἐπὶ βασιλεῖς καὶ ἡγεμόνας; cf. also 20:20 ὥστε παραδοῦναι αὐτὸν τῇ ἀρχῇ καὶ τῇ ἐξουσίᾳ τοῦ ἡγεμόνος). The third phrase ("enemies of the cross") has a close parallel in *Phil* 3:18,[51] but "the enemies" are also very much present in Luke 6:27a and the parallel in Matt. 5:44a.[52] The middle part looks like a combination of Matthew's verse 44b and Luke's verse 27b.[53]

The second half of 12.3b consists of a double final clause ("ut . . . , ut"). The keyword *perfecti* that closes the phrase points to Matt. 5:48 (pl. τέλειοι).[54] Matthew's closing phrase is anticipated already in the final clause (!) in verse 45:

ὅπως γένησθε υἱοὶ τοῦ πατρὸς ὑμῶν τοῦ ἐν οὐρανοῖς. The verse has its parallel in 6:35 in Luke (καὶ ἔσεσθε . . . , as in Matt verse 48; cf. "sitis" in 12.3b), who thus closes the section with a double reference to what Christians should aspire to in order to become the "sons of the father" who himself continuously "makes manifest" the fruits of his kindness, even to the unjust (Matthew) and the ungrateful and the selfish (Luke).[55] As is the case in *Phil.* 2.3a and 2.3b, here again the whole composition makes sense if it is looked upon as a reduced form of the parallel passage in the Sermon on the Mount/Plain, a composition, moreover, for which Luke has offered some of the wording and the core of the structure. To find one instance of such a procedure might be a coincidence; two would be a remarkable feature. Should three not therefore count as proof?[56]

Andrew Gregory has toured widely in the desert landscape of the second century. He has stopped by at all the monuments of some interest, always "looking for Luke," as the subtitle of his monograph says, but only very rarely, indeed too rarely, does he happen to stumble on it. It should not mean that Luke is not there. The experience surely is familiar. Two are admiring a work of art only to find out later on that one has somehow missed the details the other had noticed at once. The art is in the looking, as much as in the finding. It is a fact of life, it would seem, that some are looking and do not see where others seek and do find.

NOTES

1. For Paul see, among others, Andreas Lindemann, *Paulus im ältesten Christentum: Das Bild des Apostels und die Rezeption der paulinischen Theologie in der frühchristlichen Literatur bis Marcion* (BIFCS 58; Tübingen: Mohr Siebeck, 1979); Lindemann, "Der Apostel Paulus im 2. Jahrhundert," in *The New Testament in Early Christianity = La réception des écrits néotestamentaires dans le christianisme primitif* (ed. Jean-Marie Sevrin; BETL 86; Leuven: Leuven University Press, 1989), 39–67; Lindemann, "Die Sammlung der Paulusbriefe im 1. und 2. Jahrhundert," in *The Biblical Canons* (ed. Jean-Marie Auwers and Henk Jan de Jonge; BETL 163; Leuven: Leuven University Press, 2003), 321–51; E. Dassmann, *Der Stachel im Fleisch. Paulus in der frühchristlichen Literatur bis Irenäus* (Münster: Aschendorff, 1979). For Matthew see above all Édouard Massaux, *Influence de l'Évangile de saint Matthieu sur la littérature chrétienne avant saint Irénée* (Louvain and Gembloux: Duculot, 1950); repr. in BETL 75 (Leuven: Leuven University Press, 1986); English translation: *The Influence of the Gospel of Saint Matthew on Christian Literature before Saint Irenaeus* (3 vols.; Macon, Ga.: Mercer University Press, 1990–1993); Wolf-Dietrich Köhler, *Die Rezeption des Matthäusevangeliums in der Zeit vor Irenäus* (WUNT 2/24; Tübingen: Mohr Siebeck, 1987); Arthur J. Bellinzoni, "The Gospel of Matthew in the Second Century," in *Second Century* 9 (1992): 197–259. For John see Joseph N. Sanders, *The Fourth Gospel in the Early Church: Its Origin and Influence on Christian Theology up to Irenaeus* (Cambridge: Cambridge University Press, 1943); François-Marie Braun, *Jean le Théologien et son Évangile dans l'Église ancienne* (EB; Paris: Gabalda, 1959); Jean-Daniel Kaestli, Jean-Michel Poffet, and Jean Zumstein, eds., *La Communauté johannique et son histoire: Le trajectoire de l'Évangile de Jean aux deux premiers siècles*

(Geneva: Labor et Fides, 1990); Titus Nagel, *Die Rezeption des Johannesevangeliums im 2. Jahrhundert. Studien zur vorirenäische Auslegung des vierten Evangeliums in christlicher und christlich-gnostischer Literatur* (ABG 2; Leipzig: Evangelische Verlagsanstalt, 2000); Charles E. Hill, *The Johannine Corpus in the Early Church* (Oxford: Oxford University Press, 2004). Specifically for the Apostolic Fathers, cf. A Committee of the Oxford Society of Historical Theology, *The New Testament in the Apostolic Fathers* (Oxford: Clarendon, 1905); Helmut Koester, *Synoptische Überlieferung bei den Apostolischen Vätern* (TU 65; Berlin: Akademie-Verlag, 1957); Andrew F. Gregory and Christopher M. Tuckett, eds., *The Reception of the New Testament in the Apostolic Fathers* (Oxford: Oxford University Press, 2005), and *Trajectories through the New Testament and the Apostolic Fathers* (Oxford: Oxford University Press, 2005).

From among studies dedicated to one particular author, one should at least cite such twentieth-century "classics" as Arthur J. Bellinzoni, *The Sayings of Jesus in the Writings of Justin Martyr* (NovTSup 17; Leiden: Brill, 1967), and Donald A. Hagner, *The Use of the Old and New Testaments in Clement of Rome* (NovTSup 34; Leiden: Brill, 1973). On Justin see most recently also Emmanuel Luhumbu Shodu, *La mémoire des origines chrétiennes selon Justin Martyr* (Paradosis 50; Fribourg: Academic Press, 2008). The earliest history of the sayings and gospel traditions is studied in the collections of essays edited by David Wenham, *The Jesus Tradition Outside the Gospels* (Gospel Perspectives 5; Sheffield: JSOT Press, 1984); Barbara Aland and William L. Petersen, *Gospel Traditions in the Second Century: Origins, Recensions, Text, and Transmission* (Christianity and Judaism in Antiquity 3; Notre Dame, Ind.: University of Notre Dame Press, 1989); and Sevrin, *The New Testament in Early Christianity.* See further the bibliographies in Gregory and Tuckett, *Reception,* 331–46, and *Trajectories,* 433–65.

2. Though the field is not completely left open. Massaux, while primarily dealing with Matthew, has duly noted whatever material he thought to be relevant also for the other Gospels and even for Paul. Koester dealt with all of the Synoptic material as far as the Apostolic Fathers are concerned. The two Oxford projects cited in the previous note also look into the whole of the New Testament.

3. Andrew F. Gregory, *The Reception of Luke and Acts in the Period before Irenaeus: Looking for Luke in the Second Century* (WUNT 2/169; Tübingen: Mohr Siebeck, 2003). See further also Arthur J. Bellinzoni, "The Gospel of Luke in the Second Century CE," in *Literary Studies in Luke-Acts: Essays in Honor of Joseph B. Tyson* (ed. Richard P. Thompson and Thomas E. Philips, Macon, Ga.: Mercer University Press, 1998), 56–76; Bellinzoni, "The Gospel of Luke in the Apostolic Fathers: An Overview," in Gregory and Tuckett, *Trajectories,* 45–68; François Bovon, "The Reception and Use of the Gospel of Luke in the Second Century," in *Reading Luke: Interpretation, Reflection, Formation* (ed. Craig G. Bartholomew, Joel B. Green, and Anthony C. Thiselton; Scripture and Hermeneutics 6; Grand Rapids: Zondervan, 2005), 379–400. For Acts the little information there is has been touched upon by Werner Bieder, *Die Apostelgeschichte in der Historie: Ein Beitrag zur Auslegungsgeschichte des Missionsbuches der Kirche* (ThSt 61; Zürich: EVZ Verlag, 1960).

4. Cf. Bovon, "Reception," 380–81.

5. Cf. Adolf Hilgenfeld, *Kritische Untersuchungen über die Evangelien Justin's, der clementinischen Homilien und Marcion's* (Halle: Schwetschke, 1850); Wilhelm Bousset, *Die Evan-*

gelienzitate Justins des Märtyrers in ihren Wert für die Evangelienkritik (Göttingen: Vandenhoeck & Ruprecht, 1891). The former may be outdated, but the latter's conclusions have been most influential.

6. Eduard Zeller, "Die älteste Überlieferung über die Schriften des Lukas," *Theologische Jahrbücher* 7 (1848): 528–72.

7. On Irenaeus's knowledge and use of the canonical Gospels, see D. Jeffrey Bingham, *Irenaeus' Use of Matthew's Gospel in* Adversus Haereses (Traditio Exegetica Graeca 7; Leuven: Peeters, 1998); Graham N. Stanton, "Jesus Traditions and Gospels in Justin Martyr and Irenaeus," in Auwers and de Jonge, *The Biblical Canons,* 353–70; Bernhard Mutschler, *Irenäus als johanneischer Theologe: Studien zur Schriftauslegung bei Irenäus von Lyon* (STAC 21; Tübingen: Mohr Siebeck, 2004); and Mutschler, *Das Corpus Johanneum bei Irenäus von Lyon: Studien und Kommentar zum dritten Buch von Adversus Haereses* (WUNT 189; Tübingen: Mohr Siebeck, 2006). On the concept of the "fourfold gospel" cf. Graham N. Stanton, "The Fourfold Gospel," *NTS* 43/3 (1997): 317–46; repr. in Stanton, *Jesus and Gospel* (Cambridge: Cambridge University Press, 2004), 63–91.

8. Gregory makes a similar observation in his general conclusion with reference to Irenaeus and to the Muratorian Fragment: "the fact that these two witnesses to the reception of both *Luke* and *Acts* are also the first extant texts to offer any explicit and self-conscious assessment or appraisal of *Luke* and *Acts* as texts should not be overlooked" (*Reception,* 352).

9. Massaux often distinguishes between material "in which Matthean influence is definite" ("certaine"), such material "in which Matthean influence is doubtful or to be excluded" ("douteuse ou à écarter"), and "texts that come from the gospel tradition" ("textes relevant de la tradition évangélique"): see, for example, *L'Influence,* 3, 49, 82, and 86 (with regard to Justin's Dialogue with Trypho). He can be quite outspoken about the last category (for example, on p. 84, with regard to *Dial.* 88.7: "this personal and intricate work which Justin developed makes a literary dependence on Mt. so much more problematic" ("rend la dépendance littéraire de *Mt.* plus problématique"), and at times rather cautious when dealing with the first category (thus he writes on p. 81: "I believe I was able to assert that . . ." ["on a cru pouvoir affirmer que . . ."]).

10. The crucial concept is that of redaction as it was laid down in Koester's famous description of the various sorts of indications that are available for deciding on whether or not literary dependence is in play: "Es begegnen bei den AVV [Apostolic Fathers] eine ganze Reihe von Zitaten aus synoptischer Überlieferung, die zum Teil mit einer Zitationsformel ausdrücklich eingeführt werden. Es finden sich daneben aber auch mehr oder weniger bewusste Anpielungen auf synoptische Stücke, Anklänge, sowie Berührungen in der Terminologie. Zur Beantwortung der Frage, ob in den einzelnen Schriften bereits schriftliche Evangelien oder evtl. ältere Traditionen benutzt sind, müssen jeweils zunächst die Zitationsformeln und die Hinweise auf schriftliche Autoritäten untersucht warden, wobei darauf zu achten ist, unter welcher Autorität synoptische Stücke angeführt werden, unter der Autorität des 'Herrn' oder der eines schriftlichen Evangeliums, das die Geltung der 'Schrift' hatte. Trifft letzteres zu, so ist die Benutzung von Evangelien, seien es nun unsere Synoptiker oder in gleicher Geltung stehende apokryphe Evangelien, wahrscheinlich. Stehen aber die angeführten Stücke unter der Autorität des Herrn und lässt sich aus keinem der Quellenhinweise auf die Benutzung eines Evangeliums schliessen, so hängt die Frage der Benutzung davon ab,

ob sich in den angeführten Stücken Redaktionsarbeit eines Evangelisten findet" (*Synoptische Überlieferung,* 3).

11. *Reception,* 298. The evidence for Acts is less stringent, but Gregory at least allows for the possibility that (an older form of) the apocryphal *Acts of Paul, of Peter,* and *of John* might date back to the late second century (351).

12. *Reception,* 8.

13. See the critical comments on using Koester's criterion, *Reception,* 10–14.

14. And likewise it is true that a "feature might be added to the tradition by two independent redactors, and that any dependence established by this criterion need not be direct," as Gregory notes (*Reception,* 13) with reference to Christopher M. Tuckett, "Synoptic Tradition in the Didache," 197–230, in J-M. Sevrin, ed., *The New Testament in Early Christianity* (BETL 86; Leuven: Leuven University Press and Peeters, 1989). But can such an alternative be put on the same level as its counterpart? As for the limits posed by the hypothetical character of any source-critical theory, this is a factor indeed, but not more for one theory than for another, including the oral tradition theory.

15. See pp. 92–103 (the *Gospel of the Ebionites*) and pp. 153–58 (*Thomas*).

16. See pp. 136–49 (*2 Clement*).

17. See the arrangement for Justin on pp. 226–31 (*Dial.* 76.6 // Luke 10:19; *Apol.* 17.4 // Luke 12:48; *Dial.* 105.5 // Luke 23:46; *Dial.* 76.7, 100.3, 51.2 // Luke 24:7); pp. 241–53 (*Apol.* 16.13 // Luke 3:9b; *Dial.* 103.6, 125.4 // Luke 4:8; *Apol.* 16.10, 63.5 // Luke 10:16; *Apol.* 63.3, 63.13 // *Dial.* 100.1 // Luke 10:22; *Dial.* 107.1 // Luke 11:29; *Dial.* 17.4, 112.4 // Luke 11:42; *Apol.* 19.7 // Luke 12:4–5; *Apol.* 16.12 // *Dial.* 76.4, 120.6, 140.4 // Luke 13:28–29; *Dial.* 51.3 // Luke 16:16); pp. 254–63 (*Apol.* 15.8a // Luke 5:32; *Dial.* 125.1 // Luke 8:5–8; *Dial.* 51.2, 76.7, 100.3 // Luke 9:22 // Luke 24:7; *Apol.* 15.12 // Luke 9:25; *Apol.* 19.6 // Luke 18:27; *Dial.* 81.4 // Luke 20:35–36).

18. See pp. 118–24: *Did.* 16.1 (// Luke 12:35, 40) is discussed before *Did.* 1.3–2.1 (// Luke 6:27–28, 32–35), because the latter "is widely regarded as a relatively late redactional insertion" (118). Polycarp, *Phil.* 2.3a (// *1 Clem.* 13.2; Luke 6:31, 36–38) comes first because in this instance the parallel in *1 Clem.* may possibly have played a role (132). It is not clear what may have been the reason in the section on Justin.

19. On the life and work of Polycarp see Boudewijn Dehandschutter, "Polycarp's Epistle to the Philippians: An Early Example of 'Reception,'" in Sevrin, *The New Testament in Early Christianity,* 275–81, repr. in Dehandschutter, *Polycarpiana: Studies on Martyrdom and Persecution in Early Christianity. Collected Essays* (ed. Johan Leemans; BETL 205; Leuven: Leuven University Press, 2007), 154–60; and in the same volume: "Images of Polycarp: Biography and Hagiography about the Bishop of Smyrna," 271–77; Johannes B. Bauer, *Die Polykarpbriefe* (KAV 5; Göttingen: Vandenhoeck & Ruprecht, 1995), 10–12; Paul Hartog, *Polycarp and the New Testament: The Occasion, Rhetoric, Theme, and Unity of the Epistle to the Philippians and Its Allusions to New Testament Literature* (WUNT 2/134; Tübingen: Mohr Siebeck, 2002); Kenneth Berding, *Polycarp and Paul: An Analysis of Their Literary and Theological Relationship in Light of Polycarp's Use of Biblical and Extra-Biblical Literature* (VCSup 62; Leiden: Brill, 2002), 8–23. This is not the place to discuss in any detail Charles E. Hill's rather singular hypothesis about the "prolific author Polycarp" (*From the Lost Teaching of Polycarp* [WUNT 186; Tübingen: Mohr Siebeck, 2006]).

20. *Reception,* 136.

21. Ibid.

22. See the discussion of (all of the possibly) relevant parallel material in *The New Testament in the Apostolic Fathers,* 101–04; Percy N. Harrison, *Polycarp's Two Epistles to the Philippians* (Cambridge: Cambridge University Press, 1936), 285–91; Massaux, *L'Influence,* 2: 27–35; Koester, *Synoptische Überlieferung,* 112–23; Hagner, *1 Clement,* 141–43; Köhler, *Rezeption,* 97–110; Dehandschutter, "Polycarp's Epistle," 285–91 (= *Polycarpiana,* 164–70); Hartog, *Polycarp and the New Testament,* 180–86, 190–97; Berding, *Polycarp and Paul,* 53–58, 121–24; Bellinzoni, *Gospel of Luke,* 59–61; Clayton N. Jefford, *The Apostolic Fathers and the New Testament* (Peabody, Mass.: Hendrickson, 2006), 134–35. Cf. also Bauer, *Die Polykarpbriefe,* 44–45, 72–73.

23. *Influence,* 2: 29–30. Unlike Clement, Polycarp would have been familiar with and used this catechism in its "final stage." Cf. Köhler, *Rezeption,* 107: Polycarp "[zitiert] katechetisch durchgeformtes Material." The hypothesis is in any case less radical than the one proposed by W. Sanday, *The Gospels in the Second Century* (London: Macmillan, 1876), 86, who argued that Polycarp had been using a separate gospel. Zeller ("Überlieferung," 532) reckoned with "an extra-canonical writing."

24. *Synoptische Überlieferung,* 118: "[Polykarp] muss das 1. und das 3. Evangelium gekannt haben. Zwar entnimmt er die Komposition aus 1. Clem. 13,2. Aber bei der gedächtnismässigen Zitation setzt sich der Wortlaut der entsprechenden synoptischen Stellen, der Pol. ebenfalls im Gedächtnis gewesen sein muss, gegenüber dem des 1. Clem. stärker durch."

25. *Reception,* 134.

26. Speaking for many others cf. François Bovon, *Das Evangelium nach Lukas,* I (EKK, 3/1; Zürich: Benziger, 1989), 323 n. 75: "Lukas hat eine Vorliebe für γάρ und zusammengesetzte Verben (ἀντιμετρηθήσεται)." Dehandschutter ("Polycarp's Epistle," 168 n. 60) points out that the compound is also (weakly) attested in the textual tradition of Matt. 7:1 and draws attention to the fact that Clement of Alexandria (*Strom.* II.91.2) cites *1 Clem.* 13.2 with the compound verb. But probably not too much weight should be given to this relatively late attestation of what could well be the mere result of a conflation. And the same may be true for the evidence from Clement of Alexandria who also omits ἐν αὐτῷ and shows some variation also in other instances where he is quoting the same sayings.

27. Evidence of 1 Peter's influence on Polycarp is not limited to this one passage and is more substantial and structural, as Jefford shows, defining the links as "a certain sequential consistency . . . based upon the progression of Petrine texts" (*Apostolic Fathers,* 137).

28. *Phil.* 4 3 μακρὰν οὔσας πάσης διαβολῆς, καταλαλιᾶς, ψευδομαρτυρίας, φιλαργυρίας καὶ παντὸς κακοῦ.

29. The qualification εὔσπλαγχνος also in Eph. 4:32, in *1 Clem.* 29.1; 54.1, and twice also in *Phil.* (5.2 and 6.1, of ministers).

30. Cf. Luke 13:27; 16:8, 9; 18:6; Acts 1:18; 8:23. Bovon (*Lukas,* II, 435 n. 37) notes that the word does not occur that often in Luke, but it always carries "eine ausgeprägte Bedeutung." The latter is correct. As for the former part, see J. Jeremias, *Die Sprache des Lukasevangeliums: Redaktion und Tradition im Nicht-Markusstoff des dritten Evangeliums* (KEK Sonderband; Göttingen: Vandenhoeck & Ruprecht, 1980), 232 (at 13:27): "Beachtet man einerseits, dass das lk Doppelwerk den Terminus ἀνομία nicht kennt, dass Lukas dagegen

aber als einziger Synoptiker ἀδικία gebraucht, so wird man schliessen, dass ἀδικία eine der zahlreichen lukanischen Korrekturen an einem Schriftzitat ist." See also G. M. Camps and B. M. Ubach, "Un sentido bíblico de *adikos, adikia* y la interpretación de Lc 16,113," in *EstBib* 25 (1966): 75–82. On the Semitic genitive cf. Édouard Delebecque, "Le régisseur infidèle (16, 1–13)," in *Études grecques sur l'évangile de Luc. Collection d'études anciennes* (ed. Édouard Delebecque; Paris: Belles Lettres, 1976), 92 n. 1.

31. If the form of the clause may be closer to Paul, "the roots of this passage surely lie in the Christian paranetic tradition that belongs to the earliest strands of Christian tradition, and understands itself to be derived from the sayings and conduct of Jesus himself" (Paul J. Achtemeier, *1 Peter: A Commentary on First Peter* [Hermeneia; Minneapolis: Fortress, 1996], 224 [with reference to Luke 6:27–28 par. Matt.]). A similar view in Norbert Brox, *Der erste Petrusbrief* (EKK 21; Zürich, Einsiedeln, Köln: Benziger Verlag, 1979), 154, who also draws attention to a further link between 1 Peter and Luke: "In diesem Wort [Luke 6:28] begegnen immerhin die beiden Verben εὐλογεῖν und ἐπηρεάζειν aus 1Petr 3,9.16" (n. 491).

32. *Reception,* 132. Berding rightly notes that the introductory phrase does not in itself offer clear-cut proof for or against the possibility that Polycarp was holding to oral tradition (*Polycarp and Paul,* 53–54). Cf. also Dehandschutter, "Polycarp's Epistle," 169: "'remembering' does not necessarily involve an oral source."

33. "Of course it is not possible to exclude the possibility that 1 Clement has drawn on, harmonised, altered and supplemented synoptic tradition as found in the Synoptic Gospels. Yet the differences between the Synoptic parallels and the strongly stylised form of this passage, suited for oral transmisison, may be considered evidence for the use of a pre-Synoptic source" (Gregory, *Reception,* 127).

34. See James 5:12 ἵνα μὴ ὑπὸ κρίσιν πέσητε ("that you may not fall under condemnation"); 5:6 offers one of the few instances of καταδικάζω in the New Testament, apart from Luke 6:37; see further also Matt. 12:7, 37 and note the double κατακρίνω in 12:41, 42 par. Luke 11:31, 32. Cf. Bovon's comment on the close link between the two verbs: "Wenn κρίνω in V 37a noch doppeldeutig war, entfällt dies jetzt aufgrund des καταδικάζω in V 37b" (*Lukas,* I, 323–24).

35. So Gregory, *Reception,* 132; cf. also Berding, *Polycarp and Paul,* 56, and see Zeller, "Überlieferung," 532.

36. μὴ ἀπότομοι ἐν κρίσει, εἰδότες, ὅτι πάντες ὀφειλέται ἐσμὲν ἁμαρτίας. εἰ οὖν δεόμεθα τοῦ κυρίου, ἵνα ἡμῖν ἀφῇ. ὀφείλομεν καὶ ἡμεῖς ἀφιέναι. Cf. Dehandschutter, "Polycarp's Epistle," 166: "may be due also to Polycarp's intention to return to the theme of forgiveness (cf. 6, 2) with a much clearer allusion to the Gospel."

37. If one can say with Fitzmyer that "mercy in judging should lead also to generosity in giving, and so the foursome is united," one is certainly entitled to say, "to forgive (those who did harm to you) is an act of mercy." Cf. Joseph A. Fitzmyer, *The Gospel According to Luke I–IX* (Anchor Bible Commentaries; Garden City: Doubleday, 1985), 641.

38. But it would be in any case too radical a conclusion altogether to exclude Luke as a source, because "he does not have the sentence" (so Massaux, *L'Influence,* 2:29).

39. Neither οἰκτίρμων nor the variant οἰκτιρμός are found in *Phil.;* see the combined ἐλεῆμον καὶ οἰκτίρμον in *1 Clem.* 60.1.

40. The explanation that is here proposed goes beyond Berding's hypothesis because a more distinct role is given to Luke as the primary model. As a matter of fact Berding somewhat confusingly first argues that "Polycarp is aware of *1 Clement* and perhaps encouraged by 'Clement' to include such a list in his own letter but corrects the form of the text toward the written gospels," but then concludes, "in the absence of extant written documents, it seems best to argue that both Maxim # 2 and Maxim # 3 are mediated through an oral source rather than through some unknown written document, though an early document cannot be ruled out" (*Polycarp and Paul,* 56 and 57).

41. Cf. Gregory, *Reception,* 134, with reference to Schoedel, Dehandschutter, and Hartog. Cf. William R. Schoedel, *Polycarp, Martyrdom of Polycarp, Fragments of Papias* (Apostolic Fathers 5; London: Thomas Nelson, 1967), 12; Dehandschutter, "Polycarp's Epistle," 166; Hartog, *Polycarp and the New Testament,* 181–82, 193.

42. Pace Köhler, such a situation might at least explain why Polycarp, "Mt und Lk gerade so hätte 'mischen' sollen oder gar wollen" (*Rezeption,* 100).

43. "Zur Erklärung ist entweder gedächtnismässige Abweichung oder aber Einfluss der Luk.-Parallele anzunehmen" (*Synoptische Überlieferung,* 118).

44. So Gregory, *Reception,* 135. Cf. Dehandschutter, "Polycarp's Epistle," 167 n. 57.

45. In *Phil.* 5.3 the phrase βασιλεία θεοῦ stems from 1 Cor. 6:9. Dehandschutter ("Polycarp's Epistle," 167 n. 57) reckons with influence of this passage on *Phil.* 2.3b, but the phrase is not absolutely identical (τοῦ) and in this respect differs from what is said to be the more common form in the Apostolic Fathers, which happens to be the one that is found also in Luke.

46. As for the conflation with Luke I am not sure one can conclude from it that "it is the words of Jesus more than the text of Matthew and Luke that hold authority for Polycarp" (Berding, *Polycarp and Paul,* 59). For Köhler there can be no doubt about it that two macarisms have been fused together, "und also bewusst verkürzt zitiert werden" (*Rezeption,* 107).

47. The procedure had been observed by Massaux: "Finally, let me note that the words of Polycarp are a summary of the beatitudes and that he noticed that the first and the last use the same formula" (*Influence,* 2:31).

48. So Gregory, *Reception,* 135.

49. Ibid.

50. Bauer (*Polykarpbriefe,* 73) compares Polycarp's harmonizing of Matthew and Luke to what happened in the textual tradition.

51. Berding, *Polycarp and Paul,* 123: "probably dependent."

52. "The twin themes of prayer and enemies weave Phil. 12.3 together" (Hartog, *Polycarp and the New Testament,* 192).

53. That this would also be "the simplest" solution (but why would that be so?) does of course not count as an argument, as Berding is well aware (*Polycarp and Paul,* 123).

54. "Likely an allusion to Matt. 5:48" (Ibid., 124).

55. The motif of the fruit is one of those cases where the lack of the Greek original makes it very difficult to tell if Polycarp may have had a particular text in mind (1 Tim. 4:15?).

56. There are still a few other passages that could be mentioned. Gregory rejects *Phil.* 6.2 and 7.2 as possible witnesses (*Reception,* 135 n. 84) and lists one more case that is discussed

by Berding (132 n. 73: *Phil.* 4.3 and Luke 2:37). Not much can be made of the first one, but the second is now accepted by Koester (*Introduction,* vol. 2, 306) and Berding regards 4.3 as a "possible reminiscence of the widow Anna" (*Polycarp and Paul,* 199). The phrase οὗ τὸ αἷμα ἐκζητήσει ὁ θεὸς ἀπὸ τῶν ἀπειθούντων αὐτῷ in *Phil.* 2.1 might be another "reminiscence." The passage is mentioned by Hartog (*Polycarp and the New Testament,* 201 n. 19) and discussed but rejected by Berding: "Polycarp is probably in a general sense dependent upon biblical phraseology" (48). That may be true, but in the New Testament it is only Luke who reads the very same words in 11:50, which differ from Matt. 23:35 (cf. Matt. 27:25, no verb and Acts 5:28 βοῦλεσθε ἐπαγαγεῖν ἐφ' ἡμᾶς τὸ αἷμα τοῦ ἀνθρώπου τούτου). The "Lukan connection" may further be strengthened by the preceding clause in 2.1 about "the judge of the living and the dead" (ὃς ἔρχεται κριτὴς ζώντων καὶ νεκρῶν) that in this form is found in the New Testament only in Acts 10:42 (not as a noun but with a form of the verb in 2 Tim. 4:1 and 1 Pet. 4:5). The motif of "Christ the Judge" is dear to Luke, but only here and in Acts 17:31 is it made explicit: cf. Luke Timothy Johnson, *The Acts of the Apostles* (SacPag 5; Collegeville, Minn.: Liturgical Press, 1992), 193. Together these two elements form the latter half of a fourfold relative clause that defines Jesus Christ as the Lord and Judge of the whole World. The first element closely parallels 1 Cor. 15:38 (cf. Phil. 2:10 and 3:21). The second may recall Ps. 150:6. The third is mentioned in Acts in the context of Peter preaching to the Gentiles and calling Jesus Christ "Lord of all" (v. 36) and the one whom God has raised (v. 40). The latter motif is found again in Acts 2:24 in combination with that of "God loosing the pangs of death," very much in the same way as this occurs also right before in *Phil.* 1.2 (with "Hades" instead of "death," cf. Acts 2:27), a combination which succeeded in convincing even a sceptic such as Zeller that this might well be an allusion to Acts ("Überlieferung," 532). The third and fourth element of the series in 2.1 may be closer to each other than one might have thought, for in Acts 10:43 the text continues with a reference to the prophets bearing witness and preaching forgiveness of sins, a motif that occurs also in Acts 3:24 and 5:31 (cf. Luke 24:47) for "the one who believes in him" (τὸν πιστεύοντα εἰς αὐτόν, the only instance in Luke-Acts of πιστεύω with εἰς for Acts 14:23 and 19:4 are slightly different; note πιστεύσαντες εἰς in *Phil.* 2.1). These are the same prophets whose blood was shed and will now be required of "this generation" according to Luke 11:50–51. In Acts, Peter preaches the same gospel to the Gentiles as the one Jesus had preached in Luke when addressing the people of Israel and its leaders. "Die von Gott bestimmte Verkündigung hat das Volk, also Israel, als Adresse. Dies sagt Petrus also in seiner Predigt vor Nicht-Juden. Eine 'eigene' Verkündigung für Nicht-Juden gibt es nicht" (Jacob Jervell, *Die Apostelgeschichte* [KEK 17; Göttingen: Vandenhoeck & Ruprecht, 1998], 312). It is this same message Polycarp is bringing to his audience of (most probably) non-Jews. So maybe Pervo is right (and wise!) when concluding, on the basis of 2.1, that "Polycarp may have known Acts" (Richard I. Pervo, *Dating Acts: Between the Evangelists and the Apologists* [Santa Rosa, Calif.: Polebridge Press, 2006], 20).

THE BOOK OF ACTS AS A NARRATIVE COMMENTARY ON THE LETTERS OF THE NEW TESTAMENT

A Programmatic Essay

David Trobisch

This essay assesses the value of Acts as a historical source. Following the most important reading instructions presented in the text through the narrator's (Luke's) voice, the main characters (Jerusalem authorities and Paul), and the central conflict (Paul's apostleship) I shall explore the narrative within the literary context of the wider New Testament. My thesis is that the main function of Acts is to fill in the gaps in the story as it is told through the two New Testament letter collections: the Letters of Paul and the Catholic Epistles. This narrative-critical approach suggests that Acts is an excellent source to describe the inner world of second-century readers and their theological convictions. The value of Acts to reconstruct first-century events is, however, unreliable without corroboration from sources outside the New Testament.

NARRATOR'S VOICE

To tell a story one must present the audience with a setting in time and space, with characters, and with a conflict that has to be resolved. "In my first book, dear Theophilus, I wrote about everything that Jesus did and taught from the beginning to the day when he was taken up into heaven" (Acts 1:12a). In the very first sentence the readers of Acts are introduced to the narrator, whose voice will guide them through the turbulent events unfolding before their eyes. He introduces himself as the author of a previous book. Because there is only one other book in the New Testament collection addressed to Theophilus, and because that book is about "what Jesus did and taught" from "the beginning" (Jesus' birth) until "the day when he was taken up into heaven," it is clear to anyone who reads Acts in its canonical context that the author of the Acts of the Apostles is the author of the Third Gospel, whose name was given in the canonical title of that book: Luke.

As readers allow themselves to be drawn into the narrative of Acts, they discover passages written in the first person plural and learn that Luke, the narrator, was an eyewitness to some of the events he is writing about. The last of these we-passages transports the readers to Rome, where the narrator, after assuring his readers that Paul is still alive and well, falls silent. Luke concludes his second book with the words: "He lived there for two whole years in his own quarters, welcoming everyone who visited, preaching the kingdom of God, and teaching about the Lord Jesus Christ boldly and freely" (Acts 28:30–31). This last sentence provides the setting in time and space for the end of the narrative. Luke finished telling his story in Rome while Paul was still alive, thus referring the readers back to the beginning of the book, where the resurrected Jesus outlines the journey on which the readers are about to embark: "You will be my witnesses in Jerusalem [Acts 1–7], in all Judea [Acts 9–12] and Samaria [Acts 8], and to the ends of the earth [Acts 13–28]" (Acts 1:8). In Rome the apostles and readers alike have reached "the ends of the earth" as promised.

CHARACTERS

The first half of Acts is dominated by characters who have authority for the early Christian community in Jerusalem: Jesus' disciples and Jesus' family. They are introduced to readers immediately after the ascension story. The eleven disciples: "Peter, and John, and James, and Andrew, Philip and Thomas, Bartholomew and Matthew, James son of Alphaeus, and Simon the Zealot, and Judas son of James"; and the family of Jesus: "Mary the mother of Jesus, as well as his brothers" (Acts 1:13–14). In the second half of the book the main character is indisputably the apostle Paul. The overall design of Acts is thus quite clear. Jerusalem dominates the first part of the story, Paul dominates the second part of the story, and in the middle (Acts 15) both parties shake hands.[1]

LITERARY CONTEXT

The manuscript tradition of the New Testament presents the collection as one work published in four volumes. Acts precedes the Catholic Epistles in the manuscripts in the volume entitled *Praxapostolos.* The other three volumes are the Four-Gospel-Book *(Tetraeuangelion),* the Fourteen Letters of Paul *(Epistolai Paulou IΔ),* and Revelation of John *(Apokalypsis Iōannou).* All four volumes are connected to each other through an elaborate system of cross-references communicated to the readers through the editorial titles and arrangement of the books.[2]

The expression "I wrote about everything *that Jesus did*" (Acts 1:1) literally picks up the definition of a gospel-*book* as presented in the last sentence of John

(John 21:25): "But there are also many other things *that Jesus did;* if every one of them were written down, I suppose that the world itself could not contain *the books* that would be written" (John 21:25). By referring to the last sentence of John, the volume containing Acts and the Catholic Epistles *(Praxapostolos)* is linked not only to John but to the last sentence of the Four-Gospel-Book as well.

The first sentence of the Letters of Paul refers to the royal lineage of Jesus and to Jesus' resurrection (Son of David according to the flesh; Son of God through his resurrection [Rom. 1:3–4]). This sentence may be read as addressing a discrepancy between Mark, which includes neither an explanation of the royal origins of Jesus nor a resurrection appearance of Jesus, and Luke. At the same time Rom. 1:3–4 may be taken to reaffirm the reader's sentiment that Luke's Gospel is Paul's gospel for it insists on the royal origin of Jesus and gives an account of Jesus' resurrection.

The last sentences of the Letters of Paul pick up this theme again. For readers who encounter the Pauline corpus and the fourfold gospel as constitutent parts of the New Testament, Paul's reference to Mark and Luke together may be significant. The fact that Paul mentions Luke and Mark together in the same sentence (Philemon 24), albeit with Aristarchus and Demas as well, may remind readers who are sensitive to such cues that Luke knew Mark and that, on a literary level, Luke's Gospel is to be seen as an improved edition of Mark (cf. Luke's reference to previous badly organized books on Jesus [Luke 1:1–3]).

The links between Acts and the Four-Gospel-Book are apparent. In addition Acts explains to the readers of the New Testament who the authors of the two letter collections are. In its first part it introduces James, Peter, and John—the authors of six of the seven Catholic Epistles—as important characters in the story. In its second part it talks about Paul, the author of the other letters contained in the New Testament. The obvious suggestion by the editors of the New Testament is that Acts provides the narrative context to these letters. This simple insight deserves more consideration as it is quite different from most approaches to Acts. If the New Testament is taken as a literary unit, Acts functions as a narrative commentary on the letters.[3]

Acts does not quote from any letter of Paul or from any of the Catholic Epistles in the New Testament. But because Paul, James, John, and Peter are the protagonists of the plot, to the readers of the New Testament the reference to their letters might be considered just as clear as the reference to Luke's Gospel in the first sentence of Acts. By not citing expressly from the letters, Acts suggests to the readers that it provides an independent account of the same events. And by ending in Rome while Paul is still alive, Acts dates itself as contemporary to those letters that Paul and Peter wrote from Rome, specifically 2 Timothy and 2 Peter, both of which imply a situation where the authors expect their impending deaths in Rome (cf. 2 Tim. 1:17; 4:6.11; 1 Pet. 5:13; 2 Pet. 1:14, 3:1). In other words there is good reason to believe that the editors of the first edition of the New Testament wanted their readers to read Acts in the context of the Letters of Paul and the Catholic Epistles. Acts explains the letters, and the letters explain Acts.

A NARRATIVE CRITICAL ASSESSMENT

Acts needs to be read not only with attention to its canonical context but also with attention to the narrative that its author has constructed. It should not be controversial: there is no real narrative power without conflict. Conflict moves the plot, it explains why characters behave differently in comparable situations, and it captures and holds the attention of the readers. What is the central conflict of Acts?

In my view the central conflict of Acts is the tension between Paul and the Jerusalem leadership as it is documented in the Letters of Paul and the Catholic Epistles. 1 Corinthians refers to a group associated with Paul and a group associated with Peter (1 Cor. 1:12). Peter, the other apostles, and the brothers of the Lord are expressly mentioned as opponents of Paul and Barnabas (1 Cor. 9:5–6) when it comes to the question of how to finance their ministry. The Jerusalem group follows Jesus' commission to accept food and lodging from the people they visit (Matt. 10:9–11 = Mark 6:8–11 = Luke 9:3–4), whereas Paul and Barnabas earn their living with their own hands when they travel: "This is my defense to those who would examine me. Do we not have the right to our food and drink? Do we not have the right to be accompanied by a believing wife, as do the other apostles and the brothers of the Lord and Cephas? Or is it only Barnabas and I who have no right to refrain from working for a living?" (1 Cor. 9:3–6). Paul is clearly aware of Jesus' instruction: "The Lord commanded that those who proclaim the gospel should get their living by the gospel" (1 Cor. 9:14). In the eyes of Peter and the other disciples of Jesus, and in the eyes of Jesus' brothers, Paul and Barnabas break Jesus' command.

The Letter to the Galatians, which follows the Corinthian correspondence in most manuscripts of the New Testament, narrates the biographical events in the life of Paul that lead up to the escalation of his conflict with Peter during an encounter in Antioch: "But when Cephas came to Antioch, I opposed him to his face, because he stood self-condemned" (Gal. 2:11). What is written in Galatians after this point serves to explain Paul's action during the incident in Antioch and illustrates his discussion of the Mosaic law in his letter to Romans.

There is much in the Catholic Epistles that can be read as overt criticism of Paul. James seems to attack directly Paul's concept of justification by faith and not works (cf. Rom. 3:27–28; 4:5; 9:32): "You see that a person is justified by works and not by faith alone" (James 2:24). And Peter's assurance that he is in agreement with Paul makes good sense if readers are aware of a serious disagreement: "So also our beloved brother Paul wrote to you according to the wisdom given him, speaking of this as he does in all his letters. There are some things in them hard to understand, which the ignorant and unstable twist to their own destruction, as they do the other scriptures" (2 Pet. 3:15–16).

The background story of 3 John is that Diotrephes, a leader of the congregation of Gaius to which the letter is addressed, refused to feed and house itinerant preachers. For readers of the New Testament this behavior may document the discrepancy between the Pauline concept of self-support [self sufficiency?] even while traveling as an apostle and the concept of the Jerusalem leadership—in this case represented by John—to accept support from the groups they visit: "He [Diotrephes] refuses to welcome the friends, and even prevents those who want to do so and expels them from the church" (3 John 10).

Read canonically Acts functions as a narrative commentary to these and other passages. It resolves an obvious conflict. This argument also makes good sense of the overall structure of Acts, which allows roughly the same amount of text for the Jerusalem leadership as it does for Paul and his ministry. In the middle of the book they meet in Jerusalem and sign a common written statement in direct response to the incident in Antioch related to the readers in Paul's Letter to the Galatians.[4] "Then the apostles and the elders, with the consent of the whole church, decided to choose men from among their members and to send them to Antioch with Paul and Barnabas. They sent Judas called Barsabbas, and Silas, leaders among the brothers, with the following letter" (Acts 15:22–23). This tendency of Acts to construct a perfect balance between the Jerusalem leadership and Paul is also expressed in the selection of miracle stories. Everything that Peter does is repeated by Paul.

Just as Peter and John heal a lame man outside of the Jerusalem temple (Acts 3:1–10), Paul heals a lame man in Lystra (Acts 14:8–10). Peter's shadow heals the sick in Jerusalem (Acts 5:15); in Ephesus the sick are cured by touching Paul's handkerchiefs and aprons (Acts 19:12). In Jerusalem Peter casts out unclean spirits (Acts 5:16); in Ephesus Paul casts out a spirit of divination (Acts 16:18). The story of Peter healing everyone who is brought to him in Jerusalem (Acts 5:16) is paralleled by the story of Paul curing everyone who is brought to him on Malta (Acts 28:9). In Joppa Peter raises Tabitha from the dead (Acts 9:36–41), and Paul brings young Eutychus back to life in Troas (Acts 20:9–12). In Lydda Peter heals Aeneas, who was paralyzed and had been bedridden for eight years (Acts 9:33–34), while in Malta Paul cures the father of Publius, who suffered from fever and dysentery (Acts 28:8).

However, Paul never mentions his ability to heal in his letters. Worse yet, he is sick himself: "No one may think better of me than what is seen in me or heard from me, even considering the exceptional character of the revelations. Therefore, to keep me from being too elated, a thorn was given me in the flesh, a messenger of Satan to torment me, to keep me from being too elated. Three times I appealed to the Lord about this, that it would leave me, but he said to me, 'My grace is sufficient for you, for power is made perfect in weakness'" (2 Cor. 12:6–9). The word translated "weakness," *astheneia,* may also be translated as "illness." Historically speaking Paul probably did not heal and this would explain much of why his apostleship was so openly and so easily questioned. Acts, however, feels the need to counter the Pauline reading of weakness. In Acts, God's power is not "made perfect in illness."

In Samaria the power of Peter and John is stronger than the power of the magician Simon (Acts 8:18–25). In Paphos on Cyprus Paul reproaches the magician Elymas (Acts 13:6–12). When Cornelius falls down at the feet of Peter and worships him (Acts 10:25) or Paul and Barnabas are worshipped as gods in Lystra (Acts 14:11–18; cf. 28:6), Peter, Paul, and Barnabas reply with almost the same words: "I am only a mortal" (Acts 10:26) and "We are mortals just like you" (Acts 14:15). In Samaria Peter and John lay their hands on people and they receive the Holy Spirit (Acts 8:14–17; cf. 10:44). In Ephesus Paul lays his hands on the twelve disciples of John the Baptist, and the Holy Spirit comes on them (Acts 19:1–7).

In Galatians Paul insists that he was not trained by men but received the gospel of Jesus Christ through a visionary experience: "For I want you to know, brothers and sisters, that the gospel that was proclaimed by me is not of human origin; for I did not receive it from a human source, nor was I taught it, but I received it through a revelation of Jesus Christ" (Gal. 1:11–12). Acts is eager not to let Peter be outdone by Paul when it comes to revelations. A vision causes Peter to accept Gentiles into the Christian community in Joppa (Acts 10; cf. 11:5–10), just as Paul receives his commission to serve the Gentiles through a vision on his way to Damascus (Acts 9:1–22; 22:6–11; 26:12–18).

To make up for his apparent lack of apostolic healing powers, Paul insists that he has suffered more than others: "Are they ministers of Christ? I am talking like a madman—I am a better one: with far greater labors, far more imprisonments, with countless floggings, and often near death" (2 Cor. 11:23). Acts balances Paul's claim with the lives of the Jerusalem leadership: the Jerusalem leaders suffer just as much as Paul does. In Jerusalem the apostles are physically punished in front of the council (Acts 5:40); in Philippi the magistrates tear the garments off Paul and his companions and give orders to beat them with rods (Acts 16:22–23). In Jerusalem Stephen, who had been appointed by Peter and the apostles, is stoned (Acts 7:54–60); in Lystra Paul is stoned and his body is dragged out of the city, where he is left for dead (Acts 14:19–20). When the apostles are arrested in Jerusalem, an angel opens the prison doors at night (Acts 5:17–20; 12:6–11); in Philippi a great earthquake miraculously opens the prison doors and unfastens everyone's fetters, and Paul and Barnabas are set free (Acts 16:24–34). The message of Acts is clear: what Paul suffers, the Jerusalem apostles suffer as well.

Narrative criticism works best with carefully crafted narratives. Unfortunately Acts does not display a distinct love for details, plot construction, and character development. For example, the ascension of Jesus is narrated at the end of Luke's Gospel on the Mount of Olives and on Easter, but according to Acts it happened several miles away in Bethany and forty days after Jesus' resurrection. Three times the story of Paul's revelation outside of Damascus is told. The first time Paul and his companions hear God's voice (Acts 9:4–7), but in the second version only Paul hears the voice (Acts 22:7–9). The first time his companions do not see the light (Acts 9:7), but when the story is told for the third time they see it (Acts 26:13). This could have easily been corrected by a skilled editor. Another blunt example is the name change from Saul to Paul. No explanation is provided. The text simply declares "Saul, also known as Paul" (Acts 13:9) and continues to refer to the character exclusively as Paul. Linking the name change to Paul's revelation before Damascus (Acts 9) would have greatly improved the plot construction, but the author of Acts does not seem to care.

Because of the poor literary quality of Acts, it does not seem appropriate to base an argument on details but instead to concentrate on the major lines of the overall concept. I think that the structure of the book and the constructed balance between Jerusalem and Paul's ministry expresses the central redactional intention. It is the conflict between Peter and Paul that is addressed and resolved in the narrative.

HISTORICAL VALUE

Does a narrative critical assessment of Acts provide historical insights? I think it does. Acts conveys the inner world of an early Christian storyteller and his or her audience at the time of publication. Whether the book has any historical merit when it comes to describing the actual events narrated is, however, an entirely different question. The implied author of Luke knows the events he is writing about from books and from interviewing eyewitnesses and "servants of the word" (Luke 1:1–4). He is not an eyewitness. And when it comes to writing Acts the implied author's firsthand experience is limited to occasional encounters with Paul (Acts 16:10–17; 20:5–15; 21:1–18) and to accompanying Paul on his trip to Rome (Acts 27:1–28:16). The events, however, are narrated in a way that is meaningful to the readers at the time of publication.

A literary critical approach, like the narrative critical assessment of Acts presented here, is a historical critical approach. It insists that by reading the text at face value the interpreter can reconstruct the inner world of the storyteller and readers at the time of publication. Storytelling works with plausibility and therefore the characters, places, and events introduced without explanation are especially important to the interpreter. But their historical value is only for the time of publication. And more often than not literary narratives are written at great distance to the events narrated. This may be the case for Acts as well.

It is generally agreed that Acts is not referred to as a book before Irenaeus uses it extensively in his refutation of Marcion toward the end of the second century.[5] Although a lack of attestation cannot be certain proof, it does invite the possibility that Acts was not written and published in its present form until the middle of the second century. Could Acts be the last book that was included in the New Testament? The close links to the Four-Gospel-Book and to the two New Testament letter collections support such a view. In this case Acts' historical value is to document thought processes and concepts of the evolving Catholic Church in the second century. The advocated harmony between Peter and Paul reflects the all inclusive "catholic" position and may reflect the well-attested struggle between the Paul-centered Marcionite church and more Jesus-centered faith groups.

Whether Acts carries any original historical value beyond what can be corroborated in the Letters of Paul, the Catholic Epistles, and the scarce witness of contemporary historians such as Josephus should be seriously questioned rather than simply assumed. Stories often present historical fact next to poetic construction, and the implied author of Acts is not obliged to inform the audience where history ends and poetic construction begins.

Why do storytellers not simply state the events as they happened? Why do they embellish and fill in gaps by using imagination? Why do painters paint objects differently from what we ourselves see? Why do poets and musicians try to capture their experience by writing poems and songs? There is no simple answer. But when their attempts are successful we call them art, and those who capture and transform our trivial experiences of the moment into something meaningful and lasting, we call artists.

NOTES

1. David Trobisch, "The Council of Jerusalem in Acts 15 and Paul's Letter to the Galatians," in *Theological Exegesis: Essays in Honor of Brevard S. Childs* (ed. Christopher Seitz and Kathryn Greene-McCreight; Grand Rapids, Mich.: Eerdmans, 1999), 331–38.

2. David Trobisch, *The First Edition of the New Testament* (Oxford: Oxford University Press, 2000), 26–28.

3. Robert W. Wall, "The Acts of the Apostles," 10:3–370, in *The New Interpreter's Bible,* 12 vols., edited by Leander E. Keck (Nashville: Abingdon, 2002); and Robert W. Wall, "A Canonical Approach to the Unity of Acts and Luke's Gospel," in this volume, 172–191.

4. Trobisch, "The Council of Jerusalem," 331–38.

5. See Andrew F. Gregory, "The Reception of Luke and Acts and the Unity of Luke-Acts," in this volume, 82–93 (first published in *JSNT* 29 [2007]: 459–72); Ernst Haenchen, *The Acts of the Apostles: A Commentary* (ed. and trans. R. McL. Wilson; Oxford: Basil Black-

well, 1971), 9; Howard Clark Kee, *To Every Nation Under Heaven: The Acts of the Apostles* (Harrisburg, Pa.: Trinity Press, 1997), 1–2; C. K. Barrett, *A Critical and Exegetical Commentary on the Acts of the Apostles,* vol. 1 (ICC; Edinburgh: T & T Clark, 1994), 15; C. Kavin Rowe, "Literary Unity and Reception History: Reading Luke-Acts as Luke and Acts," in this volume, 74–81 (first published in *JSNT* 29 [2007], 449–57).

HEARING ACTS AS A SEQUEL TO A MULTIFORM GOSPEL

Historical and Hermeneutical Reflections on Acts, Luke, and the ΠΟΛΛΟΙ

Mikeal C. Parsons

I have found the renewed interest in and discussion of the relationship between Luke and Acts—a conversation due mostly to the persistent questions and penetrating observations of C. Kavin Rowe—to be both clarifying and illuminating. I am pleased therefore to enter into this dialogue again some fifteen or so years after Richard I. Pervo and I first took up the question.[1] The first collection of essays in the *Journal for the Study of the New Testament* appeared just as I was beginning to write the first draft to the introduction to a commentary on Acts for the Paideia series by Baker Academic; thus I had more than a passing interest in those essays, especially the ones by Rowe and Markus Bockmuehl.[2] When the second batch of essays appeared in 2007, I was nearing the completion of the commentary, and so once again relished the opportunity to follow the debate's development, since the writing of a commentary forces one to deal in very practical and pragmatic ways with what might otherwise be highly theoretical issues.[3] It was, however, only after rereading those essays in preparation for my own contribution to this current volume that I realized how much those essays had influenced my own "rethinking" regarding the unity of Luke and Acts.

This essay is an expanded version of a section from the introduction to the Paideia *Acts* commentary, with some examples taken from the exegesis of specific passages in Acts and other examples suggested here for the first time.[4] Put simply my proposal is this: Acts was *conceived and intended* to be read and heard as a sequel to a plurality of gospels, which Luke referred to as πολλοί ("many"; Luke 1:1), and of which Luke was "first among equals." That is to say, the Third Gospel provided the primary story line in terms of characters and plot (conflicts and resolutions) to which Acts provided a sequel.[5] Or to put it in a slightly different way, the "story" of Acts was heard, *from its earliest reception by the authorial audience,* also in the context of a plurality of gospels, which, by the time of Acts' publication, included Mark, Matthew, and possibly John and may have included at one point or another some now nonextant or partially preserved gospels.[6] By the time Acts was published Luke knew that the Third Gospel was being read in early Christian gatherings along with other gospels and, expecting Acts to be read in this kind of social context, wrote Acts primarily as a sequel to the Third Gospel, but with echoes and allusions (and corrections?) to these other gospels.

From a plurality of gospels would eventually emerge the notion of one gospel in four versions, indirectly attested by the longer ending of Mark, which presumes a fourfold gospel in the early second century.[7] When collectors and later canonizers placed Acts after the fourfold gospel (whether in the "Eastern" or "Western" order), they were actually *fulfilling* the *intentio operis* that Acts be read as the sequel to the "gospel" (albeit in ways Luke could not perhaps have fully anticipated) and not somehow distorting it. Thus in the case of the Acts of the Apostles, there is fundamental coherence between authorial intent and reception history. And once again the "unmaking" of Luke-Acts may be required in order to understand more fully the complex relationship of Acts to Luke and other early Christian writings.[8]

Therefore in order to read Acts "for all it's worth," or as Luke Timothy Johnson puts it, for the purpose of understanding Luke's "literary and theological voice,"[9] it is necessary to attend to the literary and theological connections not only with Luke's Gospel but also with those other narratives that recount the story of Jesus echoed in Acts.[10] In making this proposal I have found myself both in agreement and disagreement with the recent writings on the topic of the unity of Luke and Acts, particularly by Rowe, Bockmuehl, Gregory, and Johnson. I shall attempt in my explication of this hypothesis to delineate those points of dis/agreement.

COMPOSING ACTS IN LIGHT OF LUKE AND THE *Πολλοί*: A Historical Investigation

We begin with an evidentiary path that is now well known if not always well understood. Rowe is right to point out that in *Rethinking the Unity of Luke and Acts* Parsons and Pervo did little more than acknowledge the canonical "disunity" of Luke and Acts. Rowe observes: "The five and a half pages on canonical unity (a rather unclear designation) contain several interesting observations, particularly with respect to the differing textual traditions, but such observations are not developed any further. As will become clear, it is precisely these more tangible, historical matters that raise the greatest questions about the unity of Luke-Acts."[11] As Pervo responds elsewhere in this volume: "Although Parsons and Pervo noted the history of reception (including 'canonical unity,' a category that, like authorial unity, was deemed closed), they did not have the wisdom or foresight to devote a short chapter to the subject."[12] This essay may be taken as a first effort to redress this oversight.

Scrolls, Codices, Canonical Lists, the Order of Gospel Collections, and the Relationship of Luke and Acts

First I would like to offer a clarification of terms. In the chapter on narrative unity in *Rethinking the Unity of Luke and Acts,* Parsons and Pervo, drawing on the work of Seymour Chatman, distinguished between story and discourse in narrative generally, and in Luke and Acts specifically. Put simply, story is the "what" or the subject matter of what is being told, and discourse is the "way" or the literary techniques employed by the narrator to communicate the story. We further argued that at the level of story, that is, in terms of plot and characters, there may be a basic coherence between Luke and Acts, but the narrator uses different narrative or rhetorical techniques at the discourse level to convey that story. One can have coherence at the level of story while at the same time employing a variety of narrative techniques at the level of discourse that differ from one document to the next.[13] This distinction was often overlooked by reviewers but was crucial to the argument then and important to understanding the discussion now. We must also distinguish a third kind of unity, namely the view that Luke and Acts were written together on the same scroll (or codex) and if not the same scroll (due to the length of each), then two scrolls that were released or published simultaneously with the intent that they be read together.[14]

It is striking that there is, to date, *not one shred of material evidence* for this last kind of unity; that is, physical evidence that Luke and Acts circulated together, as Andrew F. Gregory puts it, in "the physical form of two parts of one literary whole."[15] The usual explanation is that Luke wrote the two documents on separate scrolls because of length limitations. Henry J. Cadbury's comments are typical:

> Books intended to be copied should conform to the customary limits of length. If the original was not too long for the usual length scroll its reproduction was feasible. It has been estimated that if written in a hand with columns like those on Codex Vaticanus the Book of Acts would have required a roll of 31 or 32 feet in length. Since the Gospel of Luke is within three per cent of the same length, the author has made possible the reproduction of both books on rolls of the same standard length. It is safe to assume that as long as scrolls were commonly employed, scrolls of this length were obtainable. Another book requiring about the same space for copying is the Gospel of Matthew.[16]

This explanation continues to be offered as a reason for the separation of Luke from Acts.[17] Cadbury's conclusions were based on the statistical analysis of

Frederick Kenyon, who set the "extreme limit" of roll length at slightly over ten meters, a conclusion he claimed was "well established on a wide basis of proof."[18]

Recent work, particularly on the papyri at Oxyrhynchus, has called into question Kenyon's analysis. William Allen Johnson has noted that Kenyon's "wide basis of proof" consists of fourteen examples.[19] Based on his own exacting analysis of the several hundred bookrolls (papyrus scrolls), Johnson concludes that the data at Oxyrhynchus (along with sample texts from Herculaneum and elsewhere) suggests "an upper limit extending at least to 15 metres, with great likelihood of odd examples extending to a length considerably beyond that."[20] Johnson further explains that scribes used prefabricated blank rolls of twenty sheets (*kollemata* of 20 to 25 cm each) that were typically 25 to 33 cm high and 4 to 5 meters in length.[21] Additional roles would be glued on in order to accommodate longer texts. Thus there was no "standard size" beyond which an author could not go, nor was the author under any pressure to "fill" the bookroll to the end, since the excess scroll could be trimmed and used at a later date. By Kenyon's and Cadbury's reckoning, a bookroll of four of these prefabricated scrolls could have easily accommodated both Luke and Acts on a single bookroll.[22] Thus there is no reason that Luke could not have written Luke/Acts on a single scroll if he had wanted; and, conversely, there is no material evidence that he did.[23]

The evidence of early Gospel collections likewise fails to support this kind of "physical" unity. The oldest copy of the fourfold gospel, P45 (ca. 200 C.E.), also contains Acts but has the Gospels in the traditional order: Matthew, Mark, Luke, and John. Codex Bezae preserves the so-called Western order of the two apostles (Matthew and John) followed by the two "apostolic companions" (Luke and Mark). Here Luke and Acts could easily have been placed together, but Mark stands between Luke and Acts. The Cheltenham Canon (ca. 360) and the stichometry of Codex Claromontanus (seventh century) places Luke last among the Gospels, but Acts comes after the Pauline Epistles in the former and at the end of the New Testament books in the latter. P74 (seventh century) puts Acts with the General Epistles.[24] This evidence (or lack of it) led Cadbury to this rather tortured opinion: "Perhaps the nearest we come to evidence that Luke and Acts were ever copied in juxtaposition is to be found in the fact that in Codex Bezae the name John (Greek Johannes) is spelled with one 'n' regularly in these two books, but with two 'n's' in Matthew, John and Mark . . . . It has been suggested that this is due to the fact that in an ancestor of Codex Bezae the same scribe copied these two books and that they were in such order that Luke came just before Acts."[25]

The inescapable conclusion is that there is absolutely no manuscript evidence to support the view that Luke and Acts ever physically appeared side by side, ready for reading as one, continuous whole. It seems, at times, that proponents of the literary unity of the documents dismiss the evidence because their preexisting hermeneutical commitments blind them to its importance. Luke Timothy

Johnson writes: "The fact that there is no evidence that Luke-Acts was received or read as a literary unity in late second-century compositions does not answer the question of how the first readers might have read and understood Luke's writing."[26] Such evidence and its historical and hermeneutical implications cannot, however, be so easily dismissed. It *is* significant that all of the known evidence—without one exception—runs counter to the standard theory; this fact should, it would seem, cause at least some pause if not outright hesitation in adopting wholeheartedly the theory of the "material" unity of Luke and Acts.

Transmission Histories and the Relationship of Luke and Acts

Another fundamental aspect of the relationship of Luke and Acts has to do with whether Luke and Acts first circulated together only to be separated in their subsequent reception or rather were circulated independently from the beginning. How one resolves this issue is also crucial for our understanding the material relationship between the Third Gospel and Acts.

It is well known that the textual transmission of Acts is distinct from that of Luke, indeed, from any other book in the New Testament. Bruce M. Metzger has noted: "The text of the book of the Acts of the Apostles circulated in the early church in two quite distinct forms, commonly called the Alexandrian and the Western."[27] There is nothing like a "Western" textual tradition for Luke's Gospel. The so-called Western text[28] is approximately 8 percent longer than the Alexandrian tradition and contains, among other things, comments of local color and interpretive glosses.[29] While the Western tradition of Acts shares with Luke (as well as the other Gospels and Pauline corpus) "minor variants that seek to clarify and explain the text and make it smooth," there are "variants of another kind, peculiar to the Western text of Acts."[30] These variants "include many additions, long and short, of a substantive nature that reveal the hand of a reviser. . . . The reviser, who was obviously a meticulous and well-informed scholar, eliminated seams and gaps and added historical, biographical, and geographical details. Apparently, the reviser did his work at an early date, before the text of Acts had come to be generally regarded as a sacred text that must be preserved inviolate."[31] The significance of Acts' distinct transmission history, however, is largely neglected or undervalued in discussions of the publication of, and literary relationship between, Luke and Acts.[32]

Regardless of how one accounts for the origins of these two textual traditions of Acts,[33] their existence provides further support for the conclusion that Acts has its own distinctive transmission history and points to a circulation of the text of Acts, independent of the Third Gospel. The cumulative weight of the distinctive textual transmission of Acts, described by Metzger above, combined with the widely observed fact that Luke and Acts never occur side by side in any canonical list, argues in favor of those who conclude that Luke and Acts never circulated together in the material form of two parts of a literary whole, and, I will contend, were never intended to.

The best explanation for Acts' independent textual transmission would seem to be spatial or temporal.[34] The spatial solution would suggest that these two distinct text forms arose because they were published or released from different locations or that they had different destinations. We know too little about the provenance of Gospel writers to entertain for long the solution that Luke published his Gospel from one place and Acts from another,[35] nor would this solution be very congenial to those holding to the view that Luke and Acts form one continuous work.

In the case of distinct destinations we actually have a "real-life" example: "Ignatius wrote seven letters almost simultaneously, six of which were sent to (relatively) local destinations in Asia Minor, and one of which was sent off to Rome; and within the Ignatian corpus, Romans does have a different transmission history."[36] Within the debate regarding whether the intended audience of Luke/Acts is a local community[37] or a more general Christian audience,[38] however, no one argues that Luke is writing to two distinct local communities, nor is he designating a local community with one text and a general audience with the other.

We are left then with the temporal solution, namely that a sufficient length of time lapsed between the release of Luke and Acts to allow for each to establish its own transmission history.[39] This hypothesis is very similar to the one advanced by Rowe over against the more traditional view that Luke and Acts circulated together and were only separated later.[40] Gregory finds both views equally plausible: "the fact that there is no early evidence for Luke and Acts circulating together may be explained *just as easily* on the basis that they were separated at so early a time that they left no traces of their prior joint circulation as on the basis that at no point did they circulate together."[41] While I agree that both are plausible, I find Rowe's explanation more probable given the cumulative weight of the separate transmission histories of Luke and Acts, as well as the separation of the two works in all known collections and lists. Such external evidence as exists favors the solution that Luke and Acts were never on the same scroll (even though, in light of what we now know of scroll lengths in antiquity, they could have been) or released together as two parts of one whole. In fact the transmission history as we have it is exactly what one would have expected to find if Luke and Acts were published at different times. Certainly Gregory is correct to argue that the absence of any trace of external evidence for the existence of Luke and Acts in the "physical form of two parts of one literary whole" could be explained by arguing that "they were separated at so early a time that they left no traces of their prior joint circulation."[42] This is a plausible argument, but is it the most probable? No. The more probable explanation, which best conforms to the evidence we have, is Rowe's "simple and elegant" hypothesis: there is no manuscript evidence for the physical unity of Luke and Acts, because Luke and Acts never circulated together.[43] Of course either *Ausgangspunkt* is *plausible,* but I conclude that it is more *probable* that the two documents were published and disseminated at different times than that an original single work was subsequently divided.

In this temporal solution one must allow for a sufficient length of time for the Third Gospel to have established its own transmission history before the publication of Acts. It is not possible to establish a *specific* length of time to qualify as "sufficient" for separate transmission histories to occur (a year? a decade?); but, it is important to note, specifying the specific lapse of time between is not necessary for our purposes. The results—total absence of any traces of a material unity of Luke/Acts—would be the same whether the lapse in publication were ten or twenty years.[44] In the intervening period the public use in Christian assemblies of a multiform Gospel would be securely in place (see below) and a collection of an indeterminate number of Paul's letters would be widely known.[45] It is within this historical framework that I place the first reception of the final form of Acts.

The Lukan Prologue and the Relationship of Luke and Acts—and the πολλοί

In terms of literary unity, the evidence of the two prologues cuts both ways and cannot be viewed as decisive evidence in either case.[46] Still the prologues, especially to the Gospel, do provide some insight into the particular shape of the literary relationship between the two documents.

The prologue to the Third Gospel (1:1–4) suggests that Luke writes in part because previous attempts at gospels have proven, in his opinion, unsuccessful in producing a rhetorically persuasive narrative.[47] On the basis of Luke's reference to "many" other attempts to write accounts of Jesus' life, it seems that a plurality of gospels was already a reality by the time the Third Gospel was written (probably in the 80s or early 90s). The number and content of these other "gospels" is unknown; the "many" (even if hyperbolic) may have included "heretics" who "used traditional material in the interest of their own perverse propaganda,"[48] though this is impossible to demonstrate. In this sense Luke may have been partially successful in replacing some of these previous attempts, of which he is apparently critical (and thus contributed to the loss of some early accounts which are no longer extant?). Luke's predecessors would almost certainly have included Mark's Gospel.

Luke probably did not think his version of the Jesus story would replace *all* other versions; after all he does identify with their efforts to some degree ("it seemed good to me also . . ."). And even if he did, he knew better by the time he published Acts.[49] His account of "the things accomplished" had taken its place alongside other versions.[50] Thus Luke writes Acts in the full knowledge that it would be read as a sequel, not just to the Third Gospel but to a plurality of narratives about Jesus, what would later be dubbed simply "the gospel" (of which there emerged four authoritative versions, but still of *one* gospel).[51] These gospels (Luke and Mark and an indeterminate number of others) were already being read together in Christian worship by the time Acts was published.[52] Modifying Daniel Marguerat's metaphor of the diptych, we have an apt description of Acts, Luke, and the "many." Hinged to the panel next to Acts (on the viewer's right) is another panel with images of these other gospel writers with St. Luke (considerably larger than the rest).[53]

We should not dismiss those other attempts at writing a gospel as possible *sources* for Acts, even if they did not rise to the level of rhetorically well formed narratives.[54] For the purposes of rhetorical argument that is concise, clear, and compelling, Luke used the Third Gospel as the primary narrative for structuring Acts, thus accounting for the many parallels between Luke and Acts.[55] In other words, with Acts Luke follows the basic plot of the Third Gospel, while presuming knowledge on the audience's part of at least some of the "many" who undertook to write a narrative about Jesus (some of which are perhaps no longer extant; cf. the agraphon in Acts 20:35). We should not be surprised then to find Acts following the basic plot and structure of the "primary" narrative, Luke, while echoing other "Jesus-stories," only some of which are still accessible to the modern reader.[56]

From the point of view of the authorial audience, Acts is read and heard as a follow up to the Jesus story. Acts is written *after* the public use of multiple gospels in early Christian gatherings but *before* this plurality of Jesus stories is textualized (reduced in number? collected and published) in the *Tetraevangelium.* In other words the fourfold gospel is the culmination of an earlier liturgical practice and theological reality of multiple gospel usage in local congregations.[57] In sum, the question of Luke's intent and the audience's reception are perhaps much closer than Rowe (and others) has allowed.

It is at this point that reception history may help shed more light on the current debate. In the face of the increasing popularity of *Wirkungsgeschichte,* some have countered that reception history is irrelevant for understanding authorial intention or how the first readers experienced a text. Luke Timothy Johnson, for example, answers negatively the question posed in his title "Literary Criticism of Luke-Acts: Is Reception-History Pertinent?", despite claiming in the opening paragraph that "I am willing to argue that biblical scholars in the future will probably find the examination of the world that the New Testament creates more fruitful than the study of the world that created the New Testament."[58]

Markus Bockmuehl, in contrast, asks, "might the earliest *reception history* actually be more relevant to the question of intention than Rowe allows?" He responds to his own question with another question and a further musing: "Is it not also the case that consistency of reception serves, more often than not, as a useful rule of thumb about the drift of ancient texts and their range of plausible meanings? . . . It would be unrealistic to expect precision here, but I wonder if being a little more explicit about the text's footprint and aftermath would allow our discussion of the potential hermeneutical 'paydirt' of *Wirkungsgeschichte* to advance beyond what has too often been seemingly eclectic and arbitrary study in the service of ulterior concerns."[59]

In agreement with Bockmuehl I suggest we revisit the evidence provided by reception history of one of the earliest extant readers of Luke and Acts, Irenaeus of Lyon.[60] Irenaeus bears witness to the common authorship of Luke and Acts, and on this everyone agrees. Rowe, however, points out that Irenaeus cannot, strictly speaking, be taken as an unambiguous witness to the literary unity of Luke-Acts, at least not in the way modern scholars use the phrase. Rather he contends that for Irenaeus: "Acts should be read not along with Luke in particular but along with the Fourfold Gospel."[61] Gregory concedes that if "recognizing the unity of Luke-Acts means reading those texts only in the light of each other and not in connection with other apostolic writings (which is certainly what many contemporary scholars seem to take it to mean) then *of course* Irenaeus did not recognize the literary unity of Luke-Acts."[62] But Gregory goes on to assert: "My contention, however, is that this modern dichotomy is unfortunate and that there is no good reason why readers (ancient or modern) who recognize the literary unity of Luke-Acts need preclude themselves from choosing to read . . . Luke in two different ways—sometimes as part of the Fourfold Gospel, and sometimes as part of Luke-Acts."[63] And specifically with regard to Irenaeus, Gregory concludes: "Thus there is no necessary reason why Irenaeus's use of [Luke] as part of his fourfold gospel and his use of Acts alongside texts other than Luke means that he could not have been cognisant of the literary unity of these two texts."[64] Gregory is also correct in surmising that Irenaeus's references to the Gospel of Luke within the immediate context of his appeal to common authorship do not rise to the level of "compelling evidence" for Irenaeus's association of Luke with Acts "as part of one literary whole."[65]

I would argue, however, that Irenaeus's use of Luke in Book 3 of *Against Heresies* is entirely consistent with the kind of usage I imagine Luke's "authorial audience" or "ideal reader" would have made of Luke and Acts.[66] Irenaeus points to a number of episodes that are unique to Luke's Gospel and comprise essential elements of Luke's plot:[67]

> but if any should reject Luke, on the ground that he did not know the truth, he plainly throws over the gospel of which he claims to be a disciple. For through him we have learned very many quite important parts of the gospel, as the birth of John and the story about Zacharias, and the coming of the angel to Mary, and the cry of Elizabeth, and the coming down of the angels to the shepherds, and the things that were spoken by them, and the testimony

of Anna and Simeon concerning the Christ . . . And everything of this kind we know through Luke alone. . . . (Irenaeus, *A.H.* 3.14.3).

Irenaeus goes on to list a great many other passages unique to Luke, including the miraculous draught of fish (Luke 5), the bent woman (Luke 7), the man with dropsy (Luke 14), the parable of the banquet (Luke 14), the anointing at Simon's house (Luke 7), the parable of the rich fool (Luke 12), the rich man and Lazarus (Luke 16), the Pharisee and the publican (Luke 18), Zacchaeus (Luke 19), the ten lepers (Luke 19), the parable of the wicked judge (Luke 18), the barren fig tree (Luke 13), and the road to Emmaus (Luke 24). All of these episodes are important to the literary patterns and theological themes so often pointed to by redaction and literary critics of Luke/Acts.

The "text's footprint," as preserved by Irenaeus, bears out Bockmuehl's intuition that reception history may be employed "as a useful rule of thumb about the drift of ancient texts and their range of plausible meanings."[68] Gregory's comment is also appropriate: "Certainly ideal readers do not have to be translated into real readers . . . , but neither is there any a priori reason why they may not be translated in this way."[69] The real reader, Irenaeus, fulfills the role of Luke's "ideal reader" (or authorial audience) by reading Acts in connection with a multiform Gospel (now authorized as the *Tetraevangelium*), while acknowledging the specific and special contours of the shape of Luke's Gospel. Likewise, at least in principle, Jaroslav Pelikan's description of his approach to his commentary on Acts is also consistent with the role of Luke's authorial audience who reads Acts both as a sequel to Luke and as a sequel to the multiform gospel. Pelikan claims that he will "in the first instance cite the Gospel of Luke where possible, and the other three Gospels as appropriate."[70]

Much of what precedes draws heavily on Rowe, Gregory, and to a lesser extent, Bockmuehl, but I would not want the reader to fail to see what I consider a crucial difference between my proposal and these others. So at the risk of being pedantic let me make clear that which distinguishes my proposal: reading Acts as a sequel to Luke *and* as a sequel to the multiform Gospel (an intertextual web in which the Third Gospel is implicated and stands as first among equals) is consistent with the role of the authorial audience imagined by the narrator (in literary terms) or with authorial intent (in historical-critical terms).

In his earlier article at least Rowe seems unable to find a way out of a kind of "bifurcated" reading that makes the interpreter choose between literary (Luke-Acts) and historical (Luke and Acts) interpretation.[71] In his later article Rowe makes a telling concession that reveals even more clearly the wedge between the literary and historical: "Thus I agree with Luke Timothy Johnson that 'a literary-critical reading . . . of Luke's entire narrative is best . . . for understanding his literary and theological voice.'"[72]

Likewise Gregory sees a kind of bifurcated reading, albeit the cables on the battery are now reversed. The "historical" reading for Gregory is to read Luke and Acts as part of a literary whole that is how Luke intended them to be read; however "for most of their history they have been read in their canonical context, as two discrete texts that relate to a range of others."[73] Both of course are most charitable to those who would choose to read these documents in ways other than in what they term the "historical" mode, though this "historical" method is apparently the preferred mode for each (for Rowe this is reception history; for Gregory, this is historical-critical).[74]

Such a bifurcation, whether of the Rowe or Gregory variety, is in my opinion a false dichotomy, at least insofar as the intention of the work we call the Acts of the Apostles is concerned: Acts was intended to be read as a sequel both to a multiform gospel *and* to the Third Gospel, which held pride of place in the intertextual milieu within which Luke expected the authorial audience to hear Acts. To cite Luke where possible and the other Gospels where appropriate (paraphrasing Pelikan) is, in my current way of thinking, the best way to begin to understand "the literary mind of the historical Luke."[75]

READING ACTS IN LIGHT OF LUKE AND THE Πολλοι: Hermeneutical Implications

What would it mean to hear Acts as a sequel to a pluriform gospel, of which Luke is "first among equals"? In other words what is the hermeneutical "paydirt"? Hearing in this way would mean, for one thing, that instead of reading Acts exclusively in light of the Third Gospel (which, as both Gregory and Rowe note, is the way in which most redaction and literary critics have interpreted Cadbury's mantra regarding the unity of Luke and Acts), the reader would explore echoes and allusions to the other Gospels as well.[76]

What follows are some brief examples taken from my Paideia Acts commentary that demonstrate exegetically what reading Acts as a sequel to a multiform gospel collection that included the other Synoptics, Mark and Matthew, might entail.[77] This feature—noting the non-Lukan materials in Acts that are parallel to the extant Gospels and their effect on the reading of Acts—is a distinctive aspect of the commentary.[78]

I have tried to include material in Acts that has lexical links (or prominently missing words; cf. Acts 1:5) and/or conceptual connections to material in Matthew and/or Mark (but not in the Third Gospel). These non-Lukan links serve to parallel (Acts 9:40; 14:21; 20:10), clarify (Acts 19:7), or extend (Acts 10:13–16, 28; 12:2) the argument of the material in Matthew and/or Mark or less frequently to correct it (cf. Acts 1:16–20).[79] Such an enterprise invites criticism at two levels at least. Have the echoes been appropriately identified? Has the role of the allusions in the argument of Acts been properly assessed? As is the case with any new endeavor I do not expect to find immediate consensus regarding my efforts either in identifying or interpreting these allusions, but if this work, however tentative and exploratory, serves in some small way to redirect scholarly energies in the interpretation of Acts to account also for alleged parallels to other Gospel traditions, then I will count it a success.

Acts 1:5 / Mark 1:8.[80] One need not read very far in Acts before encountering one of the first allusions to a non-Lukan Synoptic tradition. In Acts 1:4 Jesus tells his disciples: "John baptized with water, but you will be baptized with the Holy Spirit, not many days from now." This verse alludes to a tradition found in all three Synoptics (Mark 1:8 / Matt. 3:11 / Luke 3:16). The authorial audience recognizes that the command not to depart from Jerusalem but to wait for what the Father had promised (1:4) echoes Luke 24:49, but Jesus' note that John baptized with water, but you will be baptized with the Holy Spirit (1:5) more closely resembles the Markan form of that saying (Mark 1:8) than either Matt. 3:11 or Luke 3:16 (both of which add "and fire" to "Holy Spirit"). Here the focus is on Jesus' explanation that John the Baptist's prediction of a coming Spirit baptism was about to be fulfilled "not many days from now" (at Pentecost). Mark's version, lacking the additional reference to "baptism by fire," keeps the focus on the Spirit in a way that the Third Gospel does not. This echo (sans the fire element) also subtly suggests that the authorial audience should understand the reference to the Spirit's distribution on the disciples "as tongues of fire" as a simile and not literally, subsequent artistic depictions notwithstanding.

Acts 1:16–20 / Matt. 27:1–10.[81] In some instances Acts alludes to a tradition in order to correct or complement it; so seems to be case with Acts 1:16–20. Peter's story of Judas's demise summarizes the bare essentials of Judas's betrayal found in the Third Gospel and then adds new information presumably not known to Luke's authorial audience. The contrasts between Matthew's version of Judas's demise (Matt. 27:1–10) and Luke's account helpfully instruct regarding the distinct perspective of the Lukan Peter. Matthew's account includes: (1) Judas repented and returned the money (27:3–4); (2) the priests are responsible for buying the field for burial (27:7); (3) the name of the field is the result of the use made of the money; (4) Matthew cites Scripture (Zech. 11:12–13; Jer. 32:8–9) to explain the price of the land, not to speak of Judas's fate. Peter depicts the defection of Judas and his subsequent judgment with the use of money. In the Third Gospel (contra Matthew) Judas does not repent and return the money but rather, according to Acts 1:18, purchased a field (*chōrion*) with the betrayal money. Such a self-serving purchase not only stands in sharp contrast to the way the believers sold their fields (*chōrion*) and laid the proceedings at the apostles' feet (see 4:32–35) but also is juxtaposed to the action of the narrator of this story, Peter, who along with James and John "left everything" to follow Jesus (see Luke 5:11).

Judas has traded his inheritance (*klēros*) in the apostolic ministry (1:17) for a farm, a symbol of his apostasy from the circle of the Twelve. Ironically Judas dies on this same property, according to Acts: this man purchased a field using the money earned from his unjust deed and after becoming prostrate he burst open in the middle and all his insides poured out (1:18).

The phrase "becoming prostrate" or "falling headlong" (*prēnēs genomenos*) recalls conceptually the prophecy of Simeon that Jesus would be "set for the *fall* and rising of many in Israel" (2:34). There is no hint of suicide here (contra Matt. 27); the death is the result of divine judgment and fits into the theme of "the death of the opponent of God,"[82] and like the account of Herod (cf. Acts 12:20–23) is conveyed in vivid, "ekphrastic" language, meant as much for the eye as for the ear (see Acts 2:1–5).

Because Judas meets his death on this property it is called the Field of Blood. And just as the purchasing of a field symbolized Judas's defection, so also the fact that his property is doomed to perpetual desertion (1:20) is a sign of his judgment. The effect for the audience is to supplement or correct Matthew's explanation of the name.

Acts 9:40 / Mark 5:41.[83] In the account of Peter's resuscitation of Tabitha, Peter arrives in Joppa and is escorted to the upper room where Tabitha's corpse has been laid. Perhaps moved by the widows' weeping and mute display of Tabitha's benefaction, Peter orders everyone outside, kneels, prays, and commands, "Tabitha, get up!" (9:40). For auditors familiar with Mark the command is reminiscent of Jesus' words in Mark 5:41 (but missing from Luke), "Talitha [now Tabitha] cumi." The parallel between Jesus' action and Peter's own act is thereby strengthened. Further, Peter's miracle is not by Peter's power, a point indicated by the fact he prayed to a higher deity. Peter then presents Tabitha alive to the saints and widows (9:41).

Acts 10:13–16, 28 / Mark 7:14–23.[84] In his vision recorded in Acts 10, three times Peter is shown a sheet with all kinds of animals on it and is commanded to eat. Three times Peter refuses, claiming, "Certainly not, Lord! For I have never eaten anything that is impure and contaminated!" (10:14). The authorial audience, familiar with Mark, will also hear echoes of Jesus' teaching regarding clean and unclean foods (Mark 7:14–23, missing in Luke's Gospel)—a message ("Thus, he declared all foods clean," Mark 7:19) that Peter evidently failed to understand the first time around. In the larger argument of Acts 9:32–11:18 and 15:7–11 Peter is presented as undergoing a conversion no less radical than Cornelius's. He is led to confess, "I have truly come to understand that God does not show favoritism. Rather, in every nation, the one who fears him and does what is right is acceptable to him" (Acts 10:34–35), and later, at the Apostolic Council, he proclaims that God "made no distinction between them [the Gentiles] and us regarding our faith, but cleansed their hearts (as well as ours)" (Acts 15:9). The allusion to Mark 7, which implies that Peter has not understood (or heeded?) Jesus's proclamation that all foods are clean, deepens and enriches Acts' presentation of Peter's conversion to a more inclusive attitude regarding first food then people.[85]

Acts 12:2 / Mark 10:39 / Matt. 20:23.[86] Herod had James, the brother of John, executed by the sword (12:2). Compared to the narrative recording the martyrdom of Stephen, this notice of James's martyrdom is quite brief; however, it still serves its purpose of heightening the dramatic quality of the following story of Peter. No less important, it underscores the fact that not all of Christ's followers are divinely rescued; in this case, it is James, brother of John, one of the first of Jesus' followers to be called (Luke 5:10), one of the Twelve (Luke 6:14; Acts 1:13), and one of Jesus' "inner circle" (Luke 8:51; 9:28, 54) who meets his death. The church suffers along with its suffering messiah. The authorial audience will hear echoes of Jesus' prediction of the martyrdom of James (and John) in the Synoptic tradition: "The cup that I drink you will drink; and with the baptism with which I am baptized you will be baptized" (Mark 10:39; Matt. 20:23; but missing in Luke).

Acts 14:21 / Matt. 28:19.[87] Acts 14:21–28 begins with a reference to Paul preaching the good news in "that city" (Derbe) (14:21a), thus connecting to the previous story, which ends with Paul and Barnabas in Derbe (14:20). Not only do Paul and Barnabas preach the gospel there, they are also involved in making a substantial number of disciples (14:21b). The word translated "making . . . disciples" occurs elsewhere in the New Testament only in Matthew, most notably Matt. 28:19 (cf. also Matt. 13:52; 27:57). The authorial audience, familiar with Matthew, hears here echoes of the Great Commission, in which Jesus instructs his followers to "make disciples of all the nations." Making disciples for Luke as well as Matthew involved more than evangelism and baptism. For the Matthean Jesus "discipling" involves "teaching them whatsoever I have commanded you"; for the Lukan Paul it involves "strengthening the souls of the disciples" (14:22a).

Acts 19:7 / Mark 5:7.[88] Here in the story of Paul and the sons of Sceva (Acts 19:11–20) the echo to Mark and/or Matthew serves to clarify Luke's point regarding the connection between exorcism and magic.[89] The language used by the Jewish exorcists ("I adjure/order you by Jesus whom Paul preaches to come out" [Acts 19:13]) would be heard by the authorial audience in terms of the magical practices of antiquity. The term *adjure* is not used by Jesus or his disciples in any exorcism story in any Gospel, though the term does occur in Mark. In Mark 5:7 the words of the Gerasene demoniac to Jesus ("I adjure you by God") are an attempt to manipulate and control both Jesus and God. This term is also frequently used in magical incantations in a double command: "I adjure X by [the authority of] Y." The adjuration is an attempt to manipulate both the object of adjuration and the deity whose authority is invoked. Thus by understanding this passage in its larger cultural context and by hearing an allusion to Mark 5:7, the authorial audience understands that these Jewish exorcists/magicians are trying to use Jesus' name in a way typical of magical technique. Luke, however, makes it clear that Jesus' name is not some magical talisman vulnerable to manipulation (cf. Acts 19:15–16).[90]

Acts 20:10 / Mark 5:39.[91] Paul's "Don't worry!" (20:10) before raising the "sleeping" Eutychus echoes a similar scene in Mark's Gospel in which Jesus asks the crowd, "Why are you worrying?" before raising the "sleeping" daughter of Jairus (Mark 5:39). The term *worry* is missing from the Lukan parallel in Luke 8:52. This passage is another instance of the rich intertextual connections between Acts and the Synoptic tradition and once again prompts the authorial audience to expect Paul to resuscitate Eutychus as Jesus did Jairus's daughter.[92]

It is hoped that these few examples serve to illustrate the potential for exploring Acts as a sequel both to Luke and to a multiform gospel and to find parallels between Acts and the Third Gospel where possible and between Acts and other Gospels where appropriate.

CONCLUSION

By the time Luke composed Acts, the Third Gospel was being read and heard in early Christian gatherings in conjunction with the πολλοί, an unspecified number of other gospel accounts. Luke penned Acts (1) as a sequel to Luke with the understanding that the Third Gospel provided the baseline for his continuing development of literary plot and theological themes as part of a series of two rhetorically well formed—but not systematic—narratives, *and* (2) as a sequel to the multiform gospel in which he occasionally picked up on a literary thread or theological theme missing in the Third Gospel, either because at that point it did not serve his purposes or because at that time he was unacquainted with the writing that contained it. (3) Further, Luke also knew that Acts was self-sufficient and was "intelligible on its own."[93] Thus from the point of view of its authorial intention Acts may be read and heard on its own terms or as part of a "literary diptych," that is as a sequel to Luke, *and,* simultaneously, as a sequel to a multiform gospel, of which the Third Gospel is the primary witness.[94]

NOTES

1. And of course our contribution was in dialogue with the discussion begun by Henry J. Cadbury decades earlier. It is not my intention to deal with the reviews and responses to Mikeal C. Parsons and Richard I. Pervo's *Rethinking the Unity of Luke and Acts* (Minneapolis: Fortress, 1993; repr. with additional bibliography, 2007) that have appeared over the intervening years. Pervo has done that elsewhere in this volume ("Fourteen Years After: Revisiting *Rethinking the Unity of Luke and Acts,*" 23–40), and I find myself once again in essential agreement with the assessment and argument he presents there, though he himself may demur from the reframing and construal that I am offering here.

2. The 2005 collection included: C. Kavin Rowe, "History, Hermeneutics, and the Unity of Luke-Acts," in this volume, 43–65 (first published in *JSNT* 28/2 [2005]: 131–57); Luke Timothy Johnson, "Literary Criticism of Luke-Acts: Is Reception-History Pertinent?" in this volume, 66–69 (first published in *JSNT* 28/2 [2005]: 159–62; Markus Bockmuehl, "Why Not Let Acts Be Acts? In Conversation with C. Kavin Rowe," in this volume, 70–73 (first published in *JSNT* 28/2 [2005]: 163–66). Subsequent references are to these three essays as they appear in this volume.

3. The 2007 collection included: Michael F. Bird, "The Unity of Luke-Acts in Recent Discussion," in this volume, 3–22 (first published in *JSNT* 29/4 [2007]: 425–48); C. Kavin Rowe, "Literary Unity and Reception History: Reading Luke-Acts as Luke and Acts," in this volume, 74–81 (first published in *JSNT* 29/4 [2007]: 449–57); Andrew F. Gregory, "The Reception of Luke and Acts and the Unity of Luke-Acts," in this volume, 82–93 (first published in *JSNT* 29/4 [2007]: 459–72). Subsequent references are to these three essays as they appear in this volume.

4. Appreciation is expressed to Baker Academic for permission to use material in this essay from Mikeal C. Parsons, *Acts* (Paideia Commentaries on the New Testament; Grand Rapids: Baker Academic, 2008).

5. I am well aware of the pitfalls of the so-called fallacy of authorial intent. By using this phrase I mean no more than what we can understand of the purpose or intent of an author (in this case Luke) based on what he wrote, not on what he thought (see Pervo, "Fourteen Years After," in this volume). In this sense, then, I am equating, and in this essay using interchangeably, *authorial intent* and *intentio operis* (the "intention of the text"). I encountered this latter term used by Umberto Eco in Markus Bockmuehl, *Seeing the Word: Refocusing New Testament Study* (Grand Rapids: Baker Academic, 2006). Bockmuehl also uses the phrase in his contribution to this current discussion; cf. "Why Not Let Acts Be Acts?" 72.

6. Most of my recent writings, including the Acts commentary, have employed the term *authorial audience,* rather than *ideal* or *informed reader* as a heuristic construct. Following Rabinowitz (and others) I use the term to indicate the audience that the author had in mind when he wrote his text (cf. Peter Rabinowitz, *Before Reading: Narrative Conventions and the Politics of Interpretation* [Ithaca, N.Y.: Cornell University Press, 1987]; Warren Carter, *Matthew: Storyteller, Interpreter, Evangelist* [Peabody, Mass.: Hendrickson, 1996]; Charles H. Talbert, *Reading Luke-Acts in its Mediterranean Milieu* [NovTSup 107; Leiden: Brill, 2003]; Mikeal C. Parsons, *Luke: Storyteller, Interpreter, Evangelist* [Peabody, Mass.: Hendrickson, 2007]). The authorial audience is not a real "flesh-and-blood" audience; it is nonetheless historically circumscribed, for example, in terms of cultural knowledge of social scripts or rhetorical conventions.

7. See James Kelhoffer, *Miracle and Mission: The Authentication of Missionaries and Their Message in the Longer Ending of Mark* (WUNT 2/112; Tübingen: Mohr Siebeck, 2000).

8. For this reason since the publication of *Rethinking,* I have (when publishers and editors allowed!) replaced the hyphen in Luke-Acts with a backslash Luke/Acts—a siglum that both connects and divides and that, in the past decade or two, has become a much more recognizable and accepted symbol with the rise of Internet URLs.

9. Johnson, "Literary Criticism," 68, a phrase also echoed by Rowe in "Literary Unity," 76.

10. As we shall see some of those echoes to other Gospels may, in fact, be not only continuations of theological and literary themes but also "correctives" to the content of those other Gospels (and perhaps even in the Third Gospel). Thus the issue of "unity" is one still to be argued and not assumed.

11. Rowe, "History, Hermeneutics, 55 n. 3.

12. Pervo, "Fourteen Years After," 29–30.

13. Parsons and Pervo, *Rethinking,* 45–46, 82–83.

14. It is instructive when reading the two collections of essays in *JSNT* to ask which kind of literary unity is meant by the author. At times Rowe seems to refer to a physical unity of Luke and Acts; at other times to unity at the level of story. He does not appear to confuse the two, but the reader might not always be clear on which kind of unity is being discussed and what the relationship between the two is.

15. Gregory, "Reception," 85.

16. Henry J. Cadbury, *The Book of Acts in History* (New York: Harper & Brothers, 1955), 138.

17. Donald Juel (*Luke-Acts: The Promise of History* [Atlanta: John Knox, 1983], 12), for example, writes: "Since writing in the first century was done on scrolls, and since a limit was imposed on the length of a scroll, longer works required division into discrete 'volumes.' Scholars have determined that the Gospel of Luke and the Acts would each fill a normal scroll. Though there is some disagreement, the simplest explanation for the separation of the two volumes is size." In this volume Gregory ("Reception," 92 n. 16) writes: "I assume that Luke wrote each book on a premanufactured scroll of similar length, and that the need to fit each of his books on to such a scroll will have affected the way in which Luke planned and composed his work."

18. Frederick Kenyon, *Books and Readers in Ancient Rome and Greece* (Oxford: Oxford University Press, 1951), 54–55. By the way, Kenyon knows of much longer scrolls from Egypt but dismisses them because they were written "less for reading than for show" (*Handbook to the Textual Criticism of the New Testament* [2d ed.; London: Macmillan, 1912], 35). In his earlier work *The Making of Luke-Acts* (New York: Macmillan, 1927; repr. London: SPCK, 1961), 324 (quotation is from 1961 edition), Cadbury had alluded to "physical limitations of ancient book-making" in the composition of Luke and Acts (but without reference to Kenyon). He claims that "rolls as used in his [Luke's] time were probably limited in size." But he goes on to admit: "Of course, different lengths may have been customary at different times and places, and a roll of standard length could contain varying amounts of text in accordance with the way in which the writing was done." His discovery of Kenyon (whose first edition of the handbook appeared in 1901) allows him to quantify the limits placed on scroll production and to argue, partly on that basis, for the separation of the two works due to the limitations of ancient manuscript production.

19. William Allen Johnson, *Bookrolls and Scribes in Oxyrhynchus* (Toronto: University of Toronto Press, 2004), 10.

20. Johnson, *Bookrolls,* 149. Some "deluxe editions" reach nearly 30 meters in length; see pp. 10–13 for Johnson's explanation for reconstructing scroll height and length.

21. Johnson, *Bookrolls,* 80–143. Ostensibly the length and quality of a bookroll might seem to depend in part on whether the text was "published" and "circulated" by private individuals or by a "scribal shop." R. J. Starr (with whom Johnson concurs) concluded that the circulation of books in antiquity depended on a "series of widening concentric circles determined primarily by friendship" (see "The Circulation of Literary Texts in the Roman World," *CQ* 37/1 [1987]: 213). While it would appear that Luke would fit within the trajectory of the private individual whose text circulated among these "concentric circles," the effect of this on the bookroll's quality or length was evidently negligible: "The overwhelming bulk of bookrolls in both samples show . . . the mix of general uniformity and slight individual variation . . . that is characteristic of a well-established artisan craft. . . . For most ancient readers, the professional look and feel of the bookroll was an essential aspect of its utility, since the bookroll's sociological function as cultural icon was as important as its contents" (Johnson, *Bookrolls,* 160).

22. Corroborating evidence also comes from Herculaneum, where most scrolls are in the 10–15 meter range and the longest (*De pietate*) is 23.4 meters. Source: e-mail from Jeffrey Fish, Baylor professor of classics and member of the Herculaneum research team, 20 October 2008; used with permission.

23. This statement remains true even if, as recent studies suggest (cf. David Trobisch, *The First Edition of the New Testament* [Oxford: Oxford University Press, 2000]), the original New Testament autographs were written on codices, since, although the scroll form was easier to construct, the codex had a greater capacity to accommodate longer texts (cf. Johnson, *Bookrolls,* 86–87). It seems, then, that Luke did have the technology available—whether through a codex or scroll—to accommodate both Luke and Acts together, but there is no evidence that he took advantage of such book-making technology—further corroborating evidence that it was never Luke's intention to produce a single, continuous story, at least not in material form.

24. See Parsons and Pervo, *Rethinking,* 22.

25. Cadbury, *The Book of Acts in History,* 144, 161–62.

26. Johnson, "Literary Criticism," 66.

27. Bruce M. Metzger, *A Textual Commentary on the Greek New Testament* (2d ed.; Stuttgart: Deutsche Bibelgesellschaft / German Bible Society, 1994), 222.

28. The "Western" textual tradition is most commonly identified with, but not exclusively limited to, Codex Bezae Cantabrigiensis (D in Acts). For a description of the Western textual tradition, its relationship to Codex Bezae, and its characterization as the result of "an undisciplined and 'wild' growth of manuscript tradition and translation activity," see Bruce M. Metzger and Bart D. Ehrman, *The Text of the New Testament: Its Transmission, Corruption, and Restoration* (4th ed.; New York: Oxford University Press, 2005), 307–10.

29. Despite arguments that the Western tradition holds priority over, or at least equal footing with, the Alexandrian text (cf. A. C. Clark, *The Acts of the Apostles: A Critical Edition, with Introduction and Notes on Selected Passages* [Oxford: Clarendon, 1933]; M. E. Boismard and A. Lamouille, *Le texte occidental des Actes des apôtres: reconstitution et rehabilitation* [2 vols.; Paris: Éditions Recherche sur les civilizations, 1984]; W. A. Strange, *The Problem of the Text of Acts* [SNTSMS 71; Cambridge: Cambridge University Press, 1992]), the critical consensus continues to regard the "Western" text of Acts as generally of a secondary and

derivative nature, and generally functions—in the case of Acts—as a commentary and early witness to the reception of Acts.

30. Metzger, *Textual Commentary,* 233.

31. Ibid.

32. But it has not been ignored altogether. Rowe ("Literary Unity," 77) writes: "With respect to the former [text of Acts], we may take notice of the important fact that it is more difficult to account for the messiness of Acts' textual situation with the supposition of a neat, joint publication with Luke—*Luke-Acts*—than it is to suppose that Acts' textual situation is at least in some way intrinsically related to the manner in which it actually began to circulate" (cf. also especially Strange, *The Problem of the Text of Acts,* 181).

33. Cf. Metzger, *Textual Commentary,* 225–32.

34. Martin Dibelius's suggestion ("The Text of Acts: An Urgent Critical Text," in *Studies in the Acts of the Apostles,* 84–92 [ed. H. Greeven; trans. M. Ling and P. Schubert; New York: Charles Scribner's Sons, 1956], 89) that the poor preservation of Acts may be accounted for by the fact that Luke was used in worship and Acts was preserved only in the book trade is problematic. Elsewhere in this volume Pervo ("Fourteen Years After," 31) observes: "His view of the book trade wants correction, and his argument about the careful preservation of the Gospel text is overstated, but he understood that the distinct textual characteristics of Acts were due to a different reception."

35. Though see B. H. Streeter, *The Four Gospels: A Study of Origins, Treating of the Manuscript Tradition, Sources, Authorship, & Dates* (London: Macmillan, 1924), 534, who claims the evidence "may have corresponded to a change in residence."

36. E-mail correspondence with Michael Holmes, dated 29 August 2007; used with permission.

37. Margaret Mitchell, "Patristic Counter-evidence to the Claim that 'The Gospels were Written for All Christians,'" *NTS* 51/1 (2005): 36–79.

38. Richard Bauckham, "For Whom Were Gospels Written?" in *The Gospel for All Christians: Rethinking the Gospel Audience* (ed. Richard Bauckham; Grand Rapids, Mich.: Eerdmans, 1998), 9–48.

39. See Rowe, "Literary Unity," 78–79. A time lapse actually plays an important role for those who, like Streeter, argue for different provenances, since the shift in genre from a short, occasional letter to a longer narrative implies also a lapse of time of some indeterminate length.

40. Ibid.

41. Gregory, "Reception," 86.

42. Ibid.

43. It is not the case that there is "no indisputable evidence" for the physical unity of Luke and Acts, as Gregory (ibid.) maintains; there is simply not a *shred* of evidence discovered so far to support this view.

44. Cf. also Gregory, "Reception," 85–87. In the Paideia commentary (*Acts,* 16–17) I have argued for a *terminus ante quem* of ca. 100 C.E. (based on Acts' acquaintance with a collection of Paul's letters; see Richard I. Pervo, *Dating Acts: Between the Evangelists and the Apologists* (Santa Rosa, Calif.: Polebridge, 2006); and a *terminus ad quem* of ca. 120 C.E. (based on Polycarp's knowledge of Acts), with a most likely date for Acts of 110 C.E. Accept-

ing a date of late 80s or even early 90s for the Gospel of Luke (which has no telltale second-century marks) suggests a lapse of two decades or so between the composition and publication of the two documents.

45. In the Paideia commentary on Acts, and in ways similar to the second half of this essay in which I explore possible intertextual connections between Acts and the Synoptic Gospels, I have suggested what it might mean for the authorial audience to have heard Acts in light of knowledge of an early collection of Paul's letters. I concluded that the "overall picture of Paul in Acts is not exactly identical to the Paul of the letters (who, we do well to remember, is itself a projected rhetorical persona), but there are nonetheless similarities between the two portraits" (Parsons, *Acts,* 16); see also Parsons, *Luke: Storyteller, Interpreter, Evangelist,* 123–37. Thus I find myself in disagreement with Luke Timothy Johnson's conclusion, especially if he would be willing—as I suspect he would—to extend those comments also to the hearers of Acts: "no original hearers of Paul's letters or of the Gospels could possibly have heard them as part of a collection" (Johnson, "Literary Criticism, 66). In fact I am arguing that the authorial audience of Acts heard that text within an intertextual and hermeneutical web that included (very early, but not "canonical") collections both of the Gospels and of Paul's letters.

46. See Loveday C. A. Alexander, *The Preface to Luke's Gospel: Literary Convention and Social Context in Luke 1.1–4 and Acts 1.1* (SNTSMS 78; Cambridge: Cambridge University Press, 1993), esp. 27, 145–46, and the bibliography. In the current debate Rowe ("History, Hermeneutics, 46) has tentatively suggested that Acts 1:1–2 may imply that the audience has "already read, and presumably understood the Gospel" and that the preface "also seems to presuppose at least some chronological space between the two volumes." Johnson ("Literary Criticism," 67–68) has responded with a resounding "No!": "Nothing in the second prologue suggests the passage of time between the composition of the two volumes. Indeed the very briefness of the prologue to Acts suggests the opposite, namely that the author could assume substantial knowledge of what the first volume contains." It is not clear to me, however, how this last sentence actually refutes Rowe's suggestion. "Substantial knowledge" of the Third Gospel may have come to the audience of Acts *precisely* because of a lapse of time between the publication of the two documents. But again the issue will not be resolved on the basis of the prologues alone.

47. Parsons, *Luke: Storyteller, Interpreter, Evangelist,* 40–50.

48. Frederick W. Danker, *Jesus and the New Age: A Commentary on St. Luke's Gospel* (Philadelphia: Fortress, 1988), 24.

49. Here my view, with regard to Acts at least, is not far from Gregory's amplification of Rowe's hypothesis (although Gregory himself does not accept it): if readers of Luke were already familiar with Mark they would need at least long enough to decide that Luke's apparent wish to distinguish his narrative from other accounts of Jesus (Luke 1:1–3) did not mean that those who read Luke's work could not associate it with other texts of a similar nature. Such an association may have arisen very quickly, not least if some of Luke's early audience were more positive about the work of his predecessors than Luke himself may have been. ("Reception," 86).

My conclusion, however, differs radically from Gregory's: "Thus, Luke's preface appears to suggest that he did not want his narrative to be read alongside those of his predecessors, for their work is defective. If so, it is almost inconceivable that Luke would have envisaged his first book being read alongside three other broadly similar accounts, not least if he included among his predecessors the author of what we call the Gospel according to Mark" ("Reception," 90). I think Luke could *conceive* of it in theory because by the time he composed Acts, he had *observed* it in practice!

50. Bockmuehl makes a similar point: "To understand the historical and canonical footprint of these works as heard by their early readers, however, it matters that the Gospel is self-identified in 1.1 as one διήγησις of the Gospel events among 'many,' which very soon became one among four" ("Why Not Let Acts Be Acts?" 72).

51. I prefer the term *sequel* (also preferred in *Rethinking*), because it allows for the complexity of relationships between Acts and Luke and a multiform Gospel in ways that *continuation,* for example, does not (a term that would seem to favor a more exclusive relationship with the Third Gospel).

52. Rowe ("History, Hermeneutics," 46) makes a similar suggestion though without suggesting that Acts be read as a sequel to these "many" gospels. He proposes that a lapse of time between the publication of the two documents creates the "space which might allow the Gospel at least some time to become associated with other narratives focused explicitly on the life of Jesus (for example, Mark) and which would thus make good sense as a sort of *Ausgangspunkt* for the different treatment of Luke and Acts in the second century. The Gospel, in other words, could well have been treated as a Gospel (though of course the word would probably not have been used) prior to the 'publication,' or at least distribution, of Acts. In such an early association or grouping, Acts would not really even have had the chance to become inseparably attached to Luke."

53. Daniel Marguerat, *The First Christian Historian: Writing the "Acts of the Apostles"* (SNTSMS 121; trans. Ken McKinney, Gregory J. Laughery, and Richard Bauckham; Cambridge: Cambridge University Press, 2002), 43–64; cited and modified by Pervo, "Fourteen Years After," 32.

54. See Parsons, *Luke: Storyteller, Interpreter, Evangelist,* 40–50.

55. See Charles H. Talbert, *Literary Patterns, Theological Themes and the Genre of Luke-Acts* (SBLMS 20; Missoula: SBL and Scholars Press, 1974).

56. But even here we must proceed with caution, since the structure of Acts is closer to Mark than to Luke, at least in the sense that both begin with the Spirit and close without resolution.

57. Reconstructing the elements of early Christian gatherings is notoriously difficult, in part due to the paucity of evidence. Dennis Smith (*From Symposium to Eucharist: The Banquet in the Early Christian World* [Minneapolis: Fortress, 2003]) has offered the Greco-Roman banquet as the most likely social setting for early Christian gatherings, of which one indispensable element was "entertainment." Such entertainment, at least in the philosophical versions of the banquet, might include dramatic readings of poetry or narrative (179). Accepting Smith's basic assertion that early Christian assemblies resembled Greco-Roman banquets in form and structure (without necessarily affirming other aspects of his historical and theological analyses), one can reasonably posit that public reading and performance of early Christian texts (such as Paul's letters, the Gospels, and Acts), would have been both

edifying and entertaining (for both "profit" and "delight"). This reconstruction also conforms nicely to the later evidence of Justin who suggested that the "memoirs of the apostles" (Gospels) were read in early Christian assemblies "for as long as time permits," that is, in large stretches of narrative rather than discrete lectionary units (1 *Apol.* 67).

58. Johnson, "Literary Criticism," 66. Presumably the fruitfulness of such study for Johnson would not extend to understanding better how the original hearers would have heard the New Testament documents.

59. Bockmuehl, "Why Not Let Acts Be Acts?" 71–72. Bockmuehl (71) suggests that even Rowe has given up too much on this very point: "Rowe astutely highlights the tensions between Lukan literary-critical analysis and the actual historical footprint of his works—and between authorial intent and actual use. But might we benefit from further discussion of whether the Luke of history, as distinct from the implied author of literary criticism, did in fact 'set out to write a two-volume work'? How obvious is it either that the evangelist designed the two volumes as an integral whole from the start, or that he meant them to be read as a single work even by the time he wrote Acts?" He further wonders if Rowe "cedes unnecessary ground to the standard historical-critical construct it seems to want to question" (71).

60. I agree with Gregory ("Reception," 82) that Justin Martyr's *First Apology* 50.12 has "no convincing evidence for the use of Acts." I do not, however, find the Muratorian Fragment to hold the same weight as Irenaeus as a witness to the conceptual unity of Luke and Acts, though I am willing to concede that "the author's awareness of the separate transmission of Luke (as part of the fourfold Gospel) and of Acts does not prevent him from making links between the two books" (ibid., 85).

61. Rowe, "History, Hermeneutics," 45. Rowe credits Campenhausen with seeing that Irenaeus's two "texts" were the *Tetraevangelium* and Acts. And, as Rowe points out, for Irenaeus to read Luke isolated from the *Tetraevangelium* would make him guilty of the very same "heretical" practice of which he accuses the Marcionites! See also Pervo, "Fourteen Years After," in this volume, 30.

62. Gregory, "Reception," 83.

63. Ibid. While I am in basic agreement with Gregory's point, I am going to suggest later that, from the point of view of the "authorial audience" (or as others in this dialogue prefer, "the ideal reader"), this statement is more clearly grounded in the *intentio operis* if we speak of reading Acts in two different ways—sometimes as a sequel to the multiform gospel and more often as the sequel to the Third Gospel. Bockmuehl hints at the same point ("Why Not Let Acts Be Acts?" 72): "To understand the literary mind of the historical Luke, we may indeed benefit from reading Luke and Acts in light of each other, and perhaps especially the latter in light of the former."

64. Gregory, "Reception," 83.

65. Ibid., 85.

66. Or more precisely Irenaeus's comments are consistent with the trajectory that would run from the authorial audience at the beginning of the second century to a real reader in the last several decades of that same century.

67. Some of which are mentioned by Gregory, "Reception," 84–85.

68. Bockmuehl, "Why Not Let Acts Be Acts?" 71.

69. Gregory, "Reception," 87. Admittedly I am using Gregory's words to support Rowe's conclusion ("Literary Unity," 76–77).

70. Jaraslov Pelikan, *Acts* (Brazos Theological Commentary; Grand Rapids: Brazos Press, 2005), cited by Gregory, "Reception," 91. Despite my resonance with this methodological description, I must hasten to add that my commentary on Acts is radically different from Pelikan's in almost every respect.

71. Rowe, "History, Hermeneutics," 52–53.

72. Rowe, "Literary Unity," 76.

73. Gregory, "Reception," 90.

74. See Rowe, "History, Hermeneutics," 54; Gregory, "Reception," 90.

75. Bockmuehl, "Why Not Let Acts Be Acts?" 72.

76. Assuming the authorial audience's familiarity with some of Paul's letters, the critic might also profitably read Luke's story of Paul in light of echoes of and allusions to Paul's writings (in terms both of comparison and contrast); cf. Parsons, *Luke: Storyteller, Interpreter, Evangelist,* 123–45.

77. Although I am focusing here on the echoes between Acts and Mark and Matthew, one could, assuming Acts postdates the Fourth Gospel, also explore echoes and allusions between Acts and John from the perspective of their reception by Luke's authorial audience. I did this in only a very limited and tentative way in the commentary; for example, I suggested (*Acts,* 28) in my exegesis of Acts 1:8: "The promise of the Holy Spirit for empowering the witness of the disciples is found also in John 15:26–27." Other possible Acts/John parallels include: Acts 1:10–11 / John 20:17; Acts 2:22 / John 2:11; Acts 3:22, 7:37 / John 6:14; 7:40; Acts 7:56 / John 1:51; Acts 13:25 / John 1:20. In addition to these verbal echoes a number of conceptual and thematic parallels have been suggested (though with a plethora of varying reasons for their existence). There is a body of literature that explores the Acts-John connections, though primarily from the point of view of composition (though Matson's work is a notable exception here). That literature includes: C. K. Barrett, "The Parallels Between Acts and John," in *Exploring the Gospel of John: In Honor of D. Moody Smith* (ed. R. Alan Culpepper and C. Clifton Black; Louisville: Westminster John Knox, 1996), 220–39; Mark Matson, *In Dialogue with Another Gospel?: The Influence of the Fourth Gospel on the Passion Narrative of the Gospel of Luke* (Atlanta: Society of Biblical Literature, 2001); Pierson Parker, "When Acts Sides with John," *Understanding the Sacred Text: Essays in Honor of Morton S. Enslin on the Hebrew Bible and Christian Beginnings* (ed. John Reumann; Valley Forge, Pa.: Judson, 1972), 201–15; Parker, "The Kinship of John and Acts," *Christianity, Judaism, and Other Greco-Roman Cults: Studies for Morton Smith at Sixty* (vol. 1, *New Testament;* ed. Jacob Neusner; Leiden: Brill, 1975), 187–205; Parker, "Mark, Acts, and Galilean Christianity," *NTS* 16/3 (1969): 295–304; Parker, "The 'Former Treatise' and the Date of Acts," *JBL* 84/1 (1965): 52–58; D. Moody Smith, *John among the Gospels* (Columbia: University of South Carolina Press, 2001).

78. In the Paideia *Acts* commentary I explore some twenty allusions in Acts to non-Lukan Gospel traditions; here I deal with only seven. Of course, I view these examples as illustrative and not exhaustive. I have of necessity focused on those allusions that are found in other Gospels and *not* in Luke (that is non-Lukan in the sense that the material is entirely

missing from Luke's Gospel or the detail alluded to in Acts is present in Mark's or Matthew's (but not Luke's) version of material found in common between the two (or three).

79. There is a similarity in approach here to Richard Hays's criteria for detecting intertextual echoes, which were crafted in terms of Old Testament citations and allusions in New Testament writings, specifically Paul (see his *Echoes of Scripture in the Letters of Paul* [New Haven: Yale University Press, 1989]). For example, the echo of Mark 1:8 in Acts 1:5 yields the following results: (1) In almost any scenario the Gospel of Mark would have been *available* both to the Luke and his original readers; (2) given repetition of phrases (for example, John "baptized with water, but you will be baptized with the Holy Spirit," Acts 1:5; cf. Mark 1:8), the *volume* is quite explicit; (3) the *recurrence* of parallels and patterns between Mark and Luke (and now Acts) is well known; (4) the *thematic coherence* is likewise strong: Jesus' baptism and reception of the Holy Spirit and the beginning of his public ministry clearly parallels the apostles' reception of the Spirit and beginning of their public ministry, and the allusion to Mark's version of John the Baptist's saying strengthens this connection in ways that the Lukan version does not; (5) it is *historically plausible* that Luke intended this intertextual echo to Mark (and not Luke or Matthew) and that his readers, at least upon subsequent readings, would have recognized it; (6) in terms of the *history of interpretation,* the connection between this text in Acts and Mark has often been noted, though usually from the historical perspective of the composition of Acts (did Luke know Matthew or Mark?) rather than the hermeneutical perspective of its reception; (7) the suggested intertextual echo does illuminate the surrounding text and fits well within Luke's rhetorical argument regarding Pentecost, thus providing an aesthetically *satisfying* fit.

80. See Parsons, *Acts,* 27.

81. Ibid., 33.

82. Hans Conzelmann, *Acts of the Apostles: A Commentary on the Acts of the Apostles* (ed. Eldon Jay Epp and Christopher R. Matthews; trans. James Limburg, A. Thomas Kraabel, and Donald H. Juel; Hermeneia; Philadephia: Fortress, 1987), 11.

83. Parsons, *Acts,* 140.

84. Ibid., 146–47.

85. On these points, see ibid., 148–52, 211–12.

86. Ibid., 172.

87. Ibid., 202.

88. Ibid., 271.

89. For example, Susan Garrett, *The Demise of the Devil: Magic and the Demonic in Luke's Writings* (Minneapolis: Fortress, 1989), 154, sees the pericope drawing on language and concepts of both exorcism and magic, while Scott Shauf, *Theology as History: Paul in Ephesus in Acts 19* (New York: Walter de Gruyter, 2005), 177–224, views the passage as dealing exclusively with exorcism.

90. In significant ways this story in Acts may be heard as a specific parody of Mark 5:1–20; only there, for example, do we have instances of injuries reported.

91. See Parsons, *Acts,* 287.

92. Other potential echoes in Acts to Matthew and/or Mark include: Acts 5:29 / Mark 7:8; Acts 6:13–14 / Mark 14:56–58, 64; Acts 13:51 / Matt 10:14; Acts 20:29 / Matt 7:15.

93. Rowe, "History, Hermeneutics," 46.

94. Thus, for Acts at least, the dilemma of reading posed by Rowe is resolved. My proposal addresses Acts in relationship to Luke and other gospels, but it does not account for the Third Gospel in relationship to these other gospels. For example, although I argue that Luke knows Matthew at the time of composing Acts, did he know Matthew when he composed the Third Gospel? My proposal opens for now the possibility that Luke's Gospel "knew" Matthew's account, since these kinds of issues depend on one's solution to the Synoptic problem (although that evidence would be construed differently when viewed from the point of view of reception rather than composition). Likewise this proposal does not resolve questions of the Third Gospel's relationship to Acts, for example, does Luke anticipate Acts? In my construal at the time of the Third Gospel's publication Acts had not been written and there is no compelling evidence that it was even conceived at this point. And even if it were so conceived from the point of view of Luke's compositional purpose, that says nothing about how the authorial audience would have received it. So it remains to be seen whether one can construct a working method in which the *intentio operis* of the Third Gospel coheres with its reception history. Once again this is no mere theoretical issue for me, as I am now at work on a commentary on Luke as the Paideia companion to Acts.

LUKE, ACTS, AND THE ANCIENT READERSHIP

The Cultures of Author, Scribes, and Readers in New Testament Exegesis

Claire Clivaz

Naturally, a manuscript (Umberto Eco, *The Name of the Rose*)

New Testament scholars are not accustomed to making prophetic statements, but when I read the following "prediction" of C. Kavin Rowe in 2005, it occurred to me that he might be right. "Yet—with no claim to the prophetic gift—I will hazard a prediction: reception history of the texts of the New Testament will come to constitute a greater and greater portion of the scholarly work in the field . . . because of the ability of the text's forward history to shed substantial light on substantive issues of interpretation."[1] At that time I was considering the question of history and readership in New Testament research while writing my dissertation on Luke 22:43–44.[2] This work led me to propose a methodology that I have labeled "through the ancient readership" ("*par le lectorat antique*").[3]

This methodology allows historical results to be obtained by rejecting the notion that *Wirkungsgeschichte* functions only as an optional or supplementary step in New Testament research and, instead, by foregrounding the reader(s) as literary and historical questions in their own right. In the course of my methodological inquiry, I realized that the issues raised by the interactions between the various cultures of the author, the scribes, and the readers were currently important questions not only in Lukan exegesis or in New Testament research but also in the entire field of literary and historical studies.[4] Patrick E. Spencer was therefore right when he asserted that "reception history is the latest challenge to the unity of Luke and Acts."[5] The entirely relevant questions of reception history and readership have now led Lukan scholars into a kind of waiting room, out of which this present collection of essays will, it is hoped, help to lead us.

Andrew F. Gregory opened a helpful door by claiming that Luke and Acts and Luke-Acts were two "strategies" that have to be considered together: "Only in modern scholarship are Luke and Acts read primarily as Luke-Acts, even if that is what their author appears to have intended. One strategy is not better than the other. One strategy does not rule the other out. Each is appropriate to different circumstances and reflects different needs and interests on the part of those who employ it at any particular time."[6] This may well be the case, but we must nevertheless beware of the danger of creating an unproductive conflict within scholarly debate between the point of view of the author and that of the readers. Scholars such as Spencer and David P. Moessner, for example, continue to ask how to deal with the "tripartite hermeneutical framework of author-text-reader." For according to Spencer, not only is Rowe's "'reader' a late second-century church apologist but the other two legs to the hermeneutical stool—'author' and 'text'—are non-entities in his examination."[7] Paying attention to this criticism I will argue and propose in this article that in the field of ancient literature we need to reconstruct this triad rather as "author-scribe-reader." For between the author and the readers stand the scribes, those who actually wrote and made the texts. When we speak about texts we are in fact refering to the work of the scribe who is, at one and the same time, the final author and a reader of considerable influence. Our ancient texts are deeply marked by what Jean-Claude Mühlethaler calls "the scribal culture," hermeneutical patterns and sets of scribal practices that often prevail over authorial culture until as late as the fifteenth century.[8] As Mühlethaler puts it, "praise of the variant makes me plead for a literary history of reading and, as an inevitable corollary, for editions that, by turning the usual viewpoint on its head, do not depend on the 'very Western notion' of the creator genius, a notion that has been dominant ever since the Renaissance, leading to the cult of the original and setting it in stone for all eternity."[9] To reconsider the question of the reader(s) means, in addition, to reconsider our enduringly romantic perception of the "author," and our insufficiently pragmatic notion of the "text," the latter being the product of a scribal culture.

To explore the triad author-scribe-reader I will first demonstrate the importance of the questions raised by the reception history of Luke-Acts or of Luke and Acts and show that the question of the readers was already present in Henry J. Cadbury's 1927 *The Making of Luke-Acts.* A careful reading of this book shows also that the present seemingly endless debate about the literary genre of Luke-Acts has its origin in a cultural misunderstanding of Cadbury's work. Considering next the question of readership from a methodological point of view, I will present the methodology that I have called "through the ancient readership." Then I will examine an example of scribal culture—with its links to the culture of both author and readers—that involves a text-critical problem: Luke 24:51b, which specifies that Jesus "was carried up to heaven," leaving the disciples at the end of Luke's Gospel. Readers—and successive scribes and authors—will evaluate whether or not a way to move out of the waiting room has been found.

WHY READERS MATTER

The Readers and the Diversity of Historical Memories

The situation would seem to be clear: although Luke and Acts may have been written by a single author,[10] early witnesses show that they were not read together in the earliest days of Christianity, as is demonstrated especially by the list of canonical books included in the Codex Claromontanus.[11] This list accords a special status to Acts,[12] placing it just after Revelation and before the *Shepherd of Hermas,* the *Acts of Paul,* and the *Apocalypse of Peter.*[13] As I have noted elsewhere,[14] to Johannes Leipoldt the Coptic translations of the New Testament place Acts just before Revelation or as the last book of the canonical list when Revelation is omitted.[15] Moreover, 0189 (with Acts 5:3–21)—the earliest parchment manuscript of the New Testament and one of the five uncials that precede the development of the great text—places Acts at the beginning of a codex.[16] On the recto of the folio can be seen the number 15 (ιε), and on the verso 16 (ις). It may mean, as Philip W. Comfort and David P. Barrett assert, that "the codex originally contained only the book of Acts,"[17] but it could also mean that Acts stood at the beginning of a much longer codex. In any case, we have here a witness to Acts not preceded by the Gospel of Luke or by any of the other canonical Gospels.

Rowe[18] and Bockmuehl[19] have each drawn attention to the fact that nowhere in the surviving manuscript tradition do Luke and Acts appear one after the other. Yet whereas Stanton argued that it was the acceptance of Luke into the fourfold Gospel that led to its early separation from Acts,[20] Rowe wonders about the opposite conclusion. "Luke and Acts were not divided," he suggests, "because they were not really read together in the first place. By itself Luke was rather naturally grouped with other gospels and found its way unhindered into the fourfold gospel rather early on."[21] Rowe's suggestion, however, is an argument from silence, as Gregory suggests.[22] Since there are no earlier witnesses, the fact that our surviving manuscripts do not place Luke and Acts together is not convincing evidence that they did not once circulate in that way. Thus, given their common authorship, and the lack of any evidence that they did not circulate together prior to the emergence of the fourfold Gospel, the hypothesis that the two volumes were separated and read independently of one another at an early date remains the most plausible scenario, in accordance with Gregory's line of reasoning.[23] Consequently, with regard to the question of the conditions of publication it is wise to consider with Gregory that Luke and Acts could be read separately *and* together in the second century (cf. Irenaeus).[24] I would like to add to the debate by pointing out that scholars often have too modern a concept of "publication" precisely because they consider only the "written" step in the editorial process. Yet, as Tiziano Dorandi has demonstrated, the publication of a work in antiquity corresponded to its first public reading (πρὸς ἔκδοσιν):[25] as soon as Luke and Acts had been read in public, even if only to a circle of friends, they no longer belonged solely to their author. An excellent example are the anecdotes of Galen.[26]

In his *De ordine propriorum librorum* and *De propriis libris*[27] Galen attempted to explain to his present and future readership how to read his work, in which order his books had to be read, and which books were the most important. But the way things turned out was entirely contrary to his wishes: his more successful books appear to be precisely those that Galen viewed as preliminary drafts.[28] A canon of some of Galen's works was even established in Alexandria without any resemblance to Galen's recommendations.[29] In spite of the two texts that Galen wrote in an attempt to influence how his work was received, his readers, far from heeding him, canonized his work in a way that he certainly did not intend. In a quite similar way, Luke did not escape canonization, which resulted in something like the permanent separation of his/her twofold work. Thus did the author's claim to present what "seemed good to me"[30] undergo a crushing defeat in the process of canonization, as is also evidenced by the addition to ἔδοξε κἀμοι of *et spiritui sancto* in the Latin codices b, q, and vg manuscripts (as pointed out by Loveday C. A. Alexander).[31] This canonization of Luke's work has resulted from the history of its reception, contrary to the observation that it is "almost inconceivable that Luke would have envisaged his first book being read alongside three other broadly similar accounts,"[32] and contrary to the invitation to Theophilus "to contrast Luke's account with the others."[33]

In light of such observations I have argued that the freedom Luke had as an author was limited by the extent of the common memory or memories of his/her addressees. He/she has to evoke certain events—such as the memory of the disagreement between Paul and Barnabas—but tries to present them in his/her own way (compare Acts 15:36–40 with Galatians 2:13).[34] As long as scholars continue to view the canonical Acts as "the first history of Christianity,"[35] or to regard the πολλοί in Luke 1:1 as equivalent only to other canonical texts, we will be unable to reckon seriously with the diversity of the early Christian memories in the first and second centuries. In fact, as long we continue to think "canonically" about these matters, we reproduce materially the point of view expressed by Irenaeus when he sought to promote the Lukan Acts as the authorized story of early Christian origins. But in actual fact early Christian memories were more flexible and diversified, as may be seen in three observations that I have developed elsewhere;[36] indeed, the author of *1 Clement* is attached to Paul's memory and knows stories about him different from those found in the Lukan Acts.[37] Moreover, certain early Christians read the Lukan Acts *and* the *Acts of Paul* together, as the canonical list from the Codex Claromontanus attests. And finally,

Clement of Alexandria thinks highly of the Lukan Acts *and* incorporates other early Christian memories into his own "Christian history." Consequently, while Rowe's "'reader' [looks like] a late second-century church apologist,"[38] it may be equally affirmed that the implied reader of Luke-Acts and the alleged first audience of Luke-Acts correspond to modern readers[39] as products of scholarly minds that are shaped by a canonical reading and ignore the diversity of early Christian stories and memories. A particular methodological difficulty seems to surround the question of the reader. In order to deal with the problem it is useful to begin by considering a particularly important point in the history of the research on the matter: it was, in fact, no less a scholar than Henry J. Cadbury who, in 1927, first turned the spotlight on Luke's readers.

From Cadbury's Concern with History to the Present Question of the Readers

Cadbury was responsible for the label Luke-Acts,[40] but it is generally and wrongly assumed that he also claimed, as Spencer asserts, that "Luke-Acts is more like historiography than any other genre."[41] In point of fact, Cadbury was concerned to affirm the importance of Luke's work by describing it as belonging to the *discipline of history* and not to assign it to the literary genre of historiography.[42] The label Luke-Acts had the effect of sparking a search to identify a common literary genre for both volumes, but I would argue that such a search was born from a misreading of Cadbury's purpose. In the first place how Cadbury came to invent the label Luke-Acts needs to be noted: "Biblical books when divided were numbered, as the books of Samuel and Kings, which were named in the Greek Bible 'Kingdoms I,' 'Kingdoms II,' etc. If we applied these methods of nomenclature we should have for Luke and Acts 'Ad Theophilum I' and 'Ad Theophilum II.' We may observe further among the customs of Biblical study that even entirely independent works were associated under a common name, as the four Books of the Maccabees."[43]

In some sense the present volume owes its origin to this assertion from Cadbury: "we should have for Luke and Acts 'Ad Theophilum I' and 'Ad Theophilum II.'" These titles are what we would like to have had for Luke-Acts in ancient times, but we do not have them. In inventing the label Luke-Acts, Cadbury was consciously looking at the work from a reader's point of view and adopting a modern starting point, since no ancient readers labelled Luke's work with a shared title. Unfortunately this starting point has been too easily overlooked in research, as was Cadbury's real concern, namely, to set Luke-Acts within the discipline of history. When asserting that "No doubt Luke's work is nearer to history than to any other familiar classification,"[44] Cadbury is speaking here about "history" —not "historiography"—and about a "classification"[45] about a "genre." Later scholars—from Talbert onward[46]—have taken this to be a statement about the classification of *genre.* Marianne Palmer Bonz, to take only one of many possible examples, quotes Cadbury's sentence but adds to it the words "familiar genre." Thus she says that Cadbury concludes that "Luke-Acts is more like historiography than to any other *familiar genre* classification."[47] Why does she make this addition, which alters Cadbury's classification?

Bonz's mistake is tied to a forgetfulness that affects our inquiry as a whole, namely, that at Cadbury's time history was no longer seen as a literary genre but rather as a discipline independent from literature and therefore as a mode of research that was left unaffected by questions of style and literary features.[48] During the nineteenth century scholars adopted the Rankean idea that history can be clearly distinguished from literature: if a text really counts, according to the historicist point of view, it should belong to the discipline of history. Adopting such a stance, Cadbury had no hesitation in declaring that ancient historians and even ancient writers more generally were indifferent to literary classifications. Consequently, he was not interested in specifying the literary genre of Luke-Acts: "In referring to his predecessors, Luke is satisfied to call their work simply a "story" (διήγησις, Luke 1:1). Probably no more technical name would be felt necessary for his own work."[49] In the beginning of his book he reveals his real concern: to underline the importance of the fact that New Testament study does not "require an apology" (while, of course, producing exactly that).[50] He thus sought to place Luke's work within *the discipline* of history, troubled as he was by the "popular" aspect of Luke's writing.[51] All of Cadbury's effort was directed toward maintaining Luke and Acts—so "Luke-Acts"—within the classification and discipline of history. He could not have imagined that the numerous later attempts to identify the literary genre of Luke-Acts would be based on a (mis)reading of his analysis, since he himself considered the term of διήγησις to be a perfectly adequate literary description.

A fine article by Loveday C. A. Alexander in 1998 set things straight: she implicitly joined Cadbury in demonstrating that "we shall never solve the question of Acts' historicity by solving the genre question."[52] A fundamental difference nevertheless separates the two authors: it was no longer possible for Alexander to affirm, as Cadbury had, that the narrative form itself carries the knowledge of the past,[53] because she was conscious, as a scholar speaking at the end of the twentieth century, that markers of factuality can be subverted, especially in ancient literature.[54] This fact inevitably led her to the question of the readers: "So what, in the end, can we conclude about the status of Luke's work in the eyes of ancient readers? Would it be taken as fact or as fiction?"[55] Such considerations caused me to suggest, in *L'ange et la sueur de sang,* that the genre of Luke and Acts should be seen as a category of reception, with a link to historicity that can be perceived in various ways.[56] Evaluation of historicity necessarily involves the question of readership.

How to Approach the Question of Readership from the Standpoint of Both History and Literature

The old question of the relationship of one text to another has long involved extensive and heated methodological debates. Vernon K. Robbins proposed a sociohistorical extension to the somewhat restricted notion of verbal intertextuality with the concept of *intertexture.*[57] To look for an "intertext" means to illuminate a text by reference to literary sources without there necessarily being a direct dependence on them.[58] The notion of intertexture is not far removed from the system of transtextual relationships established by Gérard Genette, whereby the object of poetics is no longer the text but the complex network created by the "architext."[59] Nevertheless F. Gerald Downing rightly drew attention to the difficulties of intertexture, showing how intertextual links can be always developed in a "wider and in a deeper way," with no clear idea of either the limits of interpretation or of the possible means of verification.[60] These difficulties could result in a bottomless abyss between the supposed first audience of the past and the actual reader of the present. It is precisely this problem that creates the "hybrid reader" described by John A. Darr, a reader who is "a heuristic hybrid, a fusion of ancient and modern cultural horizons."[61] In other words the end result is a fictitious reader, a kind a scholarly dream or second self, suspended over a fathomless pit.

Tired of nonverifiable readers—the first audience, as well as the implied reader(s)—I have begun to work with actual ancient readers whose readings have come down to us over the ages. After all, what Clement of Alexandria or Tertullian or Origen understood from a biblical text is accessible. They expressed their responses in a cultural period closer to that of the New Testament writings—and they wrote for the earliest readers—at a time when Christianity held a diversity of memories. Moreover it is worth remembering that Plato already prized the role of the reader more highly than the effect of written speech, which "drifts all over the place . . . [and is] unable to defend or help itself"; he considered as superior to the written text the discourse that "is written with intelligence in the mind of the learner."[62] In the *Theaetetus* Socrates even advocates a division of the readership into two different categories: that of the free man who can be called a philosopher, and a lower category subject to emotions that includes women and slaves.[63] If the nature of the readership is not only a diachronic variable but also a synchronic one, it becomes necessary to uncover the point of view of this prized early reader *as well as* that of the *other readers,* whoever they are. With this in mind I have proposed that New Testament exegesis should be approached "through the ancient readership," drawing on such ancient readings as are available.[64] The search for the diversity of readers' memories opens the way to the polyphonic dimension of texts "that allows one to organize interpretations in a hierarchy" instead of choosing only one, according to the linguist Alain Rabatel.[65] Following the work of Daniel Punday and Zoltán Köveces I have posited, first, that it is the body that is the way by which the reader enters a text and, second, that it is corporeality that sets the limits for the possible interpretations and meanings.[66] I have integrated these concepts in the methodology that I have described as "through the ancient readership."

I shall now go a step further and incorporate the "author" and the "text" into this methodological approach in line with the classical triad author-text-reader referred to above. The authors can also be viewed as readers dependent on intertextual relationships, because they are preceded, surrounded, and fashioned by texts: they simply represent a special case of readers. What, however, can be said about the text? As I argue above, between the author and the readers stand the scribes, those who literally *wrote* the texts, *made* the texts. Consequently the methodology "through the ancient readership" will have to involve the three cultures of author, scribes, and readers. Standing in the middle, the scribes are at one and the same time the last authors of the text and readers with a special advantage, since they had the power to *archive* the texts.[67]

The scribal culture can be challenged at any particular moment by the author's or the readers' culture(s) but from a practical point of view this culture has a very important influence in the overall process of interpretation: it gives us texts. For example, thousands of pages by Galen have been available for centuries but, in 2007 two manuscripts—one Arabic, one Greek—allowed Véronique Boudon-Millot finally to produce a new edition of the two texts in which Galen himself comments on his work (see above). In this case the authorial culture had a significant opportunity to express itself again and to connect with a modern readership, but this opportunity itself was due to the scribal culture. The importance of the scribal culture can be symbolically summarized by the title given by Umberto Eco to the preface of his novel *The Name of the Rose:* "Naturally, a manuscript."[68] Thus I will conclude this essay by seeking to read Luke-Acts (authorial culture) and Luke and Acts (the readers' culture) through manuscripts of Luke and Acts (scribal culture).

AN EXAMPLE AT THE CROSSROADS OF AUTHORIAL, SCRIBAL, AND READERS' CULTURES: Luke 24:51b

In what follows I do not pretend to solve the enigma of the variant of Luke 24:51b. I would, however, first like to underline why Eldon Epp's proposition[69] does not seem satisfactorily to explain this variant, and, second to analyze this issue at the crossroads of the cultures of the author, scribes, and readers by keeping in mind the question of Luke-Acts, of Luke and Acts, and of the diversity of early Christian memories.

The Issue of the Western Non-interpolations and Eldon Epp's Proposition

The first problem raised by the variant of Luke 24:51b ("and he was carried up to heaven"; καὶ ἀνεφέρετο εἰς τὸν οὐρανόν) is that while it appears to belong the the so-called Western non-interpolations (WNI),[70] it does not.[71] As we know, the discovery of P[75] has very much influenced the twenty-sixth edition of Nestle-Aland, with the rehabilitation of several WNI, notably Luke 24:51b. In 1967 Kurt Aland announced this reintegration in the forthcoming twenty-sixth edition of Nestle-Aland, whereas the 1966 Greek New Testament had kept interpolations between square brackets. Since this important turn in research a few scholars have attempted to explain the WNI as later additions, but it remains difficult to understand why, for example, the WNI in Luke 24 should have been omitted in some part of the "Western"[72] textual tradition (according to Nestle-Aland). The first attempt by Mikeal C. Parsons in 1986[73] did not convince the researchers, as James Ronald Royse methodically demonstrated in *The Scribal Habits in Early Greek New Testament Papyri.*[74] Surprisingly, Royse did not consider a number of alternative views that also appeared before his own work was finally published in 2008. Royse did not, however, settle the discussion. Thus he engaged neither Bart D. Ehrman, who, in *The Orthodox Corruption of the Scriptures,*[75] regards the WNI as antidocetic interpolations, nor Michael Wade Martin, who regards them as antiseparationist.[76] Martin agrees with Parsons and Ehrman about the thematic and stylistic unity of the WNI in Luke 24, a unity that signals, according to him, an accent on Jesus' bodily existence or ascension after the resurrection.[77] But he considers that the theological *Tendenz* is "anti-separationist" rather than "anti-docetic" because this later definition cannot account for each WNI in Luke 24.[78] In my opinion Martin's is the most convincing attempt in demonstrating that the WNI in Luke 24 are interpolations because he succeeds in explaining the manuscript's data by arguing that the WNI in Luke 24 are anterior to the copy of P[75]: "The longer Alexandrian readings are not singular or subsingular readings of P[75]. Rather they are attested throughout the Alexandrian tradition, meaning that they arose separately and earlier in the history of transmission than did the singular and subsingular readings of P[75]. Otherwise one would have to account for why the entire Alexandrian tradition accepted the longer orthodox interpolations in Luke 24 but rejected the much more modest orthodox changes found elsewhere in the manuscript."[79]

Martin fails only to pay enough attention to the special case of Luke 24:51b —καὶ ἀνεφέρετο εἰς τὸν οὐρανόν—that is absent from the Sinaiticus *prima manu,*[80] from D, as well as from the ancient Latin manuscripts (a b d e ff[2] l).[81] All the other WNI in Luke 24 are mentioned in Sinaiticus: Martin signals this particularity of Luke 24:51b in a footnote but does not comment further on it.[82] The unusual character of Luke 24:51b is also confirmed by the fact that this half-verse does not have to be read either as antidocetic or as antiseparationist: indeed Irenaeus himself implicitly says as much by the fact that he actually has to argue strongly that the ascension happened *ensarkos* in order to push the scene toward an antidocetic and antiseparationist meaning; remove Irenaeus's polemic and the scene could easily admit to various other significations, even with Luke 24:51b.[83] In short Luke 24:51b does not seem to belong to the WNI and our inquiry must therefore proceed: What is the meaning of the instability of this half-verse? Could it have been omitted from the "Western" text for a particular reason, and should it be consequently considered as a Lukan verse? Such is the opinion of Epp, who proposed—in an article presented in 1978 at the annual meeting of the Society of Biblical Literature and republished without modification in 2005[84]—"the 'Western' text tended strongly to resist any description of Jesus as 'being taken up into heaven.'"[85] Epp recognizes also that "our extant witnesses to that 'Western' textual tradition do not show that this tendency was carried through with rigid consistency" but nevertheless specifies in a postscript in 2005 that he has "found no reason to modify [his] position."[86]

If we focus on the different steps of Epp's argumentation it is possible to show that he places too much stress on each of them to reach his conclusion. In point of fact neither Codex Bezae nor the "Western" textual tradition denies the heavenly ascension. Epp's arguments, which he summarizes in six points,[87] can be questioned as follows. (1) He reminds us of the absence of Luke 24:51b from the "Western" text, without specifying here that this half-verse is also absent from א*. (2) He signals the absence of ἀνελήμφθη from the "Western" text in Acts 1:2, but D mentions it.[88] (3) He notes "the use of *sublatus est* for *levatus est* in Acts 1:9" but recognizes elsewhere that this is not a powerful argument.[89] (4) He underlines "the omission of 'into heaven' in [Acts] 1:11," but this omission occurs only in Codex Bezae and not in the Latin representants of the "Western" text; moreover, in the same Codex Bezae we have in Acts 1:11 the mention ὁ ἀναλημφθεὶς ἀφ' ὑμῶν; the second argument by Epp implies that he recognizes this verb as expressing a heavenly ascension. Points (5) and (6) reflect very minor readings found in Codex Gigas, St. Augustine, and Tertullian. In conclusion the mention in Codex Bezae of ἀνελήμφθη in Acts 1:2 and of ὁ ἀναλημφθεὶς ἀφ' ὑμῶν in Acts 1:11 shows that this specific manuscript does not deny or omit the heavenly ascension of Jesus, in spite of the absence of Luke 24:51b. Moreover the other witnesses of the "Western" text all have the mention of heaven in Acts 1:11. Consequently one can affirm that no witness of the "Western" textual tradition evacuated or ignored the heavenly ascension. We must thus find another explanation for the absence of our variant in manuscripts such as א*, D, a b d e ff^2 l, or explain its presence, most notably in P^{75}. Our next step is to read Luke 24:51 through the diversity of the manuscript data, within Luke-Acts, within Luke and Acts, and among the diverse early Christian memories and stories.

Within Luke-Acts and Luke and Acts through the Manuscripts

We no longer have the autograph of Luke-Acts. We do not have any commentary on the text by the Lukan author him/herself. We have only manuscripts transmitted by scribes who are simultaneously the final authors and special readers of the text. Manuscripts are our concrete, pragmatic, and tangible starting point, and they belong to the scribal culture. We possess manuscripts that all state in Luke 24:51a that Jesus "withdrew" from the disciples (διέστη or ἀπέστη for D). Without Luke 24:51b such a description does not mean either a definitive farewell or a horizontal separation or any kind of ascension or elevation. According to ℵ*, D, it, sy^{s}, there is a very simple and clear sequence in Luke 24:51–52: Jesus withdraws from the disciples who return to Jerusalem with great joy.[90] In this version there is no clear indication that such a separation would be final: the disciples received the order to wait for a power that would come (Luke 24:49); the imperfect tense in Luke 24:53 describes a time that endures rather than a simple, punctiliar event. One element of this ongoing time could even be seen as an invitation to wait for a future encounter with Jesus: he specifies in verse 49 that he himself would send (ἐγώ) the promise of the Father, but no text of Luke—either in the Gospel or in Acts[91]—another scene in which Jesus later sends a power to the disciples. Consequently several manuscripts added ἰδού in Luke 24:49 to indicate the immediate realization of this announcement in Luke 24:50. Clearly if the reading stops at 24:51a, the end of Luke's Gospel without Luke 24:51b could have been *read* as meaning a formal goodbye but not a definitive farewell.

If, after reading Luke, we go on to read the second preface of Acts, we find an impression of a doubling of the scene whereby Acts 1:9–11 can be viewed as a second, more developed telling of the same farewell and followed this time by a scene that takes place in the ὑπερῷον (Acts 1:13), not in the temple (Luke 24:53).[92] Some scribes-readers perceived here a contradiction between the two stories and attempted to harmonize them: A*, for example, omits the mention of the temple in Luke 24:53.[93] Moreover another discrepancy occurs between Luke 24:49 and Acts 1:2: the sending of some spiritual empowerment is promised in Luke 24:49 and indicated as given in Acts 1:2, but it is not narrated between the two verses. Luke 24:50 does not mention explicitly the sending of the Spirit on the disciples, which of course happens later in Acts at Pentecost. In a similar way Acts 1:2[94] speaks about the end of the Gospel as an "ascension" by using the term ἀνελήμφθη, but Luke 24:50–52 does not use it. Thus from an authorial point of view several discrepancies between the two stories can be observed: the divergence ὑπερῷον/Temple, the disparity concerning the gift of the Spirit, and the absence in the first scene of the verb ἀναλαμβάνειν, which was used in the summary of Acts 1:2. From a reader's point of view such differences could signal and encourage interaction with other memories or stories: after all, Luke 9:51 uses a plural to describe the *days* of the ascension: τὰς ἡμέρας τῆς ἀναλήμψεως.

In relation to ἀνάλημψις the plural "days" (ἡμέρας) could obviously be seen simply as a reference to the days of the Passion-resurrection story. But it could also take on further resonance with other notions that existed among the ancient Christian readership. There were early Christian readers who understood and believed that the risen Jesus would appear again—or several times—to the disciples on the Mount of Olives. Early Christian literature has transmitted to us many testimonies concerning traditions that viewed the Mount of Olives as a special place of revelation of Jesus to the disciples,[95] especially between the resurrection and the ascension: *Pistis Sophia* 1.1, for example, relates that Jesus appeared to his disciples for eleven years before leaving them once and for all. As Anne Boud'hors points out, "the Mount of Olives is an almost conventional starting-point" (see the *Pistis Sophia*) and a place of revelation (see *The Book of the Resurrection of Jesus Christ by Bartholomew the Apostle* 18.1) from which one can go away or to which one can return (see the Coptic *Apocalypsis of Paul*).[96] According to Eusebius the importance of traditions about special revelations of the risen Jesus to some disciples is confirmed by Clement of Alexandria in the seven books of the *Hypotyposes:* "The Lord after his resurrection imparted knowledge to James the Just and to John and Peter, and they imparted it to the rest of the apostles, and the rest of the apostles to the seventy, of whom Barnabas was one."[97]

If we consider that the Gospel according to Luke could have been read independently of Acts, the open ending of Luke 24:51a read without v. 51b (as well as the plural "days" of the ascension in Luke 9:51) was likely to be connected in certain early Christian memories with other oral traditions about special revelations given by Jesus to the disciples between the resurrection and the ascension. Such a hypothesis is reinforced by two elements: first, the Gospel according to Luke was very popular in Gnostic circles, for example, among the Valentinians[98] and, second, the difficulties raised by the popularity of other special oral teachings of Jesus are clearly mentioned by Irenaeus in *A. H.* 3.2: "For [they allege] that the truth was not delivered by means of written documents, but *viva voce:* wherefore also Paul declared, 'But we speak wisdom among those that are perfect, but not the wisdom of this world' (1 Cor. 2:6)." This question is the starting point of Irenaeus's thinking that is developed in the third book of *Against Heresies,* precisely where he accords so much weight to the Lukan Acts in his understanding of early Christian history. Irenaeus thus confirms the importance of the struggle against these oral teachings for certain early Christians. Given such a proliferation of teachings it could have seemed wise to some Christians—in quite an early period—to add to Luke 24:51 the clear mention of Jesus' departure in order to present the scene as a definitive departure. The scribal tradition transmitted by P^{75} may be seen as testifying to such a reaction.

In conclusion, C. Kavin Rowe has shown that Lukan exegetes are in a waiting room associated with the question of readers and reception; Andrew F. Gregory has opened a door that enables us to move out of this room; and I have tried here to take a step out of the room by using the triad of the cultures of author, scribes, and readers. By referring to the plural "days of his taking up" in Luke 9:51, by leaving discrepancies between Luke 24:49–53 and Acts 1:2.13, the author created particularly favorable conditions for interaction between the written text and the collective memory relating to the scene of the ascension. Was this intentional or not? This is no longer a relevant question: we will never be able to get proof either way, unless we discover another text from the Lukan author commenting on his/her twofold work. What we do have are exemplars of Luke and Acts written by scribes-readers, and these exemplars attest to interactions between the variety of early Christian memories of the last scene on the Mount of Olives. Early Christian readers, such as Clement of Alexandria and Irenaeus, show in different ways that these interactions happened and continued for quite some time after the redaction of Luke-Acts, for as long as the Gospel according to Luke was able to be read with or without Acts. While authors and readers can quarrel endlessly about the interpretation of written speech—which "drifts all over the place . . . [and is] unable to defend or help itself" according to Plato—the scribe smiles in silence. Sitting in front of a papyrus the scribe writes the words and *makes* the text, listening in advance to Eco's words: "naturally, a manuscript."

NOTES

Many thanks are due to Jenny Read-Heimerdinger for revising the English version of this article.

1. C. Kavin Rowe, "History, Hermeneutics, and the Unity of Luke-Acts," in this volume, 43–65, 43 (first published in *JSNT* 28/2 [2005]: 132). Subsequent references are to this essay as it appears in this volume.

2. Now published as Claire Clivas, *L'ange et la sueur de sang (Lc 22, 43–44) ou comment on pourrait bien encore écrire l'histoire* (BiTS 7; Leuven: Peeters Press, 2010).

3. Ibid., 188–96.

4. See, for example, the works by Stephen Greenblatt (*Renaissance Self-Fashioning: From More to Shakespeare* [Chicago: University of Chicago Press, 1980]; and with Catherine Gallagher, *Practicing New Historicism* [Chicago: University of Chicago Press, 2000]); or Daniel Punday (*Narrative Bodies: Toward a Corporeal Narratology* [New York: Palgrave Macmillan, 2003]); as well as Umberto Eco's well-known *Lector in fabula. La cooperazione interpretativa nei testi narrativi* (Milan: Bompiani, 1985); or some recent suggestions for expressing the links between author, readers, and history such as those made by Jerome Meizoz (*Postures littéraires. Mises en scène modernes de l'auteur. Essai* [Genève: Slatkine, 2007]).

5. Patrick E. Spencer, "The Unity of Luke-Acts: A Four-Bolted Hermeneutical Hinge," *CBR* 5/3 (2007): 354.

6. Andrew F. Gregory, "The Reception of Luke and Acts and the Unity of Luke-Acts," in this volume, 91 (first published in *JSNT* 29/4 [2007]: 470). Subsequent references are to this essay as it appears in this volume.

7. Spencer, "The Unity," 356. He refers here to David P. Moessner, "'Managing' the Audience. Diodorus Siculus and Luke the Evangelist on Designing Authorial Intent," in *Luke and His Readers: Festschrift A. Denaux* (ed. R. Bieringer, Gilbert Van Belle, and Joseph Verheyden; BETL 182; Leuven: Leuven University Press and Peeters, 2005), 61–80.

8. Jean-Claude Mühlethaler, "Éloge de la variante: la clôture du *Testament* de Villon," in *Quant l'ung amy pour l'autre veille. Mélanges de moyen français offerts à Claude Thiry* (ed. Tania van Hemeleryck and Maria Colombo Timelli; Texte, Codex & Contexte, 5; Turnhout: Brepols, 2008), 437. He takes his title from Bernard Cerquiglini's *Éloge de la variante: Histoire critique de la philologie* (Paris: Éditions du Seuil, 1989), translated by Betsy Wing as *In Praise of the Variant: A Critical History of Philology* (Baltimore: Johns Hopkins University Press, 1999). See also Mühlethaler, "Eloge de la variante," 432: "Pourquoi ne ferions-nous pas nôtre [un] éloge de la variante? Si le point de vue du lecteur n'est pas aussi valorisé, dans notre culture, que celui de l'auteur, il a pourtant sa raison d'être. Un texte qui ne se prête pas à une lecture chaque fois renouvelée perdra vite tout intérêt et ne traversera pas les siècles. Dans le domaine musical, pour une pièce de théâtre, personne ne met en question la légitimité des différentes réalisations d'une œuvre."

9. Ibid., 437; English translation by Jenny Read-Heimerdinger.

10. See Gregory, "Reception," 89: "As Joseph Verheyden has observed, discussion on this matter is closed. . . . This need not mean, however, that hermeneutical questions that follow from agreement on the common authorship of these two texts are also closed." See also C. Kavin Rowe, "Literary Unity and Reception History: Reading Luke-Acts as Luke and Acts," in the volume, 75 (first published in *JSNT* 29/4 [2007]: 451).

11. Cod. D 06; Paris gr.107, written in the sixth century. Wilhelm Schneemelcher follows Adolf Jülicher in dating the canonical list from the fourth century (see Wilhelm Schneemelcher, ed., *New Testament Apocrypha* [vol. 1; trans. R. McL. Wilson; Westminster: John Knox Press, 2003], 37). He specifies that "it is widely assumed that here we have a Latin version of a Greek text of the third century; but this cannot be proved" (30).

12. See especially Rowe, "Literary Unity," 78. He also draws attention to the list of the *Apostolic Constitutions* ca. 85, but it is not a list in the same sense as the list included in the Codex Claromontaus.

13. See Schneemelcher, *New Testament Apocrypha*, 37.

14. See Claire Clivaz, "Reading Luke-Acts in Alexandria in the Second Century: From Clement to the Shadow of Apollos," in *Reading Acts in the Second Century* (ed. R. Ruben Dupertuis and Todd C. Penner; London: Equinox, forthcoming 2010).

15. See Johannes Leipoldt, *Geschichte des neutestamentlichen Kanons. Erster Teil. Die Entstehung* (Leipzig: J. C. Hinrichs'sche Buchhandlung, 1907), 200.

16. See Kurt Aland and Barbara Aland, *The Text of the New Testament* (Grand Rapids, Mich.: Eerdmans, 1989), 104. Unfortunately the Alands give three different dates for 0189 between the end of the second century and the beginning of the fourth: see pp. 57 and 76 (end of the second century / beginning of the third); p. 159 (third century); p. 104 (third/fourth, formerly assigned to the fourth century).

17. See Philip W. Comfort and David P. Barrett, eds., *The Text of the Earliest New Testament Greek Manuscripts* (Wheaton: Tyndale House, 2001), 643.

18. Rowe, "History, Hermeneutics," 47.

19. Markus Bockmuehl, "Why Not Let Acts Be Acts? In Conversation with C. Kavin Rowe," in this volume, 70–73 (first published in *JSNT* 28/2 [2005]: 163–64). Subsequent references are to this essay as it appears in this volume.

20. Graham N. Stanton, "The Fourfold Gospel," *NTS* 43/3 (1997): 335, cited by Rowe, "History, Hermeneutics," 47.

21. Rowe, "History, Hermeneutics," 47–48.

22. Gregory, "Reception," 86–87.

23. See Gregory, "Reception," 87.

24. See ibid., 90.

25. See Tiziano Dorandi, *Le stylet et la tablette dans le secret des auteurs antiques* (Paris: Belles Lettres, 2000), 104 and 115–16. Dorandi (115 n. 49) refers notably to Erwin Rohde (*Der griechische Roman und seine Vorläufer* [Leipzig: Breitkopf und Härtel, 1900], 327–29).

26. See Galen, *De propriis libris* prol. 1–16 and II, 6, for example. For a study of the question, see Claire Clivaz, "Peut-on parler de posture littéraire pour un auteur antique? Les exemples de Paul de Tarse, de Galien et des lecteurs du texte anonyme de l'Évangile selon Luc," *Contextes* (forthcoming 2010).

27. Two new manuscripts allowed Veronique Boudon-Millot to publish a complete edition of these texts in 2007: Véronique Boudon-Millot, ed., *Galien. Introduction générale. Sur l'ordre de ses propres livres. Sur ses propres livres. Que l'excellent médecin est aussi philosophe* (vol. 1; Paris: Belles Lettres, 2007).

28. See Boudon-Millot, *Galien,* XCIX.

29. See ibid., CXV–CXVI; for the list of Galen's works included in this "Alexandrian canon," cf. ibid., CXVIII–CXX.

30. Luke 1:3.

31. See Loveday C. A. Alexander, "What If Luke Had Never Met Theophilus?" *Biblical Interpretation* 8 (2000): 163; she adds that Luke "does not claim such direct inspiration for his own writing." Julie Paik, my research assistant, suggests that this addition could have been influenced by Acts 15:28: ἔδοξεν γὰρ τῷ πνεύματι τῷ ἁγίῳ καὶ ἡμῖν. Be that as it may, the narrative context of Acts 15:28—the letter from the apostles and elders in Jerusalem—demonstrates that the dual authorship Spirit/humans serves to reinforce the authority of a text.

32. Gregory, "Reception," 90.

33. Rowe, "Literary Unity," 77.

34. See Clivaz, *L'ange et la sueur de sang (Lc 22, 43–44),* 179–81.

35. See the monograph of Daniel Marguerat, *La première histoire du christianisme: Les Actes des apôtres* (Lectio Divina 180; 2d ed.; Genève: Labor et Fides, 2003). In the English title the "first history" becomes the "first historian": Daniel Marguerat, *The First Christian Historian: Writing the "Acts of the Apostles"* (trans. Ken McKinney, Gregory J. Laughery, and Richard Bauckham; Cambridge: Cambridge University Press, 2002).

36. See Clivaz, "Reading Luke-Acts in Alexandria in the Second Century," forthcoming.

37. See *1 Clement* 5.5–7.

38. Spencer, "The Unity of Luke-Acts," 356.

39. See Gregory, "Reception," 87: "The modern scholarly approach to Luke-Acts, which reads each volume in the light of the other and consciously excludes reference to other texts, is . . . something of a novelty in the reception of Luke-Acts."

40. See Henry J. Cadbury, *The Making of Luke-Acts* (New York: Macmillan, 1927), 11. The fact is underlined, for example, by Marguerat, *La première histoire du christianisme,* 67, and Spencer, "The Unity," 342.

41. Spencer, "The Unity," 342.

42. See Cadbury, *The Making of Luke-Acts,* 1: "Hyphenated compounds are not typographically beautiful or altogether congenial to the English language, but in order to emphasize the historic unity of the two volumes addressed to Theophilus the expression 'Luke-Acts' is perhaps justifiable."

43. Ibid., 1.

44. Ibid., 133.

45. He speaks also about a "convenient rubric" (see ibid., 132).

46. Talbert inaugurated the quest for the *literary classification* of Luke-Acts (see, for example, Charles H. Talbert, *Literary Patterns, Theological Themes and the Genre of Luke-Acts* [SBLMS 20; Missoula, Mont.: SBL and Scholars Press, 1974], 126).

47. Marianne Palmer Bonz, *The Past as Legacy: Luke-Acts and Ancient Epic* (Minneapolis: Fortress, 2000), 2, quoting Cadbury, *The Making of Luke-Acts,* 133; I have highlighted the difference with italics.

48. See for example Paul Aron, Denis Saint-Jacques, Alain Viala, and Marie-Andrée Beaudet, eds., *Le Dictionnaire du Littéraire* (Paris: PUF, 2002), 265. For a history of the relationship between history and the notion of "genre," see Clivaz, *L'ange et la sueur de sang,* 17–33.

49. Cadbury, *The Making of Luke-Acts,* 136.

50. Ibid., 1: "An attempt to bring fresh light on part of the New Testament requires no apology. Whatever else one may think of that volume, it is at least the most widely distributed of publications. Its circulation in our generation has already reached many million copies per annum. Month after month the New Testament in all its forms, with additions or subtractions, invariably heads all lists of best sellers, fiction or non-fiction. Doubtless it is not always read when received, nor heard when read, nor heeded when heard. It obtains, nevertheless, a vast amount of attention of all kinds throughout Christendom."

51. See ibid., 133–34.

52. Loveday C. A. Alexander, "Fact, Fiction, and the Genre of Acts," *NTS* 44 (1998): 394.

53. See Cadbury, *The Making of Luke-Acts,* 300.

54. See Alexander, "Fact, Fiction," 394: "In ancient literature it is evident that the conventional markers of factuality (in any genre) were easily—and regularly—subverted."

55. See ibid., 397.

56. For a presentation of genre as a category of reception, see especially Marielle Macé, *Le genre littéraire: introduction, choix de textes, commentaires, vade-mecum et bibliographie* (Paris: Flammarion, 2004).

57. See Vernon K. Robbins, *The Tapestry of Early Christian Discourse: Rhetoric, Society and Ideology* (London: Routledge, 1996) and *Exploring the Texture of the Texts: A Guide to Socio-Rhetorical Interpretation* (Valley Forge, Pa.: Trinity Press International, 1996).

58. See F. Gerald Downing, "Le problème du choix de l'intertexte: Paul s'oppose-t-il radicalement ou superficiellement à la culture de son temps?" in *Intertextualités. La Bible en échos* (ed. Daniel Marguerat and Adrian Curtis; *MoBi* 40; Genève: Labor et Fides, 2000), 237.

59. Gérard Genette, *Introduction à l'architexte* (Paris: Seuil, 1979), 90. Genette does not isolate two modes—intertextuality and hypertextuality—as Marguerat and Curtis propose (see Marguerat and Curtis, *Intertextualités,* 7).

60. See Downing, "Le problème du choix," 250 and 238.

61. See John A. Darr, "Discerning the Lukan Voice: The Narrator as Character in Luke-Acts," in *Society of Biblical Literature 1992 Seminar Papers* (ed. Eugene H. Lovering; Atlanta: Scholars Press, 1992), 259.

62. Plato, *Phaedrus* 275e and 276a.

63. Plato, *Theaetetus* 175d.

64. See Clivaz, *L'ange et la sueur de sang,* 188–96

65. See Alain Rabatel, "Point de vue et polyphonie dans les textes narratifs," in *Lire, écrire le point de vue: un apprentissage de la lecture littéraire* (ed. Philippe de Vita and Alain Rabatel; Lyon: Scérén-CRDP Académie de Lyon, 2002), 11.

66. See Punday, *Narrative Bodies,* 9; Zoltán Kövecses, *Metaphor and Emotion: Language, Culture, and Body in Human Feeling* (Cambridge: Cambridge University Press; Paris: Éditions de la Maison des Sciences de l'Homme, 2000), 185.

67. For the issue of the archive, see Jacques Derrida, *Archive Fever: A Freudian Impression* (trans. Eric Prenowitz; Chicago: University of Chicago Press, 1998).

68. These words introduce *The Name of the Rose,* preceding the preface on a non-numbered page (first English translation by William Weaver, Orlando: Harcourt Brace, 1983).

69. See Eldon Jay Epp, "The Ascension in the Textual Tradition of Luke-Acts," in *Perspectives on New Testament Textual Criticism: Collected Essays, 1962–2004* (ed. Eldon Jay Epp; NovTSup 116; Leiden and Boston: Brill, 2005), 211–25.

70. See for a list David C. Parker, *The Living Text of the Gospels* (Cambridge: Cambridge University Press, 1997), 149–50: Matt. 9:34; 21:44; Mark 2:22; 14:39; Luke 5:39; 10:41–42; 12:19, 21, 39; 22:19–20; 22:62; 24:3, 6, 12, 36, 40, 51, 52; John 3:32; 4:9.

71. See Kurt Aland, "Die Bedeutung des P75 für den Text des Neuen Testaments. Ein Beitrag zur Frage der Western non-interpolations," in *Studien zur Überlieferung des Neuen Testaments und seines Textes* (ed. Kurt Aland; *ANT* 2; Berlin: Walter de Gruyter, 1967), 158.

72. I use quotation marks in speaking about the "Western" textual tradition or text, according to Epp's suggestion (see Eldon Jay Epp, "Notes to Readers," in Epp, *Perspectives on New Testament Textual Criticism,* xxv–xxvi and 225).

73. See Mikeal C. Parsons, "A Christological Tendency in P75," *JBL* 105/3 (1986): 463–79.

74. See James Ronald Royse, *Scribal Habits in Early Greek New Testament Papyri* (Leiden and Boston: Brill, 2008), 698–703.

75. See Bart D. Ehrman, *The Orthodox Corruption of Scripture: The Effect of Early Christological Controversies on the Text of the New Testament* (New York and Oxford: Oxford University Press, 1993), 187–94.

76. See Michael Wade Martin, "Defending the 'Western Non-Interpolations': The Case for an Anti-Separationist *Tendenz* in the Longer Alexandrian Readings," *JBL* 124/2 (2005): 269–94, esp. 286. For a definition of the separationism see Ehrman, *The Orthodox Corruption,* 14: "Other Christians agreed with the adoptionists that Jesus was a full flesh and blood human and that something significant had happened to him at his baptism. For them, however, it was not that he was adopted to be God's Son; instead, at his baptism Jesus seemed to be indwelt by God. . . . This is a Christology that I will label separationist, because it posits a division between the man Jesus and the divine Christ. As we will see, it is a view that was prevalent among second-century Gnostics."

77. See Martin, "Defending the 'Western Non-Interpolations,'" 273.

78. See ibid., 286.

79. Ibid.

80. The Nestle-Aland 27 indicates a *crux deseparationis* for א* here. But a look at the manuscript on page 47b (verso) shows that Luke 24:51b stands clearly in the upper margin as a correction by another hand. See http://www.csntm.org/Manuscripts/GA%2001/GA01_047b.jpg

81. See Aland, "Die Bedeutung des P75," 158.

82. Martin, "Defending the 'Western Non-Interpolations,'" 272 n. 15.

83. See Irenaeus, *A.H.,* 1.10.1, line 10.

84. See Epp, "The Ascension," 211–25.

85. Ibid., 220.

86. Ibid., 225.

87. See ibid., 220.

88. See ibid., 216, for a detailed presentation of the manuscript data on Acts 1:2.

89. See ibid., 217.

90. D, it and sy[s] do not have the *proskunèsis* of the disciples before Jesus in Luke 24:52: καὶ ἐγένετο ἐν τῷ εὐλογεῖν αὐτὸν αὐτοὺς ἀπέστη ἀπ᾽ αὐτῶν, καὶ αὐτοὶ ὑπέστρεψαν εἰς Ἰερουσαλὴμ μετὰ χαρᾶς μεγάλης (Luke 24:51–52).

91. Jesus will not return to the disciples after the definitive farewell scene of Acts 1:6–11 if it is read as an extended doubling of Luke 24:50–52.

92. On a narrative level several other elements distinguish both scenes (see Claire Clivaz, "Douze noms pour une main: nouveaux regards sur Judas à partir de Lc 22.21–22," *NTS* 48/3 [2002]: 413–14).

93. Modern readers have also tried to harmonize these data by understanding the ὑπερῷον as a room in the temple (see, for example, Joes Rius-Camp and Jenny Read-Heimerdinger, *The Message of Acts in Codex Bezae: A Comparison with the Alexandrian Tradition.* Vol. 1. *Acts 1.1–5.42: Jerusalem* [ed. Josep Rius-Camps and Jenny Read-Heimerdinger; JSNTSup 257; London and New York: T & T Clark, 2004], 101 n. 88).

94. The issue is relevant also to D, which reads ὁ ἀναλημφθείς in Acts 1:11.

95. For a complete presentation of this question, see Clivaz, *L'ange et la sueur de sang,* 400–412.

96. Anne Boud'hors, "Éloge de Jean-Baptiste," in *Écrits apocryphes chrétiens 1* (ed. François Bovon and Pierre Geoltrain; Paris: Gallimard, 1997), 1571.

97. Clement of Alexandria, quoted in Eusebius, *Hist. Eccl.* 2:1, 2–4.

98. See Andrew F. Gregory, *The Reception of Luke and Acts in the Period before Irenaeus: Looking for Luke in the Second Century* (WUNT 2/169; Tübingen: Mohr Siebeck, 2003), 83: there is "a compelling cumulative case for Valentinian use of Luke"; Valentinians may present "the earliest evidence for a commentary on Luke."

A CANONICAL APPROACH TO THE UNITY OF ACTS AND LUKE'S GOSPEL

Robert W. Wall

The purpose of the present study is to commend a different approach to the question of the unity of Luke and Acts: namely an approach that seeks to retrieve its primary cues for defining the nature of their unity from the location of their initial reception and use as Scripture and from the phenomenology of a canonical process that divided Acts from Luke's Gospel to perform different roles within the final (that is, canonical) redaction of the New Testament.

Let me begin with an extended observation to frame this canonical approach. While the critical analysis of a narrative's literary texture and historical setting is an extraordinarily complex project, the epistemic demands we typically insinuate upon this hard work can complicate matters. In particular modernity's mythology of originality has shaped the standard approach to a biblical text that seeks after *the* meaning most likely intended by its author and apprehended as such by his audience. This "original" meaning, then, serves as the regulatory norm to measure the validity of any subsequent meaning, especially to protect the text's author from his self-serving interpreters.[1]

The powerful impress of this interpretive axiom, along with the methodological interests that facilitate it, has influenced most academic readers of the Lukan original. Henry J. Cadbury's invention of a "Luke-Acts" is the historian's observation of a single storyteller's production of a continuous narrative shaped by his particular theological grammar and historical circumstance. But once this observation is upgraded by the epistemic importance now given to an author's original, Cadbury's Luke-Acts is transformed into a powerful exegetical imperative: the very question of the "truth" of Luke and Acts demands that one study them together according to the reconstructed intentions of the story's presumptive author.[2] Tricky business, that, with so little evidence in hand!

Of course the unity of Luke and Acts conceived by the intentions of a single storyteller has been challenged from the sidelines all along. Richard I. Pervo, for example, has famously argued against their literary unity, linking Acts with the novel genre of antiquity—very different in form and function from a gospel genre.

But his study is exceptional; and recent literary and historical studies have only confirmed a unified Lukan narrative, theological program, and social location; and a range of studies has even extended Cadbury's preliminary conclusion to understand better the interconnections between Luke and Acts and between Luke-Acts and contemporary Jewish and Hellenistic traditions.

What must be said, if only for the sake of clarification, is that a canonical approach to the study of Luke and Acts need not deny this rigorous historical criticism, with all its ancillary implications. The confirmation of a "Luke-Acts," however, envisages only one kind of literary unity that depends upon certain agreements about the nature of the text itself—that is, the ancient production of a single storyteller for Theophilus. Even a historical reconstruction of this Lukan original that posits considerable distance of time and circumstance between the two volumes, although subverting any sense of their chronological unity, need not problematize the more essential claim of a narrative unity intended by the author.

Nonetheless, the effect of the church's shaping of its authoritative writings into a single biblical canon creates another kind of literary aesthetic. In this case different writings are placed together long after they are written to form a coherent and unified whole that facilitates a range of religious practices for different audiences unintended by their authors and unimagined by their first readers. Even though what I propose should not be considered a substitute for the critical constructions (or deconstructions) of a Luke-Acts, I would argue that the origins of a canonical Luke within the bounds of a fourfold gospel (rather than as Luke-Acts) and of a canonical Acts that entered the New Testament in the company of a collection of Catholic Epistles (rather than as Acts-Luke) compels the biblical interpreter to exploit the importance of this later moment when books were received by new and different audiences in their canonical form to unify the faith of "one holy catholic and apostolic church."[3]

In fact one may responsibly argue that any reconstruction of Luke's intentions in producing Luke-Acts for Theophilus may actually be less relevant to the contemporary reader than those ecclesial intentions and interpretive practices at work during the formation of the New Testament canon—which is, after all, the principal setting in which present readers receive Luke and Acts. What this reception history narrates is a kind of metamorphosis during which an authored text intended for a particular audience in the past is "transformed" into a canonical text for future audiences of readers. Luke Timothy Johnson's dismissal of evidence from the second and third century reception of a canonical Acts as irrelevant to the present discussion because it "does not answer the question of how the first readers might have read and understood Luke's writing"[4] exemplifies the reductionism of modern criticism that freezes a Lukan original in its past without admitting that it underwent substantive postproduction changes, not so much of plotline or material content but of readerly performances that cohere to the church's intentions for its biblical rule of faith. The dynamic textual history of Acts during the second century, climaxed by its posthumous publication, not only makes it difficult if not impossible to recover the Lukan original, it makes it equally difficult to dismiss the second century of Acts (and also of Luke) as unimportant.

This is especially so if Acts did not reach its final literary form until late in the second century and in an edited version more suitable for an ongoing role within the emergent Christian biblical canon to help secure the apostolic legacy of "authentic" Christianity against a variety of external and internal threats.[5] The most important early manuscripts (for example, majuscules 01–04, 1739 ms. family) not only confirm that Acts is detached from Luke from the very beginning but that it combined with a collection of Catholic Epistles to form the so-called *Apostolos* for circulation within the Eastern church to help correct a misguided use of the extant Pauline canon in support of a *sola fideism*.[6] The placement of the *Apostolos* prior to the Pauline canon in many early canon lists did not intend to displace Paul's priority within the church—the extensive use of Pauline writings within earliest Christianity make this very clear—but rather sought to frame the church's appropriation of the Pauline witness in a manner that cohered to the apostolic Rule of Faith.[7] In fact one may reasonably infer from the suggestive title given to this new literary creation, *Apostolos,* that a secondary purpose of its circulation was to correct an overly determined Paulinism instantiated in some second-century communities, not only by placing Jerusalem at the epicenter of its narrative world, but also by placing the Paul of Acts outside the bounds of the church's apostolate (cf. Acts 1:21–22).[8]

In this sense, perhaps the phenomenology of the canonical process may be thought of as a type of evolutionary mechanism. That is, new external threats present by the mid-second century and on the horizon, a change of audiences, new responsibilities that come on line to meet the internal pressures of an expanding religious movement, all forge a different ecclesial environment than Luke's to which Luke-Acts must be adapted in order for its story to survive. Put positively, subsequent readers of Acts, such as Irenaeus and Tertullian, found its narrative readily adaptable to this new environment. Again my argument is that the church's preservation, canonization (even if in edited form), and continuing use of Acts, whether in its preaching or catechesis, is predicated on the adaptability of its narrative plotline to the social and religious exigencies facing the "one holy catholic and apostolic church."

The definition of a canonical unity, different from an authorial unity, regards an alternate set of textual relationships created by the formation of the New Testament canon. Acts is separated from Luke but remains related to the fourfold gospel in which Luke is one member; and Acts is placed before two different collections of apostolic letters, Pauline and Pillars, to sound their introductory note within the biblical canon (see below). But this expansive textual unity forged by the canonical process aims at the enduring unity of the church catholic. Toward this religious end, surely the particular roles Luke intended Luke-Acts to perform for Theophilus, hinted at in Luke 1:4, are still in play for a canonical Acts, if now on a more global stage. But the church's intentions for its Scripture are different from the author's intentions for his narrative. The purpose of the present essay is to suggest what these "canonical intentions" for Acts are and how they guide the interpreter's approach into its narrative world.

THE RECEPTION OF ACTS AS SCRIPTURE

Recent studies of the precanonical reception history of Acts by Christopher N. Mount and Andrew F. Gregory are invaluable for recalibrating the relationship of Acts to Luke.[9] The central character in this historical narrative is Irenaeus who uses Acts in his polemics against so-called heresies to formulate a normative account of Christian origins. This initial use of Acts as Scripture more than any other single episode in its early *Wirkungsgeschichte* defines its subsequent role within the biblical canon.

In fact, in Mount's words, "the canonical status of Acts is the result of a late second-century apologetic for a certain form of Christianity."[10] That is, Mount understands Irenaeus's reception of Acts in relationship to the origins of Pauline Christianity, and this well suits modernity's (and especially Protestantism's) disposition to read Acts with the Pauline letters. But this move is contrary to the reception of Acts immediately following Irenaeus, which read Acts with the Catholic Epistles corpus. While Irenaeus gives no indication that he knew of the *Apostolos,* which belongs to a later stage of the canonical process in any case, he does pay considerable attention to the traditions of the Jerusalem pillars in his commentary on Acts. Of course he is mostly interested to underwrite the theological unity between the three gospels associated with the Jerusalem apostles (and by implication their "letters"[11] and the one marginal gospel linked by tradition to Paul (Luke's Gospel). The unity of a fourfold gospel tradition is not only against those who use Paul/Luke for heretical ends but against any who privilege a single gospel over its fourfold articulation; a myopia that privileges only a single apostolic tradition tends toward unprofitable ends. The central feature of Irenaeus's apologia is for the unity of a diverse fourfold whole. Acts plots a narrative of apostolic succession from a common christological fount to defend the theological unity and religious authority of a fourfold "gospels of the apostles."

The Rhetorical Design of *Against Heresies*

The design of Irenaeus's commentary on Acts in Book 3 of *Against Heresies* develops two important themes. First his commentary on the plotline of Acts is shaped by the passing exigencies of his social world and is *polemical* against the perceived "heresies" of particular people or groups—for example, Marcion, Valentinus, the Ebionites, and other second-century Gnostic movements within the church. While his reading of Acts provides us with an excellent example of patristic exegesis, his commentary hardly has normative value for the church's future. In fact we might judge his reading of Acts deficient and that other readings of Acts, especially related to James's role at the so-called Jerusalem Council (Acts 15:13–29; cf. 21:21–26), should be substituted for his. But then, second, Irenaeus's commentary is also *typological* of a way of thinking about the church's different apostolic traditions (especially Pauline and Jerusalem "pillars") in a manner that unifies them by agreement with the apostolic Rule of Faith (= RF), by common succession from the same christological fount, and in service of a common missionary purpose by virtue of a common spiritual authority derived from God. This typological appropriation of Acts had continuing purchase during the canonical process and has come even to us as a means to clarify the discrete role of Acts within the New Testament canon.

Irenaeus's Reading of Acts as Typological of the Unity between Epistolary Corpora

When read as typological of a book's continuing authority, Irenaeus's use of Acts stipulates two interrelated criteria and proffers a reading strategy that insures the book's religious profit margin that shaped the hermeneutics of the canonical process.[12] In particular it is Irenaeus's typological use of Acts (rather than his exegesis) that illumines the motive for placing Acts with the Catholic Epistles collection during the canonical process to regulate its formation and underwrite its inclusion in the New Testament canon.

The first criterion is that the substance of a book/person/tradition's teaching must cohere to the church's Rule of Faith. The second criterion, related logically to the first by Irenaeus, is that a book/person/tradition to which an appeal is made must be linked to an apostle—since the Rule of Faith comes to the catholic church from Jesus through his apostolic successors. For example, Luke's Gospel has authority despite its marginal status and use by heretic groups because of his connection with Paul. Acts upholds the religious importance of Paul for the future of the church, not only because of his Damascus Road visitation from the risen Jesus but also because of his unity in purpose and proclamation with the apostolic successors to Jesus. That is, Luke is Paul's successor who is successor to the apostles who are successors to Jesus—a succession authorized by God and imbued with the Spirit's presence. What is interesting here is that "apostolicity" is defined differently than in Acts 1:21–22, since spiritual authority is granted even to those early Christian leaders outside the apostolate, such as James and Paul—clearly a contested point even into the third century. In any case the "succession" of a Christian leader to the risen Christ underwrites the continuity of both purpose and unity of proclamation of the tradition he founded. Orthodoxy and apostolicity—so far, so good.

But herein lies the great deceit (or conceit) of heresy-making: "heresies" are clothed in ecclesial respectability, if not a presumptive theological superiority (!) by appeal to a *particular* apostle. Using his definition of Christian unity constructed by his reading of Acts, Irenaeus points out that the content and performance of any book linked to a particular apostolic tradition will be necessarily distorted because of its inherent theological myopia. The issue at stake is not so much whether a teacher appeals to an authorized "apostolic" tradition—to the memory of early Christian leaders or to their collected writings. All "heretics" did. The problem as Irenaeus understands it is that no one tradition must be used to the exclusion of all others. I would submit that this issues in a definition of canonicity predicated on notions of apostolic succession and Christian unity that assume all apostolic traditions work together in forming a completed whole greater than the sum of its particular parts. Stated in negative terms, the use of a single tradition is more easily distorted for lack of balance and incomplete revelation. Thus Marcion's use of a "mutilated" version of Luke's Gospel (even though it may have only been an earlier recension to the one used in Irenaeus's church—see Gregory) is not so much what he has edited out but that he does not use it as part of a fourfold gospel whole—the number four symbolizing holism to make this very point. Likewise, Marcion's appropriation of an incomplete Pauline canon is not so much that it is incomplete (without Pastorals, Philemon) but that in drawing upon only Luke and Paul he rejected a complete "gospels of the apostles." Irenaeus objects to a theological myopia that appeals to one particular apostolic tradition as normative to the exclusion of all the others.

While we should leave open the real possibility that such theological myopia is not intentional (the result of a conscious editing of tradition) but rather a reflection of an inchoaic canon, Irenaeus also claims that the appeal to a single tradition is often set in adversarial relation with others, thus subverting Christian unity. By quick survey of *Against Heresies,* Marcionists appealed to Paul against the Jerusalem pillars, the Montanists to John rather than to Matthew, various Gnostic/Libertine groups to Paul and John, the so-called Ebionites and other Jewish groups to James the Just (that is, to the memory of his renown piety but not yet to the Book of James which is never cited in the pseudowritings of these Jacobean groups) against Paul, and so forth.[13] This observation in turn infers an interpretive practice that resists the myopia that attaches itself to one particular apostolic tradition to the exclusion of other authorized apostolic traditions. The roots of heresy are not found in the attenuation of the apostolic tradition per se in teaching and worship; rather, it is in the privileging of one tradition above all others from which heresy springs. The use of a pluriform collection (for example, fourfold gospel), all parts of which cohere to the Rule of Faith and are linked to apostolic tradition, protects the church against theological myopia and thus heresy.

What is forged by Irenaeus's polemics is a positive *typos* of theological unity according to which every single biblical tradition is united by a common regard for the Rule of Faith. No matter to what religious tradition an appeal is made, if that tradition is apostolic, then what is expected is essential coherence with the received teachings of Jesus. But also forged is a negative definition of unity so that a departure from the Truth is not only the rejection of the Rule of Faith per se; it is also the result of considering only a single apostolic tradition to the exclusion of the full complement of apostolic traditions. In this sense, then, ecclesial unity is defined by a plurality that forges, in James A. Sanders's phrase, a "self-correcting, mutually-informing apparatus."[14] Thus the unity of the apostolic traditions is another way of speaking of its completeness, of the complementarity of its different strands (not of the harmonizing *Tendenz* of patristic hermeneutics that François Bovon claims).[15] The value of Acts is that it allowed Irenaeus to speak of the incompleteness of any single apostolic tradition that is used without benefit of all the others that draw from a common christological source and bear witness to a single Rule of Faith. By the end of the canonical process, then, the placement of Acts to bridge the four "gospels of the apostles" and their various epistolary writings envisages a dynamic and pluriform catholicity and subverts any attempt to single out one particular text or one particular teaching as normative for the whole church. All Scripture is analogical of the Rule of Faith, and it is that apostolic canon and not any one apostolic tradition that plumbs the meaning made of any biblical text.

THE PERFORMANCE OF ACTS AS SCRIPTURE

One of the most important questions raised by a canonical approach to Acts is: What do Luke's reasons for producing a sequel for Theophilus have to do with the church's reasons for publishing Acts as Scripture? A response to this question will help envisage more clearly the added-value dimension of canonical readings; the interpreter who does not deny what is already learned about Luke's Acts will still want to calibrate an approach to the canonical Acts that seeks to bridge these two interpretive horizons.[16] What follows is a series of reflections that illustrates what I have in mind.

1. Reading Acts as Scripture recognizes the importance of different literary relationships within the New Testament. The intracanonical relationships between Acts and the fourfold gospel and between Acts and the following two collections of letters (especially Pauline) are elevated in importance within the canonical context. The "canon-logic" envisaged by the arrangement of the different parts within

the New Testament whole, and sometimes even of individual writings within these canonical parts, stipulates important markers in guiding the reader's approach to the New Testament. According to this arrangement, then, the fourfold gospel (and not just the Third) is perceived as prerequisite reading for the study of Acts, and the study of Acts under the Gospel's light is then prerequisite reading for the study of the letters that follow. The implications of this canon-logic are teased out below.

2. These new intracanonical relationships forged by the canonical process are also of importance when assessing the distinctive importance of the theology of Acts within the New Testament. No longer does the biblical theologian consider the thematic interests of Acts only in terms of their congruence with those found in Luke's Gospel; rather the theological contribution that Acts makes to *biblical* theology is now measured as an indispensable part of an integral whole. Put in different words, upon consideration of the various theologies that make up the New Testament's entire theological conception, the interpreter is now pressed to imagine what a fully biblical witness to God might actually lack if not inclusive of Acts. Even more specifically, what distorted idea of the church's faith, its religious or social identity, or of its vocation in the world might result from a conversation with a body of sacred writings that did not include this book? What thin reading of the Pauline letters would result if the interpreter failed to prep herself by first reading the story of the canonical Paul of Acts? Simply put, reading Acts within its biblical setting reminds us that any theological understanding lacking the witness of Acts will distort Christian faith and life.

3. The Paul of Acts is valued more keenly from this canonical perspective than when his role is reduced to a cameo appearance in the modern quest of the historical Paul. At stake in following the story of the Paul of Acts is not so much the historical accuracy of Luke's portrait—even though this is currently being retouched—or even the important questions about his credibility within earliest Christianity. The most important issues from a canonical angle of vision are theological ones: that is, what does the Paul of Acts have to say about the future of the church and how does his story in Acts orient its readers to the implied author of the Pauline letters that follow and to the Pauline witness they enshrine?

4. The church's conflict with the synagogue at the end of the canonical process was no doubt different from Luke's assessment when he wrote Acts. What began as an intramural "Jewish problem" had become a "Judaism problem" by the end of the second century. Keen competition had developed between two "world religions," made all the more prickly by their common history and theological conception. The scribal emendations of the Western version of Acts, with a more negative characterization of unrepentant Israel, may well reflect the canonizing community's heightened sensitivity to its relationship with Judaism and its sense of the biblical canon's function to delineate the church's identity as

clearly as possible. In a different sense the portrait of Israel found in Acts clarifies the real difference between Christianity and Judaism in christological rather than in nationalistic or ethnocentric terms. Thus Acts subverts any "Christian" prejudice against Jews either on ethnic grounds (anti-Semitism) or on the mistaken presumption that God has reneged on promises made to historic Israel according to the Scriptures or that God has replaced Jews with Christians in the economy of salvation. God's faithfulness to Israel remains inviolate; therefore, today's church must become more Jewish, not less so, in order to be fully Christian in its worship and witness.

5. The "primitivism" of Acts simply reflects the ecclesial experience of the earliest church, which fashioned itself after the Diaspora synagogues and other voluntary organizations of the Roman world. Worship consisted of prayer meetings and teaching, with Christian fellowship centered in the homes of middle-class believers. The sociology of the church dramatically changed during the canonical process; these loosely confederated house-congregations became in time participants of an emerging church catholic. For this reason the ongoing interest in the images and ideas of "church" in Acts should be posited more squarely on its missionary vocation and prophetic message, its resurrection practices, and the nature of spiritual leadership—important claims on any congregation in every age—rather than replicating outward forms of governance and worship or other time-conditioned practices.

6. In this regard, reading Acts as Scripture seeks to insinuate its narrative world upon the changing "real" worlds of current readers. New layers of meaning hitherto hidden are discovered whenever sacred texts are allowed to penetrate and interpret the world of its interpreters. For example, contemporary readers will more easily discern the relevance of the Ethopian eunuch's story (see 8:26–40) for reflecting upon the relationship between the church and its homosexual members; or the example of Priscilla in Acts 18, along with other women of Acts, as role models for prophetic ministry in congregations that once were reluctant to encourage women in ministry. The vivid snapshots of the community of goods or repeated episodes that depict Paul's relations with Rome may challenge today's congregations away from civil religion or prosperity gospels and toward a more prophetic understanding of church as counterculture. By inclining its readers in this direction Acts provides an important element of a wider "canonical context" in which the faithful community gathers to reflect on those issues that either undermine or underwrite God's presence in today's world.

7. Finally, reading Acts as Scripture cultivates a fresh sense of sacred time and space. The church continues to live in "the last days," betwixt Pentecost and Parousia, when the Spirit of God empowers Christ's disciples to bear witness to the resurrection throughout the world in anticipation of God's coming triumph and creation's final restoration (see 3:20–21). The continuing authority of the

Book of Acts is to form a church that proclaims God's word and embodies a witness to its truth to herald that coming day.

THE PERFORMANCE OF ACTS WITHIN SCRIPTURE

When the New Testament Acts is received and studied within the context of the entire biblical canon (rather than as the sequel to Luke's Gospel), the reader will more naturally reflect upon the narrative as continuing Scripture's plotline of Israel's Old Testament story and Jesus' gospel story. Within its present canonical setting the sense of Acts 1:1's evocative phrase, "all that Jesus began to do and teach," is made plain by the amplified and enriched story of Jesus in the fourfold (rather than just the Third) gospel. Besides being made more alert to the importance of Israel's Scripture that Acts constantly quotes or echoes, this approach also fills in the profile of key characters that populate the narrative world of Acts. For example, the reader is better prepared to acknowledge the role performed by the Spirit-filled Peter in the opening of Acts as successor to the now departed Jesus as leader of his messianic community—a role for which the Third Gospel does not adequately prepare the reader of Acts. The Fourth Gospel provides the better seam by its concluding story of Peter's spiritual rehabilitation and the Lord's farewell injunction to his to "feed the flock" (John 21:15–17). Moreover, the reception of the Spirit promised in Jesus' farewell discourse (John 14–16) shapes the reader's anticipation of the Pentecostal community of Acts.

The relationship between the canonical Acts and the two collections of New Testament letters, while considerably more strategic in the history of interpretation, is more difficult for the interpreter to arrange: the preface to Acts signals a continuity with the gospel and the conventions of narrative literature differ from those of epistolary literature. For these reasons the differences between Acts and the following letters may seem more apparent to the reader. For example, the Paul of Acts is sometimes at odds with Paul's own self-understanding or missionary agenda evinced in the Pauline letters; neither does Luke characterize Paul as a letter writer or quote extensively from any of Paul's letters.[17] Reading Acts by the church's intentions for its biblical canon, however, would seem to compel a less adversarial relationship between the Paul of Acts and the epistolary Paul.

The potential gains of this approach to Paul may be illustrated when considering the textual seam that weaves together the final snapshot in Acts of Paul in Rome (see 28:17–31) and the opening words of Paul to the Romans, which taken together introduce biblical readers to a missionary-minded apostle who is "eager to proclaim the gospel to you also who are in Rome" (Rom. 1:15).[18] The interplay between the ending of Acts and Romans underwrites the orienting concern of a *canonical* Paul, who is not found in a secluded study writing dense Christian theology but on the city streets or in the living rooms of rented apartments relating the Christian gospel to life in practical and persuasive ways.

In this regard, among the most important roles a canonical Acts performs is to introduce the Bible's readers to the implied authors of the New Testament letters. While the historical reliability of these portraits is contested, the portraits convey a sense of their moral and religious authority that cultivates a high regard for the truth and importance of their letters for the future formation of their faithful readers. After all, these readers are the intended audience of canonical texts. In any case the salient issue that shapes Acts' narrative of Christianity's expansion into pagan territory, which is narrated with great optimism, is not its use as a historical resource but as a theological source that contributes to the church's ongoing understanding of its vocation and identity in the real world.

Acts also cultivates a sense of the personal relationships of the authors of the New Testament letters and in doing so provides a distinctive angle into the nature of the literary relationships between the Pauline and pillars letters. Similarities and dissimilarities in emphasis and theological conception found when comparing the two letter collections may actually correspond to the manner by which Acts narrates the negotiations between the reports from different missions, and of the theological convictions and social conventions required by each (for example, Acts 2:42–47; 9:15–16; 11:1–18; 12:17; 15:1–29; 21:17–26). The relations between James and Paul or between Peter and James as depicted at strategic moments in the plotline of Acts are generally collaborative rather than adversarial and frame the interpreter's approach to their biblical writings as essentially complementary (even though certainly not uniform and sometimes in conflict) in both meaning and function. If the critical consensus for a late-first-century date of Acts is accepted, which is roughly contemporaneous with the earliest, precanonical stage in the formation of the New Testament,[19] then it is likely that its collection of portraitures of early Christian leaders provides an important explanatory model for assessing the relationship between (and even within) the two emergent collections of canonical letters: The form and function of these Christian writings and their relationship to each other is another articulation of the early church's sense of the more collaborative relationship between their individual people and interpretative traditions, which is reflected then in the Book of Acts. So that, for example, if Peter and John are enjoined as partners in Acts, then we should expect to find their written traditions conjoined in an emergent Christian Bible, and that their intracanonical relations envisage the church's perception of their theological coherence. Likewise, the more difficult although finally collegial relationship between James and Paul as narrated in Acts 15 and (especially) 21 may well envisage their partnership in ecclesial formation in a manner that Protestant interpretation has sometimes subverted.

Because both the narrative world and its central characters are the literary constructions of the storyteller and are shaped by his theological commitments, the interpreter should not expect a more precise connection between, for example, the kerygma of the Peter of Acts and a Petrine theology envisaged by 1–2 Peter. Nevertheless there is evidence that Luke did indeed draw upon important traditions common to the Petrine letters when composing his narrative of the person and work of Peter. In particular 1 Peter's interpretation of Jesus as Isaiah's "Servant of God" (1 Pet. 2:21–25; cf. 1:10–12), the evident core of Petrine christology, is anticipated by four references to Jesus as "servant" in Acts (and only there in the New Testament), the first two in speeches by Peter (Acts 3:13, 26) and the last two in a prayer by the apostles led by him (4:27, 30).[20] Moreover, the God of the Petrine Epistles, who is known primarily through Jesus' resurrection (1 Pet. 1:3, 21; 3:21; cf. Acts 2:22–36) and as a "faithful Creator" (1 Pet. 4:19; cf. Acts 4:24), agrees generally with Luke's traditions of a Petrine kerygma. Even Peter's claim that the central mark of Gentile conversion is a "purity of heart" (Acts 15:9) is strikingly similar to 1 Pet. 1:22. Finally the most robust eschatology found in Acts, famous for its sparseness of eschatological thought, is placed on Peter's lips (Acts 3:20–23), thereby anticipating the keen stress posited on salvation's apocalypse in 1 Peter (cf. 2 Pet. 3:1–13).[21] A second example may be the far thinner portrait of John in Acts, who although depicted as Peter's silent partner uses his one speaking role in Acts 4:19–20 to sound a key note of the Johannine Epistles: "for we cannot but speak of what we have seen and heard" (cf. 1 John 1:1–3).[22]

When these thematic connections are rooted in the narrative world of Acts (a world in which these characters have enormous religious authority and purchase for the church's future) the epistolary expression and development of these core themes is underwritten as also important for the church's future and formation. Moreover, the certain impression of kerymatic continuity between the Lord's apostolic successors (Peter/John) and Paul, cultivated by Acts, would seem to commend a more constructive relationship between their writings. Acts performs an interpretive role, not so much to temper the diversity envisaged by the two different collections of letters but to prompt impressions of their rhetorical relationship within the New Testament. According to Acts the church that claims its continuity with the first apostles tolerates a rich pluralism even as the apostles do within Luke's narrative world, although not without controversy and confusion.[23]

ACTS 15: A Case in Canon Criticism

Although perhaps not the watershed event of Acts that some commentators insist it is, Acts 15 performs a strategic role within the biblical canon.[24] In particular it plots a unity that is typological of how the biblical interpreter might relate together the New Testament's two letter collections. The construction of this interpretive typology depends upon distinguishing more adequately between two narrative pairs that shape the story's plotline in Acts: namely, the two questions that frame the Jerusalem Council's proceedings and its two key witnesses, Peter and James, whose respective testimonies forge a normative definition of purity for the church's mission in the Diaspora.

The pair of questions, the first raised in Antioch (15:1) and the second in Jerusalem (15:5), are typically collapsed as if they are different articulations of the same theological problem regarding the salvation of repentant pagans.[25] Simply on internal grounds this seems unlikely. First, the two questions are in fact stated differently and would appear to frame different responses to Paul's mission in the Diaspora. While both concern the circumcision of repentant pagans, the Antiochene question of 15:1 expressly concerns soteriology, whether circumcision is a necessary condition of salvation. The Jerusalem question of 15:5 concerns ecclesiology, whether circumcision is a necessary condition for Christian fellowship in a congregation whose membership also includes repentant Jews.

The two questions are precisely located in notably different congregations within Acts. Syrian Antioch is the center of the church's liberalizing circumcision-free mission to the nations, while the Jerusalem church under James remains the gatekeeper of the church's Jewish legacy and its mission to the Jews (cf. Acts 21:17–26). The worry of the traditionalists, consistent with the memory of the Maccabean rebellion that asserted circumcision as a national priority (1 Macc. 2:46), is the attenuation of the church's Jewish roots—what Craig C. Hill has called the "gentilizing" of the church, a fear provoked by the successes of Paul's mission but now intensified by the prospect that Jesus' prediction of a mission at "the end of the earth" (1:8) would move the church farther and farther from the Holy City.[26]

But the agitators in Antioch are unauthorized by Jerusalem according to 15:24, and their lack of support casts suspicion on the question they provoke. Of course Luke's use of *sōzō* in 15:1 cues the reader to its earlier uses in Acts, specifically at the first Jerusalem Council following Cornelius's conversion when their question had already been answered. That is, the agitators are unauthorized precisely because their question has become irrelevant.

Second, there is nothing in Acts that would lead us to believe that the question provoked by the Jerusalem Pharisees is either unauthorized or uncivil. In fact their question occasions a council's compromise rather than a congregation's conflict. By the time the deeply Jewish fear registered in Antioch travels down the interstate to Jerusalem, the perceived worry about Paul's mission has been moderated—at least from the perspective of the Jerusalem church, which warmly welcomes Paul and Barnabas (15:4). The question of 15:5, which mentions circumcision but not as a condition of salvation, anticipates a middle ground brokered by James on ecclesiological rather than on soteriological grounds—that is, on *being* a member of the covenant community rather than on *becoming* a member. Indeed while the Antiochene response envisages a conservative overreaction to a perceived gentilizing tendency, Jerusalem Council convenes under the presumption of the earlier verdict hammered out in Acts 11 and is rather more concerned about *halakhah:* how will the Jewish church welcome repentant pagans into its fellowship in the same manner that it welcomed Paul and Barnabas upon their return to Jerusalem.

Toward this end the Acts' narrative fashions a dialogue between a second narrative pair: the Peter and the James of Acts. Again most commentators collapse the two, supposing that the Book of James confirms and then extends Peter's witness. But again this overlooks evident differences in their testimonies.

For example, in response to the question of purity appropriately raised by the Pharisees, the Peter of Acts famously makes Paul's case by defining purity as a matter of the heart cleansed by faith (15:9). The James of Acts responds by alerting the council to what Simeon first related about God's visitation of the nations. While most take *Simeon* as a likely reference and so confirmation of *Simon* Peter's earlier testimony, could this Simeon rather be a reference to the Jewish prophet whose *Nunc Dimittis* prophecy in Luke 2:29–32 first heralded the visitation of God's salvation to the nations at the messiah's birth? If so, then James is not confirming either Barnabas's or Paul's testimony, which he does not mention, nor Peter's, but rather the fulfillment of Simeon's prophecy of Gentile inclusion.[27]

More significant, the purity code he insists upon (15:20, 29), which is confirmed by the Spirit, hardly affirms uncritically the "purity of the heart by faith" formula. Almost certainly James thinks Peter's response to the Pharisees' question concedes too much to Antioch's more liberal position. While circumcision is no longer required of repentant pagans, whether for salvation or Christian fellowship, the Book of James believes that a code of public practices must be enforced to delineate a covenant community's purity before God in a pagan world. In this regard the prohibitions against idolatry and sexual immorality, addressed subsequently by Paul in 1 Corinthians, are probably more apropos of the Diaspora mission than is Gentile circumcision. In any case the point is that Peter's "purity of the heart by faith" is a necessary but insufficient condition of a repentant pagan's identification with the restored Israel scripted by Amos's prophecy. What James seeks is a compromise, not a concession, which will insure a more robust definition of Jewish purity for the future mission to the Gentile converts of the Diaspora. The code of purity practices insists on an embodied faith for all to see beyond Jerusalem.

And indeed, beyond Jerusalem the Paul of Acts is exemplary of a more Jewish definition of purity (cf. 24:16–21). For example, he is arrested in Philippi for being a Jew (16:20–21) and he earlier circumcises Timothy (16:3; cf. Gal. 2:3!), not only as testimony to his personal loyalty to his young associate but also to his ancestral religion (cf. 21:23–26). The role Timothy performs in Acts contrasts to Titus in Galatians 2. Timothy is of mixed parentage, Jewish and Gentile; and in prospect of the Diaspora church Paul circumcises him in order to preserve his mother's Jewish inheritance.[28] He stands as a symbol of Paul's missiological intent in Acts, which is to found Christian congregations in the Diaspora with a mixture of Jewish and Gentile converts but whose faith and practices are deeply rooted in the church's Jewish legacy.

It should be pointed out that the repetition of familiar Pauline themes in the Pillars letter collection, even though perhaps idealized for rhetorical purposes, acquires a thickened meaning when read in light of a prior reading of Acts. The reader will be put on the alert that an increasingly gentilized church, which might seek to build a covenant-keeping community even though opting out of purity practices, must consider the nature of religious observance according to the norms of Jerusalem's canonical heritage. As such their public profession of faith must be embodied in the community's public practices.[29] The full experience of God's righteousness is by performance of works and not by *sola fide.*

There is a sense in which the role a canonical Acts best performs is to explain rather than to temper the very diversity envisaged by the two collections of biblical letters. According to Acts the church that claims its continuity with the first apostles tolerates a rich pluralism even as the apostles did—and not without controversy. What is achieved at the Jerusalem Council may be more a theological *understanding* rather a theological *consensus.* The divine revelation given to the apostles according to Acts forms a pluralizing monotheism which in turn informs two discrete missions and appropriate proclamations, Jewish *and* Gentile (cf. Gal. 2:7–10). Sharply put, Acts supplies the Bible's reader with a narrative that helps to contextualize the instruction of *both* collections of letters, Pauline and pillars: on the one hand, the Pauline canon reflects the gospel of a Gentile mission, while the pillars collection reflects the gospel of a Jewish mission. However, rather than causing division within the church, such a theological diversity is now perceived as normative and necessary for the work of a God who calls both Jews and Gentiles to be the people of God. As a context for theological reflection Acts forces us to interpret the letters in the light of two guiding principles: first we should expect to find kerygmatic diversity as we move from Pauline to Catholic letters; and second we should expect such a diversity to be useful in forming a single people for God. Against a critical hermeneutics which tends to select a "canon within the Canon" from among the various possibilities, the Bible's own recommendation is for an interpretive strategy characterized by a mutually illuminating and self-correcting conversation between biblical theologies.

How then does this kind of catholicity deepen our understanding of God's people? The canonical approach to Acts (and by analogy to Luke's Gospel set now within a fourfold canon) presumes a series of literary relationships that envisage a more complementary than adversarial whole. In this case the Pauline church, which may be inclined to accommodate itself to the mainstream of the world system in order to spread the gospel more effectively (cf. 1 Cor. 9:12b-23), is reminded by the witness of the Jerusalem pillars that it must take care not to be corrupted by the values and behaviors of the world outside of Christ (cf. James 1:27).[30] That is, the synergism affected by the orienting concern suggests that the diverse theologies that make up the whole biblical canon compose a dynamic self-correcting apparatus, which prevents the reader from theological distortion. In fact the verdict of the James of Acts that a purity of the heart by faith in Christ is a necessary but insufficient condition for maintaining membership within a covenant-keeping community sounds the very cautionary note that illumines the reason the pillars collection is added to the biblical canon to join a conversation that already includes the Pauline witness. It should not surprise us, then, to note that it is the Diaspora letter of the Book of James that embraces the James of Acts most warmly when stipulating that a pure and undefiled religion is not characterized by professions of an orthodox faith apart from works, but only when faith is publicly embodied in the performance of God's "perfect law of liberty" (James 2:14–26).

NOTES

1. The same reasoning, of course, could be used to justify the use of *any* particular point in the prehistory or history of a biblical text as the plumb line to measure future readings. Rarely does one find a more robust defense of originalism that includes theological or epistemological justifications; the reasons given are mostly practical and concern the preservation of critical orthodoxy. At least the fundamentalist (and hopelessly muddled) doctrine of "verbal plenary inspiration," according to which biblical authors were selected and inspired by God to produce a propositional medium of divine revelation (albeit in their own voices) does attempt to underwrite modernity's originalism with a theological warrant. Perhaps the best one can do is follow Andrew F. Gregory's lead in admitting to different readers with different interests in a text; so the scholar's approach to a biblical text and her attention to historical and literary matters will not be the approach of the ordinary believer whose reading may serve theological purposes and for theological reasons.

2. This point is succinctly made by John Barton who writes, "The concern [of the historical-critical method] was always to place texts in their historical context, and to argue that we misunderstand them if we take them to mean something they could not have meant for their first readers. . . . The original meaning was the true meaning, and the main task of biblical scholars was to get back to this meaning, and to eliminate the false meanings that unhistorical readers thought they had found in the text." ("Historical-critical approaches" in *The Cambridge Companion to Biblical Interpretation* [ed. John Barton; Cambridge: Cambridge University Press, 1998], 10–11.)

3. The principal subtext of the present study is the proposal of a second "point of origin" (or "original meaning") that studies an authored text when it is first received and used as Scripture (or "canonical" if this carries a different sense than "Scripture"). The structure of my defense in granting elevated importance to the canonical origins of a text, with its ancillary claims of canonical (rather than authorial) intent or meaning, is similar to modernity's defense of a text's "original meaning." That is, Barton's definition of a critical orthodoxy (see

note 2 above) can be reappropriated for defining the interpretive constraints given a text's canonization, except now the first readers of a canonical text are located differently both in relationship to their social worlds and in relationship to the literary text. The church now replaces Luke, Irenaeus replaces Theophilus, the late-second-century church requiring instruments to facilitate its catholic unity to counter its own splinter groups replaces Luke's church and its problems with supersessionism, and so on. In fact we may know more about this second point of origin than the first, making it an even more effective critical measure than the reconstruction of an authorial original in protecting the sanctity of the text against abuse. But my primary justification project is metatheological and not prudential or an ethics of reading. That is, by indexing a text's "original meaning" or intent to its initial reception as Scripture, the interpreter receives and renders the text within its current and I would argue its most relevant context—the biblical canon.

4. Luke Timothy Johnson, "Literary Criticism of Luke-Acts: Is Reception-History Pertinent?" in this volume, 66 (first published in *JSNT* 28/2 [2005]: 160).

5. See W. A. Strange, *The Problem of the Text of Acts* (SNTSMS 71; Cambridge: Cambridge University Press, 1992).

6. See David R. Nienhuis, *Not by Paul Alone* (Waco, Tex.: Baylor University Press, 2007), esp. 85–90.

7. K-W. Niebuhr and Robert W. Wall, *The Catholic Epistles and Apostolic Traditions: The New Perspective on James and Other Studies* (Waco, Tex.: Baylor University Press, 2009).

8. No explanation is given in the patristic sources for the eventual dissolution of this *Apostolos* and for the role of a canonical Acts to bridge the fourfold gospel with the Pauline canon. Nienhuis argues that the most likely explanation is the dominance of the West (and its Vulgate) and its claim of Pauline priority (87). But the phenomenology of the canonical process includes a normal settling process that fixed a final literary form that facilitated the practices of a biblical canon. The evidence of the early reception of Acts as part of this *Apostolos* sounds a cautionary note to contemporary scholars who presume that the canonical Acts (and probably a Luke-Acts) intends from the outset a proprietary connection with the Pauline canon. The manucsripts and early canon lists suggest that a closer connection existed between Acts and the letters of the Jerusalem pillars. My own intuition is that the creation of this collection was to help the church battle the heretics and antinomianism dependent upon the Pauline canon, which may have been settled or replaced by other battles by the end of the canonical process.

9. See especially Andrew F. Gregory, "The Reception of Luke and Acts and the Unity of Luke-Acts," in this volume, 82–93 (first published in *JSNT* 29/4 [2007]: 459–72). The reception history of Acts during the patristic period is an obvious interest of Henry J. Cadbury's *The Book of Acts in History* (London: A & C Black, 1955) given that his hypothesis of a unified Luke-Acts may be challenged by the history of their canonization, which suggests a disunified Luke and Acts (see my brief comment below). Cadbury does confirm the ancient observation of the strategic role that Acts subsequently performs in giving shape and structure of a Gospel-Letters canon as a literary bridge between them—an observation that is contextualized and expanded by David Trobisch in his important study *Die Endredaktion des Neuen Testaments* (NTOA 31; Göttingen: Vandenhoeck & Ruprecht, 1996). In any case, their studies along with others have been evaluated (and on occasion corrected) by Gregory,

The Reception of Luke and Acts in the Period before Irenaeus (WUNT 2/169; Tübingen: Mohr Siebeck, 2003), 299–351, who concludes (against C. K. Barrett's optimism) that Irenaeus is the first to show the "influence" of Acts—I would rather observe that Irenaeus is the first to use Acts as "Scripture"—in his *Against Heresies,* even though not alone in his knowledge of Acts (350–51). In this regard I would only mention in passing—though with keen interest—that several of the clearest allusions to traditions used in Acts are found in the writings of groups linked to James and other Jerusalem pillars. Again this implicit use of Acts within the Jacobean community may well anticipate a future role of Acts in the formation and canonization of a "pillars collection" with the Book of James as its frontispiece. In my opinion two other monographs, by David E. Smith, *The Canonical Function of Acts: A Comparative Analysis* (Collegeville, Minn.: Liturgical Press, 2002), and to a lesser degree by Christopher N. Mount, *Pauline Christianity: Luke-Acts and the Legacy of Paul* (NovTSup 104; Leiden: Brill, 2002), are more useful for the purposes of this study since each seeks to understand Irenaeus's theological motive and hermeneutics in using Acts as a piece with the very idea of a biblical canon. In this sense the use of Acts in Irenaeus's polemics defines its prospective canonical role—that is, the raison d'être for its admission into the biblical canon and its use by Scripture's faithful readers.

10. Mount, *Pauline Christianity,* 57.

11. Irenaeus does not seem alert to contemporary tensions between tradents of the Jerusalem apostles evinced in the Nag Hammadi tractates, between those loyal to the memories (and secrets) of the "Beloved Disciple" and those communicants attached to the catholic church that idealized Peter, or between Pauline Christians and those who lionized the spiritual authority of James and considered Paul an opponent.

12. Mount argues that Ireaenus's use of Acts "invents" a version of Christian unity for use in early catholic polemics that subverts the intentions of both storytellers and the historical record of Christianity's origins. My point is rather that it is precisely this more poetic use of Acts that affords it canonical status and that defines its canonical role—not Luke's motive for writing Acts, whatever that is, nor the historical record of the church's beginnings, however that is reconstructed.

13. Similarly the Pauline canon consisting only of nine or ten letters rather than thirteen, the Petrine tradition remembered by only 1 Peter without 2 Peter, or 1 John without 2 and 3 John, or Jude without the Book of James (since Jude 1:1 mentions James) is incomplete and lacking a robust apostolicity.

14. This is a phrase I have heard Sanders use frequently in public lectures, seminars, and private conversation. For his elaboration of what it means, see James A. Sanders, "The Issue of Closure in the Canonical Process," in *The Canon Debate* (ed. Lee M. McDonald and James A. Sanders; Peabody, Mass.: Hendrickson, 2002), 252–63.

15. See the collection of essays found in François Bovon, *Studies in Early Christianity* (Grand Rapids, Mich.: Baker Academic, 2003), 195–301, esp. "The Synoptic Gospels and the Non-Canonical Acts of the Apostles," 209–25.

16. This is an orienting concern of my commentary on Acts in volume 10 of *The New Interpreter's Bible* (ed. Leander E. Keck; Nashville: Abingdon Press, 2002), 3–370.

17. But see Steve Walton, *Leadership and Lifestyle: The Portrait of Paul in the Miletus Speech and 1 Thessalonians* (SNTSMS 108; Cambridge: Cambridge University Press, 2000),

who challenges this consensus by noting several allusions to a likely proto-Pauline canon. For a comprehensive listing and analysis of the intertextual echoes of Pauline letters in Acts, see David Wenham, "Acts and the Pauline Corpus," in *The Book of Acts in Its Ancient Literary Setting* (ed. Bruce W. Winter and Andrew D. Clarke; Grand Rapids, Mich.: Eerdmans, 1993), 215–58;

18. See Robert W. Wall, "Romans 1:1–15: An Introduction to the Pauline Corpus of the New Testament," in *The New Testament as Canon* (ed. Robert W. Wall and Eugene E. Lemcio; JSNTSup 76; Sheffield: JSOT Press, 1992), 142–60.

19. David Trobisch, *Die Endredaktion.* But now see Richard I. Pervo, *Dating Acts: Between the Evangelists and the Apologists* (Santa Rosa, Calif.: Polebridge Press, 2006), and Joseph B. Tyson, *Marcion and Luke-Acts: A Defining Struggle* (Columbia, S.C.: University of South Carolina Press, 2006), who date the earliest version of Acts to the early second century; and W. A. Strange, *The Problem of the Text of Acts* (SNTSMS 71; Cambridge: Cambridge University Press, 1992), which follows Cadbury and K. Lake in dating the canonical version of Acts to the late second century. But none of these reconstructions, even if accurate, undermines my essential claim.

20. Cf. Oscar Cullmann, *Peter: Disciple, Apostle, Martyr: A Historical and Theological Essay* (London: SCM, 1953), 63–69.

21. See Robert W. Wall, "The Canonical Function of 2 Peter," *BibInt* 9/1 (2001): 77–79.

22. See Paul N. Anderson, *The Christology of the Fourth Gospel* (Valley Forge, Pa.: Trinity Press International, 1997), 274–77, who suggests that at the one point in Acts where Peter and John speak with one voice (4:19–20)—Peter alone speaks when they are teamed elsewhere in this narrative world—the narrator has constituted a saying that combines Petrine (4:19) with Johannine (4:20) traditions. Their pairing in Acts in both work and speech may well envisage an emerging consensus within the ancient church that their traditions, both personal and theological, are complementary parts of an integral whole.

23. The late Brevard Childs explores some of these same issues in the final book of a brilliant career, *The Church's Guide for Reading Paul: The Canonical Shaping of the Pauline Corpus* (Grand Rapids, Mich.: Eerdmans, 2008). While grateful that Childs engages my efforts to develop a "critical methodology when interpreting Acts that is shaped by attention to canonical form and function" (222), his criticism of my assessment of the relationship between Acts and Luke's Gospel and the Pauline letters within a canonical context is misplaced; in fact I think we are somewhat closer than he supposes, especially as is made clear by the present essay. For example, he claims that I approach Acts "as Luke's intentional commentary on the Gospel" (233), when what I actually argue in my commentary is that a canonical Acts provides its audience with a canonical setting by which the *fourfold* gospel of the New Testament canon is thickened and extended—whether in the kerygmatic portions of the speeches or more allusively in the christological shaping of several key episodes in Acts. Earlier Childs claims that I use Acts "to bind Paul and the Gospels together" (225–26), which he then links with Adolf von Harnack's misguided analysis of the canonization of Acts as a political bid to unify the early catholic church. I actually pay scant attention to this idea in my work and never as an interpretive cue for reading Acts. In fact I take it that the principal role of the biblical Acts is to introduce and frame the two canonical collections of letters that follow—a point surely unintended by its narrator.

24. This section revises the concluding portion of my "The Jerusalem Council (Acts 15:1–21) in Canonical Context," in *From Biblical Criticism to Biblical Faith: Essays in Honor of Lee Martin McDonald* (ed. William. H. Brackney and Craig A. Evans; Macon, Ga.: Mercer University Press, 2007), 93–101.

25. See, for example, John Painter, *Just James: The Brother of Jesus in History and Tradition* (2d ed.; Columbia: University of South Carolina Press, 2004). Painter argues that the narrative in Acts is plotted in such a way, especially when glossed by Gal. 2:11–14, that Antioch's conflict becomes Jerusalem's question. As such the issue of full membership in the covenant community is never resolved in Acts whose readers are left with the mediating position of James who does not require circumcision as a covenant marker—a position that Painter does not think historically accurate.

26. So Craig C. Hill, *Hellenists and Hebrews: Reappraising Division within the Earliest Church* (Minneapolis: Fortress, 1992), 103–47.

27. Stephen Fowl first alerted me to this possibility in an unpublished paper presented at Princeton Theological Seminary; see also Rainer Riesner, "James' Speech (Acts 15:13–21), Simeon's Hymn (Luke 2:29–32), and Luke's Sources," in *Jesus of Nazareth: Lord and Christ* (ed. Joel B. Green and Max Turner; Grand Rapids, Mich.: Eerdmans, 1994), 263–78.

28. The Jewish cast of Paul's story in Acts is a principal exegetical interest of my commentary on Acts.

29. Of course the Pauline letters would not disagree with this conclusion. I would argue, however, that for the Pauline tradition these social, moral, and religious practices, which mark out a people as "Christian" are the natural yield of "being in Christ" and that "being in Christ" is the result of profession that "Jesus is Lord" (Rom 10:9). A Pauline redemptive calculus, whether understood politically or personally, is concentrated by the beliefs of the Pauline gospel rather than by the practices of the Pauline churches. It is this essential difference of logic that fashions—I think from the early church—a different spirituality, which is centered by orthodox confession, than that found in the congregations of the Catholic Epistles traditions.

30. I seek to develop this point more fully in "Toward a Unifying Theology of the Catholic Epistles: A Canonical Approach," in *Catholic Epistles and the Tradition* (BETL 176; ed. Jacques Schlosser; Leuven: Peeters, 2004), 43–71; and it will be a principal dimension of a "new perspective on James" introduced in the recent collection, *The Catholic Epistles and Apostolic Traditions* (eds. K-W. Niebuhr and Robert W. Wall; Waco, Tex.: Baylor University Press, 2009).

WORKS CITED

Essays included in this volume are marked with *.

Achtemeier, Paul J. *1 Peter: A Commentary on First Peter.* Hermeneia. Minneapolis: Fortress, 1996.

Aland, Barbara. "Welche Rolle spielen Textkritik und Textgeschichte für das Verständnis des Neuen Testaments? Frühe Leserperspektiven." *NTS* 52 (2006): 303–18.

Aland, Barbara, and William L. Petersen. *Gospel Traditions in the Second Century: Origins, Recensions, Text, and Transmission.* Christianity and Judaism in Antiquity 3. Notre Dame, Ind.: University of Notre Dame Press, 1989.

Aland, Kurt. "Die Bedeutung des P75 für den Text des Neuen Testaments. Ein Beitrag zur Frage der Western non-interpolations." In *Studien zur Überlieferung des Neuen Testaments und seines Textes,* 155–71. Edited by Kurt Aland. *ANT* 2. Berlin: Walter de Gruyter, 1967.

Aland, Kurt, and Barbara Aland. *The Text of the New Testament.* Grand Rapids, Mich.: Eerdmans, 1989.

Alexander, Loveday C. A. *The Preface to Luke's Gospel: Literary Convention and Social Context in Luke 1.1–4 and Acts 1.1.* SNTSMS 78. Cambridge: Cambridge University Press, 1993.

———. "Ancient Book Production and the Circulation of the Gospels." In *The Gospels for All Christians: Rethinking the Gospel Audiences,* 71–112. Edited by Richard Bauckham. Grand Rapids, Mich.: Eerdmans, 1998.

———. "Fact, Fiction and the Genre of Acts." *NTS* 44 (1998): 380–99.

———. "Reading Luke-Acts from Back to Front." In *The Unity of Luke-Acts,* 419–46. Edited by Joseph Verheyden. BETL 142. Leuven: Leuven University Press, 1999.

———. "What If Luke Had Never Met Theophilus?" *Biblical Interpretation* 8 (2000): 161–70.

———. *Acts in Its Ancient Literary Context: A Classicist Looks at the Acts of the Apostles.* Library of New Testament Studies 298. London: T & T Clark, 2005.

Allen, O. Wesley. *The Death of Herod: The Narrative and Theological Function of Retribution in Luke-Acts.* SBLDS 158. Atlanta: Scholars, 1997.

Anderson, Paul N. *The Christology of the Fourth Gospel.* Valley Forge, Pa.: Trinity Press International, 1997.

Aron, Paul, Denis Saint-Jacques, Alain Viala, and Marie-Andrée Beaudet, eds. *Le Dictionnaire du Littéraire.* Paris: PUF, 2002.

Aune, David E. *The New Testament in Its Literary Environment.* LEC 8. Philadelphia: Westminster, 1987.

Barrett, C. K. *Luke the Historian in Recent Study.* London: Epworth, 1961.

———. "Acts and Christian Consensus." In *Context: Essays in Honour of Peder Johan Borgen,* 19–33. Edited by Peter W. Bøckman and Roald E. Kristiansen. Trondheim: Tapir Press, 1987.

———. "The Third Gospel as a Preface to Acts? Some Reflections." In *The Four Gospels 1992: Festschrift Frans Neirynck,* 1451–66. Vol. 2. Edited by F. Van Segbroek et al. BETL 100. Leuven: Leuven University Press, 1992.

———. *A Critical and Exegetical Commentary on the Acts of the Apostles.* Vol. 1. ICC. Edinburgh: T & T Clark, 1994.

———. "The First New Testament?" *NovT* 38 (1996): 94–104.

———. "The Parallels Between Acts and John." In *Exploring the Gospel of John: In Honor of D. Moody Smith,* 220–39. Edited by R. Alan Culpepper and C. Clifton Black. Louisville: Westminster John Knox, 1996.

———. *A Critical and Exegetical Commentary on the Acts of the Apostles.* Vol. 2. ICC. Edinburgh: T & T Clark, 1998.

Barton, John. "Historical-critical approaches." In *The Cambridge Companion to Biblical Interpretation,* 9–20. Edited by John Barton. Cambridge: Cambridge University Press, 1998.

Barton, Stephen C. "Can We Identify the Gospel Audiences?" In *The Gospels for All Christians: Rethinking the Gospel Audiences,* 173–94. Edited by Richard Bauckham. Grand Rapids, Mich.: Eerdmans, 1998.

Bauckham, Richard. "The Acts of Paul as a Sequel to Acts." In *The Book of Acts in Its Ancient Literary Setting,* 105–52. Edited by Bruce W. Winter and Andrew D. Clarke. *BIFCS 1.* Grand Rapids, Mich.: Eerdmans, 1993.

———. "For Whom Were Gospels Written?" In *The Gospels for All Christians: Rethinking the Gospel Audiences,* 9–48. Edited by Richard Bauckham. Grand Rapids, Mich.: Eerdmans, 1998.

Bauer, Johannes B. *Die Polykarpbriefe.* KAV 5. Göttingen: Vandenhoeck & Ruprecht, 1995.

Bellinzoni, Arthur J. *The Sayings of Jesus in the Writings of Justin Martyr.* NovTSup 17. Leiden: Brill, 1967.

———. "The Gospel of Matthew in the Second Century." *Second Century* 9 (1992): 197–259.

———. "The Gospel of Luke in the Second Century CE." In *Literary Studies in Luke-Acts: Essays in Honor of Joseph B. Tyson,* 59–76. Edited by Richard P. Thompson and Thomas E. Phillips. Macon, Ga.: Mercer University Press, 1998.

———. "The Gospel of Luke in the Apostolic Fathers: An Overview." In *Trajectories through the New Testament and the Apostolic Fathers,* 45–68. Edited by Andrew F. Gregory and Christopher M. Tuckett. Oxford: Oxford University Press, 2005.

Berding, Kenneth. *Polycarp and Paul: An Analysis of Their Literary and Theological Relationship in Light of Polycarp's Use of Biblical and Extra-Biblical Literature.* VCSup 62. Leiden: Brill, 2002.

Bieder, Werner. *Die Apostelgeschichte in der Historie. Ein Beitrag zur Auslegungsgeschichte des Missionsbuches der Kirche.* ThSt 61. Zürich: EVZ-Verlag, 1960.

Bingham, D. Jeffrey. *Irenaeus' Use of Matthew's Gospel in* Adversus Haereses. Traditio Exegetica Graeca 7. Leuven: Peeters, 1998.

Bird, Michael F. "The Unity of Luke-Acts in Recent Discussion." *JSNT* 29/4 (2007): 425–48.*

Bockmuehl, Markus . "Why Not Let Acts Be Acts? In Conversation with C. Kavin Rowe." *JSNT* 28/2 (2005): 163–66.*

———. *Seeing the Word: Refocusing New Testament Study.* Grand Rapids: Baker Academic, 2006.

Boismard, M. E., and A. Lamouille. *Le texte occidental des Actes des apôtres: reconstitution et rehabilitation.* 2 vols. Paris: Éditions Recherche sur les civilizations, 1984.

Bonz, Marianne Palmer. *The Past as Legacy: Luke-Acts and Ancient Epic.* Minneapolis: Fortress, 2000.

Borgman, Paul. *The Way According to Luke: Hearing the Whole Story of Luke-Acts.* Grand Rapids, Mich.: Eerdmans, 2006.

Botha, Pieter J. J. "Community and Conviction in Luke-Acts." *Neotestamentica* 29/2 (1995): 145–65.

Boud'hors, Anne. "Éloge de Jean-Baptiste." In *Écrits apocryphes chrétiens I,* 1553–78. Edited by François Bovon and Pierre Geoltrain. Paris: Gallimard, 1997.

Boudon-Millot, Veronique, ed. *Galien. Introduction générale. Sur l'ordre de ses propres livres. Sur ses propres livres. Que l'excellent médecin est aussi philosophe.* Vol. 1. Paris: Belles Lettres, 2007.

Bousset, Wilhelm. *Die Evangelienzitate Justins des Märtyrers in ihren Wert für die Evangelienkritik.* Göttingen: Vandenhoeck & Ruprecht, 1891.

Bovon, François. *De Vocatione Gentium. Histoire de l'interprétation d'Act. 10, 1–11, 18 dans les six premiers siècles.* BGBE 8. Tübingen: Mohr Siebeck, 1967.

———. *Das Evangelium nach Lukas, Lk 1,1–9,50. I 3,1.* EKK. Zürich: Benziger, 1989.

———. *Luke 1. A Commentary on the Gospel of Luke 1:1–9:50.* Edited by Helmut Koester. Translated by Christine M. Thomas. Hermeneia. Minneapolis: Fortress, 2002.

———. "The Reception and Use of the Gospel of Luke in the Second Century." In *Reading Luke: Interpretation, Reflection, Formation,* 379–400. Edited by Craig G. Bartholomew, Joel B. Green, and Anthony C. Thiselton. Scripture and Hermeneutics 6. Grand Rapids: Zondervan, 2005.

———. *Luke the Theologian.* 2d ed. Waco, Tex.: Baylor University Press, 2006.

———. "The Reception of the Book of Acts in Antiquity." In *Contemporary Studies in Acts.* Edited by Thomas E. Phillips. Macon, Ga.: Mercer University Press, 2009.

Braun, François-Marie. *Jean le Théologien et son Évangile dans l'Église ancienne.* EB. Paris: Gabalda, 1959.

Brown, Raymond E. *An Introduction to the Gospel of John.* Edited by Francis J. Moloney. New York: Doubleday, 2003.

Brox, Norbert. *Der erste Petrusbrief.* EKK 21. Zürich, Einsiedeln, Köln: Benziger Verlag, 1979.

Buckwalter, H. Douglas. *The Character and Purpose of Luke's Christology.* SNTSMS 89. Cambridge: Cambridge University Press, 1996.

Bultmann, Rudolph. *Theology of the New Testament.* Translated by K. Grobel. 2 vols. New York: Charles Scribner's Sons, 1951, 1955.

Cadbury, Henry J. *The Making of Luke-Acts.* New York: Macmillan; repr. London: SPCK, 1961.

———. *The Book of Acts in History.* London: A & C Black, 1955.

Campenhausen, Hans von. *The Formation of the Christian Bible.* Translated by J. A. Baker. Philadelphia: Fortress, 1972.

Camps, G. M., and B. M. Ubach. "Un sentido bíblico de adikos, adikia y la interpretación de Lc 16, 1–13." *EstBíb* 25 (1966): 75–82.

Carroll, John T. "The God of Israel and the Salvation of the Nations." In *The Forgotten God: Perspectives in Biblical Theology: Essays in Honor of Paul J. Achtemeier on the Occasion of his Seventy-fifth Birthday*, 91–106. Edited by A. Andrew Das and Frank J. Matera. Louisville: Westminster John Knox, 2002.

Carter, Warren. *Matthew: Storyteller, Interpreter, Evangelist.* Peabody, Mass.: Hendrickson, 1996.

Cerquiglini, Bernard. *Éloge de la variante: Histoire critique de la philologie.* Translated by Betsy Wing. Paris: Éditions du Seuil, 1989.

———. *In Praise of the Variant: A Critical History of Philology.* Baltimore: John Hopkins University Press, 1999.

Cerro, G. del. "Los hechos apócrifos de los Apósteles. Su género literario." *EstBíb* 51 (1993): 207–32.

Chen, Diane G. *God as Father in Luke-Acts.* New York: Peter Lang, 2006.

Childs, Brevard S. *The New Testament as Canon: An Introduction.* Philadelphia: Fortress, 1984.

———. *The Church's Guide for Reading Paul: The Canonical Shaping of the Pauline Corpus.* Grand Rapids, Mich.: Eerdmans, 2008.

Clark, A. C. *The Acts of the Apostles: A Critical Edition, with Introduction and Notes on Selected Passages.* Oxford: Clarendon, 1933.

Clivaz, Claire. "Douze noms pour une main: nouveaux regards sur Judas à partir de Lc 22.21–22." *NTS* 48/3 (2002): 413–14.

———. *L'ange et la sueur de sang (Lc 22, 43–44) ou comment on pourrait bien encore écrire l'histoire. BiTS.* Leuven: Peeters, 2009.

———. "Peut-on parler de posture littéraire pour un auteur antique? Les exemples de Paul de Tarse, de Galien et des lecteurs du texte anonyme de l'Évangile selon Luc." *Contextes* (forthcoming 2010).

———. "Reading Luke-Acts in Alexandria in the Second Century: From Clement to the Shadow of Apollos." In *Reading Acts in the Second Century.* Edited by R. Dupertuis and Todd C. Penner. London: Equinox, forthcoming 2010.

Comfort, Philip W., and David P. Barrett, eds. *The Text of the Earliest New Testament Greek Manuscripts.* Wheaton: Tyndale House, 2001.

A Committee of the Oxford Society of Historical Theology. *The New Testament in the Apostolic Fathers.* Oxford: Clarendon, 1905.

Conzelmann, Hans. *The Theology of Saint Luke.* Translated by Geoffrey Buswell. London: Faber & Faber, 1961.

———. *Acts of the Apostles: A Commentary on the Acts of the Apostles.* Edited by Eldon Jay Epp and Christopher R. Matthews. Translated by James Limburg, A. Thomas Kraabel, and Donald H. Juel. Hermeneia. Philadephia: Fortress, 1987.

Cullmann, Oscar. *Peter: Disciple, Apostle, Martyr: A Historical and Theological Essay.* London: SCM, 1953.

Cunningham, Scott Smith. *'Through Many Tribulations': The Theology of Persecution in Luke-Acts.* JSNTSup 142. Sheffield: Sheffield Academic Press, 1997.

Dahl, N. A. "The Story of Abraham in Luke-Acts." In *Studies in Luke-Acts,* 139–58. Edited by Leander E. Keck and J. Louis Martyn. Nashville: Abingdon, 1966.

Danker, Frederick W. *Jesus and the New Age: A Commentary on St. Luke's Gospel.* Philadelphia: Fortress, 1988.

Darr, John A. "Discerning the Lukan Voice: The Narrator as Character in Luke-Acts." In *Society of Biblical Literature 1992 Seminar Papers,* 255–65. Edited by Eugene H. Lovering. Atlanta: Scholars, 1992.

Dassmann, E. *Der Stachel im Fleisch. Paulus in der frühchristlichen Literatur bis Irenäus.* Münster: Aschendorff, 1979.

Davies, John G. *He Ascended into Heaven.* London: Lutterworth Press, 1958.

Dehandschutter, Boudewijn. "Polycarp's Epistle to the Philippians: An Early Example of 'Reception.'" In *The New Testament in Early Christianity,* 275–81. Edited by Jean-Marie Sevrin. BETL 86. Leuven: Leuven University Press, 1989.

———. "Images of Polycarp: Biography and Hagiography about the Bishop of Smyrna." In his *Polycarpiana. Studies on Martyrdom and Persecution in Early Christianity. Collected Essays,* 271–77. Edited by Johan Leemans. BETL 205. Leuven: Leuven University Press, 2007.

———. *Polycarpiana. Studies on Martyrdom and Persecution in Early Christianity. Collected Essays.* Edited by Johan Leemans. BETL 205. Leuven: Leuven University Press, 2007.

Delebecque, Édouard. "Le régisseur infidèle (16, 113)." In *Études grecques sur l'évangile de Luc. Collection d'études anciennes.* Edited by Édouard Delebecque. Paris: Belles Lettres, 1976.

Denova, Rebecca I. *The Things Accomplished Among Us: Prophetic Traditions in the Structural Pattern of Luke-Acts.* JSNTSup 141. Sheffield: Sheffield Academic Press, 1997.

Derrida, Jacques. *Archive Fever: A Freudian Impression.* Translated by Eric Prenowitz. Chicago: University of Chicago Press, 1998.

Dibelius, Martin. *From Tradition to Gospel.* Translated by B. Woolf. New York: Charles Scribner's Sons, 1935.

———. "Style Criticism of the Book of Acts." In *Studies in the Acts of the Apostles,* 1–25. Edited by H. Greeven. Translated by M. Ling and P. Schubert. New York: Charles Scribner's Sons, 1956.

———. "The Text of Acts: An Urgent Critical Text." In *Studies in the Acts of the Apostles,* 84–92. Ed. H. Greeven. Translated by M. Ling and P. Schubert. New York: Charles Scribner's Sons, 1956.

Dorandi, Tiziano. *Le stylet et la tablette dans le secret des auteurs antiques.* Paris: Belles Lettres, 2000.

Downing, F. Gerald. *Doing Things with Words in the First Christian Century.* JSNTSup 200. Sheffield: Sheffield Academic Press, 2000.

———. "Le problème du choix de l'intertexte: Paul s'oppose-t-il radicalement ou superficiellement à la culture de son temps?" In *Intertextualités. La Bible en échos,* 237–50. Edited by Daniel Marguerat and Adrian Curtis. *MoBi* 40. Genève: Labor et Fides, 2000.

Dupont, Jacques. "La conclusion des Actes et son rapport à l'ensemble de l'ouvrage de Luc." In *Les Actes des Apôtres: Traditions, redaction, théologies,* 359–404. Edited by Jacob Kremer. BETL 43. Leuven: Leuven University Press 1979.

Eco, Umberto. *The Name of the Rose.* Translated by William Weaver. Orlando, Fla.: Harcourt Brace, 1983.

———. *Lector in fabula. La cooperazione interpretativa nei testi narrative.* Milan: Bompiani, 1985.

Ehrman, Bart D. *The Orthodox Corruption of Scripture: The Effect of Early Christological Controversies on the Text of the New Testament.* New York and Oxford: Oxford University Press, 1993.

Elliott, J. K. Review of Andrew F. Gregory, *The Reception of Luke and Acts in the Period before Irenaeus. NovT* 48/1 (2006): 201–2.

Epp, Eldon Jay. "The Ascension in the Textual Tradition of Luke-Acts." In *Perspectives on New Testament Textual Criticism: Collected Essays, 1962–2004,* 211–25. Edited by Eldon Jay Epp. NovTSup 116. Leiden and Boston: Brill, 2005.

Epp, Eldon Jay, and Gordon D. Fee, eds. *New Testament Textual Criticism: Its Significance for Exegesis.* Oxford: Clarendon Press, 1981.

Esler, Philip F. *Community and Gospel in Luke-Acts: The Social and Political Motivations of Lucan Theology.* SNTSMS 57. Cambridge: Cambridge University Press, 1987.

———. "Community and Gospel in Early Christianity: A Response to Richard Bauckham's *Gospels for All Christians.*" *SJT* 51 (1998): 235–48.

Fitzmyer, Joseph A. *The Gospel According to Luke.* 2 vols. Garden City: Doubleday, 1981–1985.

Gamble, Harry Y. *Books and Readers in the Early Church: A History of Early Christian Texts.* New Haven: Yale University Press, 1995.

Garrett, Susan. *The Demise of the Devil: Magic and the Demonic in Luke's Writings.* Minneapolis: Fortress, 1989.

Gasque, W. Ward. *A History of the Criticism of the Acts of the Apostles.* BGBE 17. Tübingen: Mohr Siebeck, 1975.

Gaventa, Beverly Roberts. *Acts.* ANTC. Nashville: Abingdon, 2003.

Genette, Gérard. *Introduction à l'architexte.* Paris: Seuil, 1979.

Gilbert, Gary. "Roman Propaganda and Christian Identity in the Worldview of Luke-Acts." In *Contextualizing Acts: Lukan Narrative and Greco-Roman Discourse,* 233–56. Edited by Todd C. Penner and Caroline Vander Stichele. SBJSS 20. Atlanta: Society of Biblical Literature, 2003.

Gilmore, S. McL. "The Gospel According to St. Luke." In *The Interpreter's Bible,* 8:1–434. New York: Abingdon, 1952.

Green, Joel B. *The Theology of Luke.* NTT. Cambridge: Cambridge University Press, 1995.

———. "Internal Repetition in Luke-Acts: Contemporary Narratology and Lucan Historiography." In *History, Literature and Society in the Book of Acts,* 283–99. Edited by Ben Witherington. Cambridge: Cambridge University Press, 1996.

———. "Acts of the Apostles." In *Dictionary of the Later New Testament and Its Developments,* 7–24. Edited by Ralph P. Martin and Peter H. Davids. Downers Grove, Ill.: Inter-Varsity Press, 1997.

———. *The Gospel of Luke.* NICNT. Grand Rapids, Mich.: Eerdmans, 1997.

Green, Joel B., and Michael C. McKeever, eds. *Luke-Acts and New Testament Historiography.* IBR Bibliographies 8. Grand Rapids: Baker, 1994.

Greenblatt, Stephen. *Renaissance Self-Fashioning: From More to Shakespeare.* Chicago: University of Chicago Press, 1980.

Greenblatt, Stephen, and Catherine Gallagher. *Practicing New Historicism.* Chicago: University of Chicago Press, 2000.

Gregory, Andrew F. *The Reception of Luke and Acts in the Period before Irenaeus: Looking for Luke in the Second Century.* WUNT 2/169. Tübingen: Mohr Siebeck, 2003.

———. "Looking for Luke in the Second Century: A Dialogue with François Bovon." In *Reading Luke: Interpretation, Reflection, Formation,* 401–13. Edited by Craig G. Bartholomew, Joel B. Green, and Anthony C. Thiselton. Scripture and Hermeneutics 6. Grand Rapids, Mich.: Zondervan, 2005.

———. "The Reception of Luke and Acts and the Unity of Luke-Acts." *JSNT* 29/4 (2007): 459–72.*

———. "Irenaeus and the Reception of Luke and Acts in the Second Century." In *Contemporary Studies in Acts.* Edited by Thomas E. Phillips. Macon, Ga.: Mercer University Press, 2009.

Gregory, Andrew F., and Christopher M. Tuckett, eds. *The Reception of the New Testament in the Apostolic Fathers.* Oxford: Oxford University Press, 2005.

———. *Trajectories through the New Testament and the Apostolic Fathers.* Oxford: Oxford University Press, 2005.

Haenchen, Ernst. *The Acts of the Apostles: A Commentary.* Edited and translated by R. McL. Wilson. Oxford: Basil Blackwell, 1971.

Hagner, Donald A. *The Use of the Old and New Testaments in Clement of Rome.* NovTSup 34. Leiden: Brill, 1973.

Hahneman, Geoffrey M. *The Muratorian Fragment and the Development of the Canon.* Oxford: Clarendon Press, 1992.

Harms, Richard B. *Paradigms from Luke-Acts for Multicultural Communities.* New York: Peter Lang, 2001.

Harnack, Adolf von. *The Origin of the New Testament and the Most Important Consequences of the New Creation.* London: Williams & Northgate, 1925.

Harrison, Percy N. *Polycarp's Two Epistles to the Philippians.* Cambridge: Cambridge University Press, 1936.

Hartog, Paul. *Polycarp and the New Testament: The Occasion, Rhetoric, Theme, and Unity of the Epistle to the Philippians and Its Allusions to New Testament Literature.* WUNT 2/134. Tübingen: Mohr Siebeck, 2002.

Hays, Richard. *Echoes of Scripture in the Letters of Paul.* New Haven: Yale University Press, 1989.

Hengel, Martin. *The Four Gospels and the One Gospel of Jesus Christ: An Investigation of the Collection and Origin of the Canonical Gospels.* Translated by John Bowden. London: SCM, 2000.

Hilgenfeld, Adolf. *Kritische Untersuchungen über die Evangelien Justin's, der clementinischen Homilien und Marcion's.* Halle: Schwetschke, 1850.

Hill, Charles E. *The Johannine Corpus in the Early Church.* Oxford: Oxford University Press, 2004.

———. *From the Lost Teaching of Polycarp.* WUNT 186. Tübingen: Mohr Siebeck, 2006.

Hill, Craig C. *Hellenists and Hebrews: Reappraising Division within the Earliest Church.* Minneapolis: Fortress, 1992.

Hills, Julian. "The Acts of the Apostles in the *Acts of Paul.*" In *SBLSP* 33, 24–54. Edited by E. Lovering. Atlanta: Scholars, 1994.

Hur, Ju. "The Unity, Genre and Purpose of Luke-Acts Revisited." *Korea Theological Journal* 3 (2000): 227–58.

———. *A Dynamic Reading of the Holy Spirit in Luke-Acts.* JSNTSup 211. Sheffield: Sheffield Academic Press, 2001.

Jefford, Clayton N. *The Apostolic Fathers and the New Testament.* Peabody, Mass.: Hendrickson, 2006.

Jeremias, J. *Die Sprache des Lukasevangeliums. Redaktion und Tradition im Nicht-Markusstoff des dritten Evangeliums.* KEK Sonderband. Göttingen: Vandenhoeck & Ruprecht, 1980.

Jervell, Jacob. *The Theology of the Acts of the Apostles.* Cambridge: Cambridge University Press, 1996.

———. *Die Apostelgeschichte.* KEK 17. Göttingen: Vandenhoeck & Ruprecht, 1998.

Johnson, Luke Timothy. "On Finding the Lukan Community: A Cautious Cautionary Essay." In *1979 Seminar Papers,* 87–100. Edited by Paul J. Achtemeier. SBL. Missoula, Mont.: Scholars, 1979.

———. *The Gospel of Luke.* SacPag 3. Collegeville, Minn.: Liturgical Press, 1991.

———. *The Acts of the Apostles.* SacPag 5. Collegeville, Minn.: Liturgical Press, 1992.

———. "The Christology of Luke-Acts." In *Who Do You Say That I Am? Essays on Christology,* 49–65. Edited by Mark Allan Powell and David R. Bauer. Louisville: Westminster John Knox, 1999.

———. "Literary Criticism of Luke-Acts: Is Reception-History Pertinent?" *JSNT* 28/2 (2005): 159–62.*

Johnson, William Allen. *Bookrolls and Scribes in Oxyrhynchus.* Toronto: University of Toronto Press, 2004.

Jones, F. Stanley. *An Ancient Jewish Christian Source on the History of Christianity: Pseudo-Clementine Recognitions 1.21–71.* SBLTT 37. Atlanta: Scholars, 1995.

———. "A Jewish Christian Reads Luke's Acts of the Apostles: The Use of the Canonical Acts in the Ancient Jewish Christian Source behind Pseudo-Clementine *Recognitions* 1.27–71." SBLSP 34. Atlanta: Scholars, 1995.

Juel, Donald. *Luke-Acts: The Promise of History.* Atlanta: John Knox, 1983.

Kaestli, Jean-Daniel, Jean-Michel Poffet, and Jean Zumstein, eds. *La Communauté johannique et son histoire: Le trajectoire de l'Évangile de Jean aux deux premiers siècles.* Geneva: Labor et Fides, 1990.

Keck, Leander E. *New Interpreter's Bible.* 12 vols. Nashville: Abingdon, 2002.

Keck, Leander E., Paul Schubert, and J. Louis Martyn, eds. *Studies in Luke-Acts.* Nashville: Abingdon, 1966.

Kee, Howard Clark. *To Every Nation Under Heaven: The Acts of the Apostles.* Harrisburg: Trinity Press International, 1997.

Kelhoffer, James. *Miracle and Mission: The Authentication of Missionaries and Their Message in the Longer Ending of Mark.* WUNT 2/112. Tübingen: Mohr Siebeck, 2000.

———. "'How Soon a Book' Revisited: ΕΥΑΓΓΕΛΙΟΝ as a Reference to 'Gospel' Materials in the First Half of the Second Century." *ZNW* 95/12 (2004): 134.

Kenyon, Frederick. *Handbook to the Textual Criticism of the New Testament.* 2d ed. London: Macmillan, 1912.

———. *Books and Readers in Ancient Rome and Greece.* Oxford: Oxford University Press, 1951.

Kloppenborg, John S. *Excavating Q: The History and Setting of the Sayings Gospel.* Minneapolis: Fortress, 2000.

Klutz, Todd. *The Exorcism Stories in Luke-Acts: A Sociostylistic Reading.* SNTSMS 129. Cambridge: Cambridge University Press, 2004.

Koester, Helmut. *Synoptische Überlieferung bei den Apostolischen Vätern.* TU 65. Berlin, Akademie-Verlag, 1957.

———. *Ancient Christian Gospels: Their History and Development.* Philadelphia: Trinity Press International, 1990.

Köhler, Wolf-Dietrich. *Die Rezeption des Matthäusevangeliums in der Zeit vor Irenäus.* WUNT 2/24. Tübingen: Mohr Siebeck, 1987.

Korn, Manfred. *Die Geschichte Jesu in veränderter Zeit: Studien zur bleibenden Bedeutung Jesu im Lukanischen Doppelwerk.* WUNT 2/51. Tübingen: Mohr Siebeck, 1993.

Kövecses, Zoltán. *Metaphor and Emotion: Language, Culture, and Body in Human Feeling.* Cambridge: Cambridge University Press; Paris: Éditions de la Maison des Sciences de l'Homme, 2000.

Kurz, William. "Promise and Fulfillment in Hellenistic Jewish Narratives and in Luke and Acts." In *Jesus and the Heritage of Israel: Luke's Narrative Claim upon Israel's Legacy,* 147–70. Edited by David P. Moessner. Harrisburg: Trinity Press, 1999.

Lampe, Peter. *From Paul to Valentinus: Christians at Rome in the First Two Centuries.* Minneapolis: Fortress, 2003.

Lane, Thomas J. *Luke and the Gentile Mission: Gospel Anticipates Acts.* New York: Peter Lang, 1996.

Lawson, John. *The Biblical Theology of Saint Irenaeus.* London: Epworth, 1948.

Leipoldt, Johannes. *Geschichte des neutestamentlichen Kanons. Erster Teil. Die Entstehung.* Leipzig: J. C. Hinrichs'sche Buchhandlung, 1907.

Lindemann, Andreas. *Paulus im ältesten Christentum: Das Bild des Apostels und die Rezeption der paulinischen Theologie in der frühchristlichen Literatur bis Marcion.* BHTh 58. Tübingen: Mohr Siebeck, 1979.

———. "Der Apostel Paulus im 2. Jahrhundert." In *The New Testament in Early Christianity = La réception des écrits néotestamentaires dans le christianisme primitive,* 39–67. Edited by Jean-Marie Sevrin. BETL 86. Leuven: Leuven University Press, 1989.

———. "Die Sammlung der Paulusbriefe im 1. und 2. Jahrhundert." In *The Biblical Canons,* 321–51. Edited by Jean-Marie Auwers and Henk Jan de Jonge. BETL 163. Leuven: Leuven University Press, 2003.

Litwak, Kenneth D. *Echoes of Scripture in Luke-Acts: Telling the History of God's People Intertextually.* JSNTSup 282. London: T & T Clark, 2005.

Longenecker, Bruce. "Lukan Aversion to Humps and Hollows: The Case of Acts 11.27–12.25." *NTS* 50/2 (2004): 185–204.

Luhumbu Shodu, Emmanuel. *La mémoire des origines chrétiennes selon Justin Martyr.* Paradosis 50. Fribourg: Academic Press, 2008.

Luz, Ulrich. *Matthew 1–7: A Commentary.* Hermeneia. Minnneapolis: Fortress, 2007.

Macé, Marielle. *Le genre littéraire: introduction, choix de textes, commentaires, vade-mecum et bibliographie.* Paris: Flammarion, 2004.

Maddox, Robert L. *The Purpose of Luke-Acts.* SNTW. Edinburgh: T & T Clark, 1982.

Malherbe, Abraham. *Social Aspects of Early Christianity.* Philadelphia: Fortress, 1983.

Marguerat, Daniel. "Luc-Actes: une unité à construire." In *The Unity of Luke-Acts,* 57–81. Edited by Joseph Verheyden. BETL 142. Leuven: Leuven University Press, 1999.

———. *The First Christian Historian: Writing the "Acts of the Apostles."* Translated by Ken McKinney, Gregory J. Laughery, and Richard Bauckham. SNTSMS 121. Cambridge: Cambridge University Press, 2002.

———. *La première histoire du christianisme: les Actes des apôtres.* Lectio Divina 180. 2d ed. Genève: Labor et Fides, 2003.

Marshall, I. Howard. *Luke: Historian and Theologian.* 3d ed. Exeter: Paternoster, 1988.

———. *The Acts of the* Apostles. NTG. Sheffield: Sheffield Academic Press, 1992.

———. "Acts and the 'Former Treatise.'" In *The Book of Acts in Its First Century Setting: Volume 1—Ancient Literary Setting,* 163–82. Edited by Bruce W. Winter and Andrew D. Clark. Grand Rapids, Mich.: Eerdmans, 1993.

———. "'Israel' and the Story of Salvation: One Theme in Two Parts." In *Jesus and the Heritage of Israel: Luke's Narrative Claim upon Israel's Legacy,* 340–57. Edited by David P. Moessner. Harrisburg: Trinity Press, 1999.

———. *New Testament Theology: Many Witnesses, One Gospel.* Downers Grove, Ill.: Inter-Varsity Press, 2004.

———. Review of Andrew Gregory, *The Reception of Luke and Acts in the Period before Irenaeus. SJT* 59/1 (2006): 121–24.

Marshall, I. Howard, and David Peterson, eds. *Witness to the Gospel: The Theology of Acts.* Grand Rapids, Mich.: Eerdmans, 1998.

Martin, Michael Wade. "Defending the 'Western Non-Interpolations': The Case for an Anti-Separationist *Tendenz* in the Longer Alexandrian Readings." *JBL* 124/2 (2005): 269–94.

Massaux, Édouard. *Influence de l'Évangile de saint Matthieu sur la littérature chrétienne avant saint Irénée.* Louvain and Gembloux: Duculot, 1950. Repr. in BETL 75. Leuven: Leuven University Press, 1986.

———. *The Influence of the Gospel of Saint Matthew on Christian Literature before Saint Irenaeus.* 3 vols. Macon, Ga.: Mercer University Press, 1990–93.

Matera, Frank J. *New Testament Christology.* Louisville: Westminster John Knox, 1999.

Matson, Mark. *In Dialogue with Another Gospel?: The Influence of the Fourth Gospel on the Passion Narrative of the Gospel of Luke.* Atlanta: Society of Biblical Literature, 2001.

Meeks, Wayne. *The First Urban Christians.* New Haven: Yale University Press, 1983.

Meizoz, Jerome. *Postures littéraires. Mises en scène modernes de l'auteur. Essai.* Genève: Slatkine, 2007.

Metzger, Bruce M. *A Textual Commentary on the Greek New Testament.* 2d ed. Stuttgart: Deutsche Bibelgesellschaft / German Bible Society, 1994.

———. *The Canon of the New Testament: Its Origin, Development and Significance.* Oxford: Clarendon, 1997.

Metzger, Bruce M., and Bart D. Ehrman. *The Text of the New Testament: Its Transmission, Corruption, and Restoration.* 4th ed. New York: Oxford University Press, 2005.

Mitchell, Margaret. "Patristic Counter-evidence to the Claim that 'The Gospels were Written for All Christians.'" *NTS* 51/1 (2005): 36–79.

Mittelstadt, Martin W. *The Spirit and Suffering in Luke-Acts: Implications for a Pentecostal Pneumatology.* New York: T & T Clark, 2004.

Moessner, David P. *Lord of the Banquet: The Literary and Theological Significance of the Lukan Travel Narrative.* Minneapolis: Augsburg Fortress, 1989.

———. "'Managing' the Audience. Diodorus Siculus and Luke the Evangelist on Designing Authorial Intent." In *Luke and His Readers: Festschrift A. Denaux,* 61–80. Edited by R. Bieringer, Gilbert Van Belle, and Joseph Verheyden. BETL 182. Leuven: Leuven University Press and Peeters, 2005.

———, ed. *Jesus and the Heritage of Israel: Luke's Narrative Claim upon Israel's Legacy.* Harrisburg: Trinity Press, 1999.

Moessner, David P., and David L. Tiede. "*Two* Books but *One* Story?" In *Jesus and the Heritage of Israel: Luke's Narrative Claim upon Israel's Legacy,* 1–4. Edited by David P. Moessner. Harrisburg: Trinity Press, 1999.

Mount, Christopher N. *Pauline Christianity: Luke-Acts and the Legacy of Paul.* NovTSup 104. Leiden: Brill, 2002.

Mühlethaler, Jean-Claude. "Éloge de la variante: la clôture du *Testament* de Villon." In *Quant l'ung amy pour l'autre veille. Mélanges de moyen français offerts à Claude Thiry,* 425–37. Edited by Tania van Hemeleryck and Maria Colombo Timelli. Texte, Codex & Contexte 5. Turnhout: Brepols, 2008.

Mutschler, Bernhard. *Irenäus als johanneischer Theologe: Studien zur Schriftauslegung bei Irenäus von Lyon.* STAC 21. Tübingen: Mohr Siebeck, 2004.

———. *Das Corpus Johanneum bei Irenäus von Lyon: Studien und Kommentar zum dritten Buch von Adversus Haereses.* WUNT 189. Tübingen: Mohr Siebeck, 2006.

Nagel, Titus. *Die Rezeption des Johannesevangeliums im 2. Jahrhundert: Studien zur vorirenäischen Aneignung und Auslegung des vierten Evangeliums in christlicher und christlich-gnostischer Literatur.* ABG 2. Leipzig: Evangelische Verlagsanstalt, 2000.

Nave, Guy D. *The Role and Function of Repentance in Luke-Acts.* Atlanta: Scholars, 2002.

Neagoe, Alexandru. *The Trial of the Gospel: An Apologetic Reading of Luke's Trial Narratives.* SNTSMS 116. Cambridge: Cambridge University Press, 2002.

Niebuhr, K-W., and Robert W. Wall. *The Catholic Epistles and Apostolic Traditions: The New Perspective on James and Other Studies.* Waco, Tex.: Baylor University Press, 2009.

Nienhuis, David R. *Not by Paul Alone.* Waco, Tex.: Baylor University Press, 2007.

O'Neill, J. C. *The Theology of Acts in Its Historical Setting.* 2d ed. London: SPCK, 1970.

Pagels, Elaine. "Visions, Appearances and Apostolic Authority: Gnostic and Orthodox Tradition." In *Gnosis: Festschrift für Hans Jonas,* 415–30. Edited by Barbara Aland. Göttingen: Vandenhoeck & Ruprecht, 1978.

Paget, James Carleton. Review of Andrew Gregory, *The Reception of Luke and Acts in the Period before Irenaeus. JEH* 55/4 (2004): 742–44.

Painter, John. *Just James: The Brother of Jesus in History and Tradition.* 2nd ed. Columbia: University of South Carolina Press, 2004.

Pao, David W. *Acts and the Isaianic New Exodus.* WUNT 2/130. Tübingen: Mohr Siebeck, 2000.

Parker, David C. *The Living Text of the Gospels.* Cambridge: Cambridge University Press, 1997.

Parker, Pierson. "The 'Former Treatise' and the Date of Acts." *JBL* 84/1 (1965): 52–58.

———. "Mark, Acts, and Galilean Christianity." *NTS* 16/3 (1969): 295–304.

———. "When Acts Sides with John." In *Understanding the Sacred Text: Essays in Honor of Morton S. Enslin on the Hebrew Bible and Christian Beginnings,* 201–15. Edited by John Reumann. Valley Forge, Pa.: Judson, 1972.

———. "The Kinship of John and Acts." In *Christianity, Judaism, and Other Greco-Roman Cults: Studies for Morton Smith at Sixty.* Vol. 1, *New Testament,* 187–205. Edited by Jacob Neusner. Leiden: Brill, 1975.

Parsons, Mikeal C. "A Christological Tendency in P75." *JBL* 105/3 (1986): 463–79.

———. *The Departure of Jesus in Luke-Acts: The Ascension Narratives in Context.* JSNTS 21. Sheffield: Sheffield Academic Press, 1987.

———. "The Unity of Lukan Writings: Rethinking the *Opinio Communis.*" In *Steadfast Purpose: Essays on Acts in Honor of Henry Jackson Flanders,* 29–53. Edited by N. H. Keathley. Waco, Tex.: Baylor University Press, 1990.

———. *Luke: Storyteller, Interpreter, Evangelist.* Peabody, Mass.: Hendrickson, 2007.

———. *Acts.* Paideia Commentaries on the New Testament. Grand Rapids: Baker Academic, 2008.

Parsons, Mikeal C., and Richard I. Pervo. *Rethinking the Unity of Luke and Acts.* Minneapolis: Fortress, 1993. Repr. with additional bibliography, 2007.

Pelikan, Jaroslav. *Acts.* Brazos Theological Commentary on the Bible. Grand Rapids, Mich.: Brazos Press, 2005.

Penner, Todd. "Contextualizing Acts." In *Contextualizing Acts: Lukan Narrative and Greco-Roman Discourse.* Edited by Todd C. Penner and Caroline Vander Stichele. SBLSS 20. Leiden: Brill, 2004.

———. "Madness in the Method? The Acts of the Apostles in Current Study." *Currents in Biblical Research* 2/2 (2004): 223–93.

Pervo, Richard I. *Profit with Delight: The Literary Genre of the Acts of the Apostles.* Philadelphia: Fortress, 1987.

———. "Must Luke and Acts Belong to the Same Genre?" *SBLSP* (1989): 309–16.

———. "A Hard Act to Follow: *The Acts of Paul* and the Canonical Acts." *Journal of Higher Criticism* 2/2 (1995): 3–32.

———. "Israel's Heritage and Claims Upon the Genre(s) of Luke and Acts: The Problems of a History." In *Jesus and the Heritage of Israel: Luke's Narrative Claim upon Israel's Legacy,* 127–43. Edited by David P. Moessner. Harrisburg: Trinity Press, 1999.

———. *Dating Acts: Between the Evangelists and the Apologists.* Santa Rosa, Calif.: Polebridge, 2006.

———. "Direct Speech in Acts and the Question of Genre." *JSNT* 28/3 (2006): 285–307.

Phillips, Thomas E. *Acts and Ethics.* NTMon 9. Sheffield: Sheffield Phoenix Press, 2005.

———. "The Genre of Acts: Moving Towards a Consensus." *CBR* 4 (2006): 365–96.

———, ed. *Contemporary Studies in Acts.* Macon, Ga.: Mercer University Press, 2009.

Plato. *Phaedrus.* Translated by H. R. M. Lamb. Loeb Classical Library. Cambridge: Harvard University Press, 1914–1990.

Plato. *Theaetetus.* Translated by H. N. Fowler. Loeb Classical Library. Cambridge: Harvard University Press, 1921–1987.

Pokorný, Petr. *Theologie der lukanischen Schriften.* FRLANT 174. Göttingen: Vandenhoeck & Ruprecht, 1998.

Poupon, Gérard. "Les 'Actes de Pierre' et leur remaniement." *ANRW* II.25.6 (1988): 4363–83.

Price, Robert M. *The Widow Traditions in Luke-Acts: A Feminist-Critical Scrutiny.* SBLDS 155. Atlanta: Scholars, 1997.

Punday, Daniel. *Narrative Bodies: Toward a Corporeal Narratology.* New York: Palgrave Macmillan, 2003.

Rabatel, Alain. "Point de vue et polyphonie dans les textes narratifs." In *Lire, écrire le point de vue: un apprentissage de la lecture littéraire,* 7–24. Edited by Philippe de Vita and Alain Rabatel. Lyon: Scérén-CRDP Académie de Lyon, 2002.

Rabinowitz, Peter. *Before Reading: Narrative Conventions and the Politics of Interpretation.* Ithaca, N.Y.: Cornell University Press, 1987.

Rese, Martin. "Das Lukas-Evangelium. Ein Forschungsbericht." *ANRW* II.25.3 (1985): 2258–2328.

Riesner, Rainer. "James' Speech (Acts 15:13–21), Simeon's Hymn (Luke 2:29–32), and Luke's Sources." In *Jesus of Nazareth: Lord and Christ,* 263–78. Edited by Joel B. Green and Max Turner. Grand Rapids, Mich.: Eerdmans, 1994.

Rius-Camps, Josep, and Jenny Read-Heimerdinger, eds. *The Message of Acts in Codex Bezae: A Comparison with the Alexandrian Tradition.* Vol. 1. *Acts 1.1–5.42: Jerusalem.* JSNTSup 257. London and New York: T&T Clark, 2004.

Robbins, Vernon K. *Exploring the Texture of the Texts: A Guide to Socio-Rhetorical Interpretation.* Valley Forge, Pa.: Trinity Press International, 1996.

———. *The Tapestry of Early Christian Discourse: Rhetoric, Society and Ideology.* London: Routledge, 1996.

Robinson, James M., Paul Hoffmann, and John S. Kloppenborg, eds. *The Critical Edition of Q.* Hermeneia. Minneapolis: Fortress, 2000.

Rohde, Erwin. *Der griechische Roman und seine Vorläufer.* Leipzig: Breitkopf und Härtel, 1900.

Rordorf, Willy. "Actes de Paul." In *Écrits apocryphes chrétiens 1,* 1115–77. Edited by François Bovon and Pierre Geoltrain. Paris: Gallimard, 1997.

Roth, S. John. *The Blind, The Lame, and the Poor: Character Types in Luke-Acts.* JSNTSup 144. Sheffield: Sheffield Academic Press, 1997.

Rothschild, Clare K. *Luke-Acts and the Rhetoric of History: An Investigation of Early Christian Historiography.* WUNT 2/175. Tübingen: Mohr Siebeck, 2004.

Rousseau, Adelin and Louis Doutreleau. *Irenée de Lyon Contre les Hérésies Livre III.* S.C. 211. Paris: Éditions du Cerf, 1974.

Rowe, C. Kavin. "History, Hermeneutics, and the Unity of Luke-Acts." *JSNT* 28/2 (2005): 131–57.*

———. "Literary Unity and Reception History: Reading Luke-Acts as Luke and Acts." *JSNT* 29/4 (2007): 449–57.*

Royse, James Ronald. *Scribal Habits in Early Greek New Testament Papyri.* Leiden and Boston: Brill, 2008.

Sanday, William. *The Gospels in the Second Century.* London: Macmillan, 1876.

Sanday, William, and Cuthbert H. Turner. *Novum Testamentum Sancti Irenaei Episcopi Lugdunensis.* Oxford: Clarendon Press, 1923.

Sanders, Joseph N. *The Fourth Gospel in the Early Church: Its Origin and Influence on Christian Theology up to Irenaeus.* Cambridge: Cambridge University Press, 1943.

Schneemelcher, Wilhelm, ed. *New Testament Apocrypha.* Vol. 1. Translated by R. McL. Wilson. Westminster: John Knox, 2003.

Schneider, Gerhard. *Die Apostelgeschichte.* 2 vols. HTK 5. Freiburg: Herder & Herder, 1980–1982.

Schoedel, William R. *Polycarp, Martyrdom of Polycarp, Fragments of Papias.* Apostolic Fathers 5. London: Thomas Nelson, 1967.

Sevrin, Jean-Marie, ed. *The New Testament in Early Christianity.* BETL 86; Leuven: Leuven University Press, 1989.

Shauf, Scott. *Theology as History: Paul in Ephesus in Acts 19.* New York: Walter de Gruyter, 2005.

Shepherd, Massey H., and Sherman E. Johnson, eds. *Munera Studiosa.* Cambridge, Mass.: Episcopal Theological School, 1946.

Shepherd, William H. *The Narrative Function of the Holy Spirit as a Character in Luke-Acts.* SBLDS 147. Atlanta: Scholars, 1994.

Sim, David C. "The Gospels for All Christians? A Response to Richard Bauckham." *JSNT* 24/2 (2001): 3–27.

Smith, David E. *The Canonical Function of Acts: A Comparative Analysis.* Collegeville, Minn.: Liturgical Press, 2002.

Smith, Dennis E. *From Symposium to Eucharist: The Banquet in the Early Christian World.* Minneapolis: Fortress, 2003.

Smith, D. Moody. "When Did the Gospels Become Scripture?" *JBL* 119/1 (2000): 3–20.

———. *John among the Gospels.* Columbia: University of South Carolina Press, 2001.

Souter, Alexander. *The Text and Canon of the New Testament.* New York: Charles Scribner's Sons, 1920.

Spencer, F. Scott. *Acts.* Sheffield: Sheffield Academic Press, 1997.

Spencer, Patrick E. "The Unity of Luke-Acts: A Four-Bolted Hermeneutical Hinge." *CBR* 5/3 (2007): 341–66.

Squires, John T. *The Plan of God in Luke-Acts.* SNTSMS 76. Cambridge: Cambridge University Press, 1993.

Stanton, Graham N. "The Fourfold Gospel." *NTS* 43/3 (1997): 317–46.

———. "Jesus Traditions and Gospels in Justin Martyr and Irenaeus." In *The Biblical Canons,* 353–70. Edited by Jean-Marie Auwers and Henk Jan de Jonge. BETL 163. Leuven: Leuven University Press, 2003.

———. *Jesus and Gospel.* Cambridge: Cambridge University Press, 2004.

Starr, R. J. "The Circulation of Literary Texts in the Roman World." *CQ* 37/1 (1987): 213–23.

Stenschke, Christoph W. "The Need for Salvation." In *Witness to the Gospel: The Theology of Acts,* 125–44. Edited by I. Howard Marshall and David Peterson. Grand Rapids, Mich.: Eerdmans, 1998.

Sterling, Gregory E. "'Opening the Scriptures': The Legitimation of the Jewish Diaspora and the Early Christian Mission." In *Jesus and the Heritage of Israel: Luke's Narrative Claim upon Israel's Legacy,* 199–217. Edited by David P. Moessner. Harrisburg: Trinity Press, 1999.

Strange, W. A. *The Problem of the Text of Acts.* SNTSMS 71. Cambridge: Cambridge University Press, 1992.

Strauss, Mark L. *The Davidic Messiah in Luke-Acts: The Promise and Its Fulfilment in Luke's Christology.* JSNTSup 110. Sheffield: Sheffield Academic Press, 1995.

Streeter, B. H. *The Four Gospels: A Study of Origins, Treating of the Manuscript Tradition, Sources, Authorship, & Dates.* London: Macmillan, 1924.

Stuehrenberg, P. F. "The Study of Acts before the Reformation: A Bibliographical Introduction." *NovT* 29/2 (1987): 100–136.

Sundberg, Albert C., Jr. "Canon Muratori: A Fourth-century List." *HTR* 66/1 (1973): 1–41.

Talbert, Charles H. *Literary Patterns, Theological Themes and the Genre of Luke-Acts.* SBLMS 20. Missoula, Mont.: SBL and Scholars Press, 1974.

———. *Reading Acts: A Literary and Theological Commentary on the Acts of the Apostles.* New York: Crossroads, 1997.

———. "Prophecies of Future Greatness: The Contributions of Greco-Roman Biographies to an Understanding of Luke 1:5–4:1." In *Reading Luke-Acts in its Mediterranean Milieu,* 65–77. NovTSup 107. Leiden: Brill, 2003.

———. *Reading Luke-Acts in its Mediterranean Milieu.* NovTSup 107. Leiden: Brill, 2003.

Talbert, Charles H., and J. H. Hayes. "A Theology of Sea Storms in Luke-Acts." In *Jesus and the Heritage of Israel: Luke's Narrative Claim upon Israel's Legacy,* 267–83. Edited by David P. Moessner. Harrisburg: Trinity Press, 1999.

Talbert, Charles H., and Perry Stepp. "Succession in Luke-Acts and in the Lukan Milieu." In *Reading Luke-Acts in its Mediterranean Milieu,* 19–55. NovTSup 107. Leiden: Brill, 2003.

Tannehill, Robert C. *The Narrative Unity of Luke-Acts: A Literary Interpretation.* 2 vols. Minneapolis: Fortress, 1986, 1990.

———. "The Story of Israel within the Lukan Narrative." In *Jesus and the Heritage of Israel: Luke's Narrative Claim upon Israel's Legacy,* 325–39. Edited by David P. Moessner. Harrisburg: Trinity Press, 1999.

Thielman, Frank. *Theology of the New Testament: A Canonical and Synthetic Approach.* Grand Rapids: Zondervan, 2005.

Thomas, Christine M. *The* Acts of Peter, *Gospel Literature, and the Ancient Novel: Rewriting the Past.* New York: Oxford University Press, 2003.

Thompson, Michael B. "The Holy Internet: Communication Between Churches in the First Christian Generation." In *The Gospels for All Christians: Rethinking the Gospel Audiences,* 49–70. Edited by Richard Bauckham. Grand Rapids, Mich.: Eerdmans, 1998.

Trobisch, David. *Die Endredaktion des Neuen Testaments.* NTOA 31. Gottingen: Vandenhoeck & Ruprecht, 1996.

———. "The Council of Jerusalem in Acts 15 and Paul's Letter to the Galatians." In *Theological Exegesis: Essays in Honor of Brevard S. Childs,* 331–38. Edited by Christopher Seitz and Kathryn Greene-McCreight. Grand Rapids, Mich.: Eerdmans, 1999.

———. *The First Edition of the New Testament.* Oxford: Oxford University Press, 2000.

Trocmé, Étienne. *Le livre des Actes et l'histoire.* Paris: Presses Universitaires de France, 1957.

Tuckett, Christopher M. *Luke.* NTG. Sheffield: Sheffield Academic Press, 1996.

———. "Synoptic Tradition in the Didache." In J-M. Sevrin, ed., *The New Testament in Early Christianity,* 197–230, BETL 86. Leuven: Leuven University Press and Peeters, 1989.

Tyson, Joseph B. *Marcion and Luke-Acts: A Defining Struggle.* Columbia: University of South Carolina Press, 2006.

Verheyden, Joseph, ed. *The Unity of Luke-Acts.* BETL 142. Leuven: Leuven University Press, 1999.

———. "The Unity of Luke-Acts. What Are We Up To?" In *The Unity of Luke-Acts,* 3–56. Edited by Joseph Verheyden. BETL 142. Leuven: Leuven University Press, 1999.

———. "The Canon Muratori: A Matter of Dispute." In *The Biblical Canons,* 487–556. Edited by Jean-Marie Auwers and Henk Jan de Jonge. BETL 163. Leuven: Peeters, 2003.

Vielhauer, P. "On the 'Paulinism' of Acts." In *Studies in Luke-Acts; Essays Presented in Honor of Paul Schubert,* 33–51. Edited by Leander E. Keck and J. Louis Martyn. Nashville: Abingdon, 1966.

Wall, Robert W. "The Acts of the Apostles in Canonical Context." In *The New Testament as Canon.* Edited by Robert W. Wall and Eugene E. Lemcio. JSNTSup 76. Sheffield: JSOT Press, 1992.

———. "Romans 1:1–15: An Introduction to the Pauline Corpus of the New Testament." In *The New Testament as Canon,* 142–60. Edited by Robert W. Wall and Eugene E. Lemcio. JSNTSup 76. Sheffield: JSOT Press, 1992.

———. "The Canonical Function of 2 Peter." *BibInt* 9/1 (2001): 64–81.

———. "The Acts of the Apostles." In *New Interpreter's Bible,* 10: 3–370. Edited by Leander E. Keck. 12 vols. Nashville: Abingdon, 2002.

———. "Toward a Unifying Theology of the Catholic Epistles: A Canonical Approach." In *Catholic Epistles and the Tradition,* 43–71. BETL 176. Edited by Jacques Schlosser. Leuven: Peeters, 2004.

———. "The Jerusalem Council (Acts 15:1–21) in Canonical Context." In *From Biblical Criticism to Biblical Faith: Essays in Honor of Lee Martin McDonald,* 93–101. Edited by William. H. Brackney and Craig A. Evans. Macon, Ga.: Mercer University Press, 2007.

Walters, Patricia. *The Assumed Authorial Unity of Luke and Acts: A Reassessment of the Evidence.* SNTSMS 145. Cambridge: Cambridge University Press, 2009.

Walton, Steve. *Leadership and Lifestyle: The Portrait of Paul in the Miletus Speech and 1 Thessalonians.* SNTSMS 108. Cambridge: Cambridge University Press, 2000.

Wasserberg, Günter. *Aus Israels Mitte - Heil für die Welt: Eine narrativ-exegetische Studie zur Theologie des Lukas.* BZNW 92. Berlin: Walter de Gruyter, 1998.

Weatherly, Jon A. *Jewish Responsibility for the Death of Jesus in Luke-Acts.* JSNTSup 106. Sheffield: Sheffield Academic Press, 1994.

Wedderburn, A. J. M. "Zur Frage der Gattung der Apostelgeschichte." In *Geschichte, Tradition, Reflexion: Festschrift für Martin Hengel zum 70*, 303–22. Edited by Hubert Cancik, Hermann Lichtenberger, and Peter Schäfer. Tübingen: Mohr Siebeck, 1996.

Wenham, David. *The Jesus Tradition Outside the Gospels.* Gospel Perspectives 5. Sheffield: JSOT Press, 1984.

———. "Acts and the Pauline Corpus." In *The Book of Acts in Its Ancient Literary Setting*, 215–58. Edited by Bruce W. Winter and Andrew D. Clarke. Grand Rapids, Mich.: Eerdmans, 1993.

Wenk, Matthias. *Community-Forming Power: The Socio-Ethical Role of the Spirit in Luke-Acts.* Sheffield: Sheffield Academic Press, 2000.

Witherington, Ben. *The Acts of the Apostles: A Socio-Rhetorical Commentary.* Grand Rapids, Mich.: Eerdmans, 1998.

Woods, Edward J. *The 'Finger of God' and Pneumatology in Luke-Acts.* JSNTSup 205. Sheffield: Sheffield Academic Press, 2001.

Zeller, Eduard. "Die älteste Überlieferung über die Schriften des Lukas." *Theologische Jahrbücher* 7 (1848): 528–72.

Zwiep, A. W. *The Ascension of the Messiah in Lukan Christology.* NovTSup 87. Leiden: Brill, 1997.

CONTRIBUTORS

Michael F. Bird is lecturer in systematic theology at the Bible College of Queensland. His publications include *Jesus and the Origins of the Gentile Mission* (2007), *The Saving Righteousness of God* (2007), *A Bird's-Eye View of Paul* (2008), *Are You the One Who Is to Come? The Historical Jesus and the Messianic Question* (2009), and *Crossing over Sea and Land: Jewish Missionary Activity in the Second Temple Period* (2009).

Markus Bockmuehl is professor of biblical and early Christian studies at the University of Oxford and Fellow of Keble College. His publications include *Seeing the Word: Refocusing New Testament Study* (2007) and, as editor, with Alan Torrance, *Scripture's Doctrine and Theology's Bible: How the New Testament Shapes Christian Dogmatics* (2008) and, with James Carleton Paget, *Redemption and Resistance* (2007).

François Bovon is Frothingham Professor of the History of Religion at Harvard Divinity School and formerly professor at the University of Geneva. His publications include a four volume critical commentary on the Gospel of Luke (published in German in the Evangelisch-katholischer Kommentar [1989–2009], in French in the Commentaire du Nouveau Testament [1991–2009] and in English in the Hermeneia series [2002–]) and, with Bertrand Bouvier and Frédéric Amsler, a critical edition of the Greek Acts of the apostle Philip (1999).

Claire Clivaz is assistant professor in New Testament and early Christian literature at the University of Lausanne (Switzerland). Her publications include *L'ange et la sueur de sang (Lc 22,43–44) ou comment on pourrait bien encore écrire l'histoire* (BiTS 7), (2010).

Andrew Gregory is chaplain and fellow of University College, Oxford, and a member of the theology faculty of the University of Oxford. His publications include *The Reception of Luke and Acts in the Period before Irenaeus* (2003) and (as editor or as coeditor and as a contributor), *The New Proclamation Commentary on the Gospels* (2007), *The Reception of the New Testament in the Apostolic Fathers* (2005), and *Trajectories through the New Testament and the Apostolic Fathers* (2005). He has also contributed chapters to a number of other academic books, and he has published articles in *Expository Times*, *Journal for the Study of the New Testament* and *New Testament Studies.*

Luke Timothy Johnson is Robert W. Woodruff Professor of New Testament and Christian Origins at the Candler School of Theology, Emory University. His recent publications include *Brother of Jesus: Friend of God* (2004), *Hebrews: A Commentary* (2006), and *Among the Gentiles* (2009).

Mikeal C. Parsons is professor and Kidd L. and Buna Hitchcock Macon Chair in religion at Baylor University. His publications include *Body and Character in Luke and Acts: The Subversion of Physiognomy in Early Christianity* (2006), *Luke: Storyteller, Evangelist, Interpreter* (2007), and *The Acts of the Apostles* (2008).

Richard I. Pervo is retired in St. Paul, Minnesota. His recent publications include *Dating Acts* (2006), *Acts: A Commentary* (edited by Harold W. Attridge; 2009) and *The Making of Paul: Constructions of the Apostle in Early Christianity* (2010).

C. Kavin Rowe is assistant professor of New Testament at Duke University Divinity School. In addition to multiple scholarly articles in a wide variety of scholarly journals, he is the author of two books: *World Upside Down: Reading Acts in the Graeco-Roman Age* (2009), and *Early Narrative Christology: The Lord in the Gospel of Luke* (2006). He has been a Fulbright Scholar, a Lilly Faculty Fellow, and a recipient of a grant from the Louisville Institute. In 2009 he was one of twelve scholars worldwide to be awarded the John Templeton Prize for Theological Promise.

David Trobisch has taught New Testament at the University of Heidelberg, Germany, Missouri State University, Yale Divinity School, and Bangor Theological Seminary in Maine. His publications include *The First Edition of the New Testament* (2000).

Joseph Verheyden is Professor of New Testament at the Catholic University of Leuven (Belgium). He has published many articles, including contributions on synoptic studies, textual criticism of the New Testament, intertestamental and noncanonical literature, and the reception history of the New Testament. His books include *De vlucht van de christenen naar Pella: onderzoek van het getuigenis van Eusebius en Epiphanius* (1988) and, as editor, *The Unity of Luke-Acts* (1999).

Robert Wall is the Paul T. Walls Professor of Scripture and Wesleyan Studies at Seattle Pacific University. His recent books include, with Anthony Robinson, *Called to Be Church* (2006) and, coedited with Karl-Wilhelm Niebuhr, *The Catholic Epistles and the Apostolic Tradition* (2009).

INDEX OF SCRIPTURE CITATIONS

INDEX OF ANCIENT AUTHORS

INDEX OF MODERN AUTHORS